THE COURT
AS ARCHIVE

THE COURT AS ARCHIVE

EDITED BY ANN GENOVESE, TRISH LUKER
AND KIM RUBENSTEIN

Published by ANU Press
The Australian National University
Acton ACT 2601, Australia
Email: anupress@anu.edu.au

Available to download for free at press.anu.edu.au

ISBN (print): 9781760462703
ISBN (online): 9781760462710

WorldCat (print): 1085371650
WorldCat (online): 1085371719

DOI: 10.22459/CA.2019

This title is published under a Creative Commons Attribution-NonCommercial-NoDerivatives 4.0 International (CC BY-NC-ND 4.0).

The full licence terms are available at
creativecommons.org/licenses/by-nc-nd/4.0/legalcode

Cover design and layout by ANU Press.
Cover photograph by National Archives of Australia.

This edition © 2019 ANU Press

Contents

Acknowledgements vii

Introduction 1
Ann Genovese, Trish Luker and Kim Rubenstein

Part 1—Public Law and Citizenship

1. Court Records, Archives and Citizenship. 25
   Kim Rubenstein and Andrew Henderson

2. Aspects of Citizen Access to Court Archives 47
   Ernst Willheim

3. When the Carnival is Over: The Case for Reform of Access
   to Royal Commission Records 67
   Hollie Kerwin and Maya Narayan

Part 2—Histories and Jurisprudence of Australia

4. A Matter of Records: The Federal Court, The National Archives
   and 'The National Estate' in the 1970s .99
   Ann Genovese

5. Framing the Archives as Evidence: A Study of Correspondence
   Documenting the Place of Australia's Original High Court
   in a New Commonwealth Polity. 123
   Susan Priest

6. Accessing the Archives of the Australian War Crimes Trials
   after World War II. 145
   Narrelle Morris

Part 3—Institutional Experience and Responsibility for Records

7. A Conversation with Warwick Soden (Principal Registrar
   and Chief Executive Officer, Federal Court of Australia) 167
   Interviewed by Kim Rubenstein and Ann Genovese

8. A Conversation with Louise Anderson and Ian Irving
   (Former Native Title Registrars, Federal Court of Australia).....189
   Interviewed by Ann Genovese and Kim Rubenstein

9. Providing Public Access to Native Title Records:
   Balancing the Risks Against the Benefits...................213
   Pamela McGrath

10. Archiving Revolution: Historical Records Management
    in the Massachusetts Courts............................239
    Andrew Henderson

11. Sentencing Acts: Appraisal of Court Records in Canada
    and Australia.......................................263
    Trish Luker

Postscript: A Memorandum to the Federal Court of Australia......287

Contributors..293

Acknowledgements

Many individuals and a number of organisations have assisted us during the course of the The Court as Archive Project and in the development and production of this collection. In particular, we would like to thank our respective institutional homes (the University of Melbourne, the University of Technology Sydney and The Australian National University) and the Australian Research Council for collectively funding and supporting the project; all the contributors to this edited collection; the research assistants who worked with us on the project with such commitment and care: Andrew Henderson, Peter Moore and Holly Kerwin; and the Federal Court of Australia, in particular Justice Susan Kenny and Warwick Soden and Lyn Nasir for their interest and engagement with the motivation for this research from its inception and in the development of this book; the National Archives of Australia; the ANU Press Publication Subsidy committee for providing funds for proofreading; and colleagues at ANU Press.

We would also like to thank all the friends and scholars who have engaged with us in conversations about the project over its lifetime, with special thanks to those who have hosted us at their institutions.

Finally, we would like to thank those who support us to do our work closer to home. Ann would like to thank Paul, Joseph and Samuel; Trish would like to thank Georgine; and Kim thanks Garry, Cohava and Eli.

Introduction

Ann Genovese, Trish Luker and Kim Rubenstein

Until the late 20th century, 'an archive' generally meant a repository for documents, as well as the generic name for the wide range of documents the repository might hold. An archive could be visited, and then also searched, to discover past actions or lives that had meaning for the present. While historians and historiographers have long understood the contests that archives contain, and represent, the very idea of 'the archive' has, over the last 40 years, become the subject and object of widening, and intensified, consideration. This consideration has been intellectual (from scholars in a wide range of disciplines) and public (from communities and individuals whose stories are held captive, or sometimes hidden or excluded from official archives), as well as institutional. It has involved scrutiny and critique of official archives' limitations and practices, as well as symbolic, affective and theoretical expansion and heightened expectation of what 'the archive' is, or should be. The very language of 'the archive' now carries freight as administrative practice, normative value, metaphor, description and aspiration in different ways than it did in the 20th century (or even 10 years ago, when we began our collaboration).

The Court as Archive offers a unique contribution to these reinvigorated—and sometimes new—conversations about what an archive might be, what it can do as a consequence and to whom it bears custodial responsibilities. In particular, this collection addresses what it means for contemporary Australian superior courts of record not only to have constitutional and procedural duties to documents as a matter of law, but also to acknowledge obligations to care for those materials in a way that understands their public meaning and public value for the Australian people, in the past, in the present and for the future.

The Court as Archive Project

This collection began its life in a prosaic manner: from a sense of practical frustration—unique perhaps to scholars who work with documents generated and located in courts—with the difficulties that occur in attempting to access these rich materials. These difficulties, although neither uniform across jurisdictions or academic pursuits, nor new, are strikingly similar when scholars step back from their research to share with each other experiences of restriction and inaccessibility of court materials, and the implications of these experiences for their research. Indeed, the grounding for this book, and the subsequent project collaboration, had its genesis in such a conversation in 2008 at a workshop hosted by the Centre for International and Public Law (CIPL) at The Australian National University (ANU). Kim Rubenstein, then director of CIPL, invited scholars from history and law to engage with the book *Rights and Redemption: History, Law, and Indigenous People*.[1] This book analysed and examined the use and production of historical expert evidence in Australian litigation involving Indigenous parties in the late 1990s and early 2000s. The Rights and Redemption Project involved direct engagement with the Federal Court of Australia, examining (under court order) the historical materials adduced in those matters at a time when there was a genuine sharpness to public debate surrounding the status of Indigenous litigants' claims against the past and present Australian state.

The difficulties of access to court material emerged as a common theme in the CIPL workshop. Each of the presenters had encountered roadblocks in scholarly research due to a lack of access to key material held by the court. For example, Trish Luker, who had completed a PhD on the Stolen Generations case *Cubillo v The Commonwealth*,[2] and Kim Rubenstein, in seeking the transcript of the David Hicks Federal Court matter concerning questions of citizenship.[3] Whether it be transcripts of evidence, submissions of parties or a range of other material that could help enlighten our respective research, we had all been interested to draw insights from the court experience around the ways that individual citizens had challenged the exercise of state power within the judicial context and what that may mean in a range of scholarly interventions.

---

[1] Ann Genovese, Ann Curthoys and Alexander Reilly, *Rights and Redemption: History, Law, and Indigenous People* (UNSW Press, 2008).
[2] *Cubillo v Commonwealth* (2000) 103 FCR 1; Trish Luker, *The Rhetoric of Reconciliation: Evidence and Judicial Subjectivity in Cubillo v Commonwealth* (PhD Thesis, LaTrobe University, 2007).
[3] *Hicks v Ruddock* (2007) 156 FCR 574.

At the CIPL workshop, we also discussed how the Federal Court recognised that it was at a formative moment in its own institutional history and practice regarding its responsibilities as a court and, potentially, as an archive. This recognition is encapsulated by former Native Title Registrars of the court, Louise Anderson and Ian Irving, in an interview we conducted for our research, which appears as Chapter 8 in this book. In particular, the arrival of native title litigation and the legal necessity for Indigenous peoples to tender enormous amounts of evidentiary proof of 'continuity' to country resulted in exponential funding and growth of cognate disciplinary research about Indigenous experience on country. It also led to the production and preservation of Indigenous parties' law, including testimonial evidence recorded in on country hearings, artworks and other material objects tendered as evidence. These materials, although fraught, given they were produced for a legal proceeding, were nevertheless understood by the court (as well as Indigenous parties and scholars) as carrying a weight and purpose for which the court assumed a significant responsibility. In that context, the court became acutely aware of its ill-defined function as an archival repository. However, it also realised that coming to terms with those native title holdings made visible its role as custodian of law stories not only confined to that jurisdiction. It reminded the court, and those scholars meeting at the CIPL workshop, about the nature, status, access, preservation and location of all of the materials courts hold that are of value to the Australian citizenry and public more broadly.

So began a series of regular meetings, over the course of five years, which led ultimately to the Australian Research Council (ARC) Discovery grant that took that research interest seriously. In 2013, we began our investigation on general questions about Chapter III courts as archives, centred on the paradigmatic example of the Federal Court of Australia.[4] One of our purposes has been very practical: to think alongside the Federal Court about how, as an institution of law and of the state, it might also function

---

4   The Federal Court of Australia provides an ideal site for investigation of the contested issues associated with the civic role of courts in administering legal archival records of national significance. Established as an innovative response at a key moment in the development of Australian administrative law (Commonwealth, *Commonwealth Administrative Review Committee Report 1971*, Parl Paper No 144 (1971) ('Kerr Report')), the court has a unique mandate and jurisdictional scope, specifically in adjudicating disputes between citizens and the state. It is a court established under Chapter III of the *Australian Constitution* and by statute, thereby illuminating core issues concerning the judicial power of the Commonwealth. As a superior court of record (SCOR), the Federal Court makes determinations that are binding and conclusive, unless or until set aside on appeal. Further, it has an expanding jurisdiction and legislative responsibility.

as an archival repository. That question goes beyond, and potentially complicates, its status as a court of record (a legal status we explain in the following section). To address the question methodologically, we deliberately chose to examine the Federal Court's archive of administrative practices, rather than an exploration of the rich litigation materials the court holds. This approach holds firmly to Australian public law principles and, at the same time, relates these to the broad innovations occurring in research institutionally situated and focused on and in 'the archive'. We describe our method, and how it exists in conversation with current fields of related inquiry, in more detail below; however, note here that this approach has enabled us as a research team to examine, through a range of diverse records and sources, how the Federal Court has conceived its own citizenship and its own place and role in shaping a modern democratic nation.

Alongside close empirical and analytical work of our own, the Court as Archive Project was also envisaged as a way to extend a key insight of our earlier meeting: the necessity of collaboration, cross-disciplinary and cross-institutional dialogue when addressing difficult questions of law and public meaning. The problems that come into view once a court of record is conceived of, and engaged with, as an archive are complex. They do not lend themselves to analysis situated solely within universities, government agencies, courts, or diverse public communities—nor are they limited to Australia. We interviewed court officials facing similar problems, in similar jurisdictions, with similar histories. For example, in 'Sentencing Acts: Appraisal of Court Records in Canada and Australia', Trish Luker includes Canadian and Australian jurisdictional approaches to the sentencing of court records and in 'Archiving Revolution: Historical Records Management in the Massachusetts Courts', our research assistant, Andrew Henderson, highlights the values of international comparison.

Most significantly for the genesis of this book, our project design was predicated on convening a symposium, which was again held at CIPL, in 2016. We invited collaborators and interlocutors who had diverse official and scholarly duties to archives and their use to consider with us how to recognise the implications of a court of record's responsibilities to the materials it holds and the communities it serves. A core outcome of the symposium was clarification of a key point: this work requires close networked thinking to engage well with practical questions of custodianship, access, legal and constitutional requirements, and preservation and future use of court materials. As we elaborate below, this book is a direct reflection of the symposium.

INTRODUCTION

The Court as Archive Project: Methods in Scholarly Conversation

Before we introduce the chapters in this book, it is important to briefly set the scholarly scene. Our grounding objectives in the Court as Archive Project have been to interpret and clarify the institutional purpose and civic responsibilities of courts through their archival role; to consider explicitly, and for the first time in Australia, the unique role of the Federal Court as a site of production of significant national archives since its establishment in 1976, and to develop principles through empirical research to inform the administration of materials held by Australian superior courts of record as responsive civic institutions in 21st-century Australia. In designing a method to join and undertake these objectives, it was important to situate our objectives and institutional approach in relation to theoretical and empirical scholarship around archives and public law jurisprudence on superior courts.

The Archival Turn in Law

In the Court as Archive Project, we are joining the contemporary scholarly interest in, and interventions into, how archives are perceived and used.[5] The shared challenge in this diverse work is to make visible and scrutinise the 19th-century presumption that state archives exist to sustain and promulgate the nation and, in the process, to underwrite a particular account of history.[6] This redirection in archival thinking includes paying attention to materiality and material culture, including documentary theory and practices of documentation.[7] In settler colonial contexts like Australia, the scrutiny and rethinking of archives and documentation

---

5   See Chapters 1, 4 and 11, this volume. For leading examples across the scholarly and disciplinary spectrum, see Antoinette Burton (ed), *Archive Stories: Facts, Fictions, and the Writing of History* (Duke University Press, 2005); Ann Laura Stoler, *Along the Archival Grain: Epistemic Anxieties and Colonial Common Sense* (Princeton University Press, 2009); Jacques Derrida, *Archive Fever: A Freudian Impression* (University of Chicago Press, 1996); Carolyn Steedman, *Dust: The Archive and Cultural History* (Rutgers University Press, 2002); Matthew S Hull, *Government of Paper: The Materiality of Bureaucracy in Urban Pakistan* (University of California Press, 2012); Arlette Farge, *The Allure of the Archives* (Yale University Press, 2013); Francis X Blouin Jr and William G Rosenberg, *Processing The Past: Contesting Authority in History and The Archives* (Oxford University Press, 2011); Cornelia Vismann, *Files: Law and Media Technology* (Stanford University Press, 2008).
6   See, for example, Derrida, above n 5; Steedman, above n 5; Blouin Jr and Rosenberg, above n 5; Stoler, above n 5; and Chapter 4, this volume.
7   Vismann, above n 5; Annelise Riles, 'Anthropology, Human Rights, and Legal Knowledge: Culture in the Iron Cage' (2006) 108 *American Anthropologist* 991.

is also a matter of justice and politics: it is understood by Indigenous scholars, communities and institutions as an engagement in political relationships that have been driven by Indigenous peoples as an assertion of their sovereignty and a performance of their citizenship.[8]

In the time since we began our research, interest in archives and archival theory and its relationship with law and jurisprudence has grown.[9] In a critical legal context, it has been described as a 'counter-archival' practice, taking up a long-established tradition in historiography and directing it to law: reading legal texts against the grain; revealing lacunae, silences and omissions in the archive; or exposing layers of meaning in archival documents.[10] Alternatively, a close reading of transcripts of trials and court records may identify bias, discrimination or deference to flawed knowledge.[11] Other projects are creating and re-creating archives of law and of legal lives. This includes oral history projects enlarging the archive on women lawyers reflecting on their lives, their own sense of active citizenship and their contributions to the state.[12] In Australia, the National Library of Australia now houses over 50 full life oral histories of 'trailblazing women lawyers' who have practised in Australia and internationally,[13] with parallel projects in other countries.[14] It also includes rewriting conspicuous and established legal archives. In addition, feminist judgments projects have emerged in a number of common law jurisdictions to produce imagined judicial decisions that serve to correct the archive

---

8   For recent examples, see Tahu Kukatai and John Taylor (eds), *Indigenous Data Sovereignty*, CAEPR Research Monograph No 38, (ANU Press, 2016), doi.org/10.22459/CAEPR38.11.2016; Darren Jorgensen and Ian McLean (eds), *Indigenous Archives: the Making and Unmaking of Australian Art* (UWA Press, 2017); Kim Rubenstein, 'Power, Control and Citizenship: The Uluru Statement from the Heart As Active Citizenship' (Speech delivered at the Transnational, International and Comparative Law and Policy Network Biennial Interdiscplinary Conference, Bond University, 26 May 2017).

9   Renisa Mawani, 'Law's Archive' (2012) 8 *Annual Review of Law and Social Science* 337; Katherine Biber and Trish Luker (eds), *Evidence and the Archive: Ethics, Aesthetics and Emotion* (Routledge, 2017); Stewart Motha and Honni van Rijswijk (eds), *Law, Memory, Violence: Uncovering the Counter-Archive* (Routledge, 2016), doi.org/10.4324/9781315737157.

10   Motha and van Rijswijk, above n 9; Trish Luker, 'Animating the Archive: Artefacts of law', cited in Motha and van Rijswijk, above n 9.

11   Emma Cunliffe, *Murder, Medicine and Motherhood* (Hart Publishing, 2011).

12   See The Trailblazing Women and the Law Project (ARC Linkage LP120200367) <www.tbwl.esrc.unimelb.edu.au> and the online exhibition as one output of the project at <http://www.womenaustralia.info/lawyers/>.

13   See the full list at <http://www.womenaustralia.info/lawyers/browse_oralhistories.html>.

14   In the United States of America, the American Bar Association houses a Trailblazing Women Lawyers oral history collection at <www.americanbar.org/groups/senior_lawyers/women_trailblazers_project_listing/> and in Canada there are women lawyers oral histories in <https://www.osgoodesociety.ca/oral-history/>.

of common law jurisprudence.[15] Rather than engaging a critical outsider position, participants in these projects take on a performative 'drag' that serves to parody the judicial subject, while simultaneously correcting the archive of judicial decisions.

At the same time, legal historians are conducting projects where they interrogate the operation of legal authority and legal procedure by rethinking, recovering and reanimating a range of court archives.[16] Others, working as historians of jurisprudence, are attending to the writing of jurisprudence itself in official and unofficial forms, styles and genres to question the conduct of lawful relationships and the expectations of what an archive of and for law might look like, and for whom.[17] Further, and building on long-held traditions of empirical scholarship in court and public administration and legal ethnography, court records have become sites for analysis in different ways, with attention to documentary meaning-making practices,[18] as well as public law jurisprudence.[19]

As legal scholars with interests and training in other disciplines, we have been actively participating in these developments. However, it was clear to us that further work was necessary to consider the questions of courts' duties to the people they serve, through the question of how their records are preserved, curated or accessed. In particular, we recognised that it was necessary to connect the innovations in thinking about how scholars might address 'an archive' with long-standing legal principles about a superior court's role and function. For us, as a research team, it seemed clear that

---

15   Heather Douglas, Francesca Bartlett, Trish Luker and Rosemary Hunter (eds), *Australian Feminist Judgments: Righting and Rewriting Law* (Hart Publishing, 2015).
16   See, for example, Shaunnagh Dorsett, *Juridical Encounters: Maori and the Colonial Courts 1840–1852* (Auckland University Press, 2017); Mark Finnane, Andy Kaladelfos, Alana Piper, Yorick Smaal, Robyn Blewer and Lisa Durnian, *The Prosecution Project Database* (17 July 2016) <https://prosecutionproject.griffith.edu.au/prosecutions>; ANU College of Law, *Dr Heather Roberts receives DECRA for judicial research* (10 November 2017) <https://law.anu.edu.au/news-and-events/news/dr-heather-roberts-receives-decra-judicial-research>.
17   Ann Genovese and Shaun McVeigh, 'Nineteen Eighty Three: A Jurisographic Report on *Commonwealth v Tasmania*' (2015) 24(1) *Griffith Law Review* 68; Ann Genovese, Shaun McVeigh and Peter D Rush, 'Lives Lived with Law: An Introduction' (2016) 20 *Law Text Culture* 1; Ann Genovese, 'About Libraries: A Jurisographer's Notes on Lives Lived With Law' (2016) 20 *Law Text Culture* 33.
18   Bruno Latour, *The Making of Law: An Ethnography of the Conseil d'Etat* (Wiley, 2010); Vismann, above n 5.
19   Judith Resnik, Dennis E Curtis and Allison Tait, 'Constructing Courts: Architecture, the Ideology of Judging, and the Public Sphere', cited in Richard Sherwin and Anne Wagner (eds), *Law, Culture & Visual Studies* (Springer Publishing Company, 2013); Judith Bellis, 'Public Access to Court Records in Australia: An International Comparative Perspective and some Proposals for Reform' (2010) 19(4) *Journal of Judicial Administration* 197.

by returning to core questions of public law scholarship—namely, who is the court for, as much as what it must do—we would be able to begin to think about the court as an institution that records contemporary Australian life for the future.

Public Law and Courts of Record

Our questions circulated around superior courts of record because they have an institutional mandate to maintain a conclusive 'testimony of all that has taken place'.[20] As a matter of common and constitutional law, courts of record can unmake and redecide decisions that are otherwise determinative, and the 'record' of their own proceedings is limited by, and subject to, legal requirements.[21] Superior courts of record are guided by the civil law principle of 'open court', which encourages the public to witness the court's functions to promote the rule of law so that justice can be seen to be done. Federal superior courts of record are also subject to other constitutional imperatives, such as the principle of separation of powers. However, they must also respond to competing legal imperatives that arise because of the diverse accrued national jurisdictions, notably the right of individual litigants to privacy; the need to respect Indigenous control of cultural knowledge; the maintenance of legal professional privilege; and the protection of copyright. These matters of jurisdiction carry deeper public law issues underlying the institutional role of federal superior courts of record that are civic, as well as constitutional. When resolving disputes between parties (whether between individual citizens or between a citizen and the state), a federal superior court of record inevitably has an impact beyond those parties, through the democratic values it espouses and pronounces, the methods of administrative and judicial decision-making undertaken, as well as its engagement as one arm of government in the overall constitutional make-up of the state. The documents produced by and for federal superior courts of record as a result of litigation, which must be recorded, clearly have significance beyond the resolution of disputes. They are also rich records of public interest and importance about the relationship between the individual

---

20 Frederick Pollock and Frederic William Maitland, *The History of English Law Before the Time of Edward I* (Cambridge University Press, 1898), vol 1, 688.
21 Historically, only certain decision-making bodies create a 'record' for the purposes of judicial review. See *Craig v State of South Australia* (1995) 184 CLR 163; *Kirk v Industrial Court of New South Wales* (2010) 239 CLR 531; and *Automotive, Food Metals, Engineering, Printing and Kindred Industries Union v ALS Industrial Australia Pty Ltd* (2015) 234 FCR 305.

and the state that are not readily accessible elsewhere, as the 'archival turn' across scholarship in legal history and theory has demonstrated. However, through our experience as researchers, we were also aware that there is no comprehensive, national approach or principled framework to administer or recognise how the preservation of a court's documents and records may also act as an archive of Australian jurisprudence, of Australian citizenship and of Australian civic life.[22]

It was these issues and contradictions that we had to place centrally, rather than to the side, while considering appropriate methods for the project. For example, while the principle of open court is well established in Australia, there is no common law right of access to court records.[23] Significantly, court records are also exempt from the operation of the *Archives Act 1983* (Cth) (*'Archives Act'*), despite a recommendation to the contrary.[24] The complex, inconsistent and restrictive regime governing public access to court records across Australian jurisdictions has attracted concern, and different kinds of response, from public lawyers and scholars

---

22   Despite urgent and repeated calls for action (see, for example, Bellis, above n 19; Ernst Willheim, 'Are Our Courts Truly Open?' (2002) 13(3) *Public Law Review* 191; Ernst Willheim, 'Australian legal procedures and the protection of secret Aboriginal spiritual beliefs: a fundamental conflict' in Peter Cane, Carolyn Evans, and Zoe Robinson (eds), *Law and Religion in Theoretical and Historical Context* (Cambridge University Press, 2008), doi.org/10.1017/CBO9780511493843.010; Justine Twomey, 'Legal and practical considerations in managing access to materials held by NTRBs and Land Councils' (Speech delivered at the National Native Title Conference 2007, Cairns, 6–8 June 2007) <http://ntru.aiatsis.gov.au/collections/pdfs/AIATSIS%20Native%20Title%20Conference%20 Materials%20Access%20Policy%20J%20Twomey.pdf>), no comprehensive, national approach or principled framework for administering access to court records exists. Preliminary work towards a state access regime in Victoria was initiated in 2005 (County Court of Victoria, *Discussion Paper: Access to Court Records* (2005)), without large impact on public access rights. In NSW, the *Court Information Act 2010* (NSW) was passed in July 2010, but is still not in force, with acknowledgement by the relevant standing committee that the root of the delay lies in the unresolved 'contradiction in the act between open information and privacy' (Richard Coleman, quoted in Nicola Shaver, 'How privacy hobbles push for open justice', *The Australian* (online) 3 June 2011 <https://www.theaustralian.com.au/business/legal-affairs/how-privacy-hobbles-push-for-open-justice/news-story/fe622d88862f6cd810f6f0512a8ff940?sv=7cb3819c07653fff99a97c9ca992109d>). At the same time, no specific consideration has been given to the structural or practical implications of the mounting judicial records of Indigenous knowledge on file. As Willheim points out, Australian law has 'failed to resolve a fundamental conflict between, on the one hand basic common law values including openness and transparency in public administration ... and on the other hand, Aboriginal religious value, in particular, the secret nature of much Aboriginal religious belief'. This research will assist in developing that principled framework for federal SCORs and will also be of value to broad conceptual and practical application in other jurisdictions.
23   *Public Service Board (NSW) v Osmond* (1986) 159 CLR 656.
24   A recent discussion of the development of the *Archives Act* and which documents would be exempt can be seen in the judgment of Griffith J in *Hocking v Director-General of National Archives of Australia* [2018] FCA 340, [29]–[36] in the context of assessing access to certain documents of the office of the Governor-General.

of court administration,[25] the judiciary,[26] government[27] and the media.[28] In general, these responses argue that without the ability to meaningfully witness the judicial process, the operation of open justice—famously called the 'hallmark of the common law system'[29]—is significantly curtailed, and the institutional legitimacy[30] and public confidence[31] held in these superior courts is compromised. The absence of public access to the records of 'public interest claims' under adjudication[32] also has detrimental consequences for understanding the court's role in promoting the rule of law and judicial process, as well as societal norms and behavioural standards.

There are also procedural problems, perhaps less publicly debated, that complicate these questions. Court procedures designed to enhance the efficiency of judicial administration now commonly require evidence in chief by way of affidavit. Written submissions are filed without oral explanation and pleadings are not ordinarily read in full.[33] Even meaningful public access to oral evidence is frequently now sought via the written record as few people now attend judicial proceedings,[34] and the severe truncation of spoken evidence has made 'the adjudicative process less and less comprehensible to the person in the public gallery'.[35] Similarly, substantive media and academic access has been curtailed, further limiting public access to information about courts' daily business. Therefore, the complexity for courts to uphold their constitutional duties and, at the same time, recognise the function the records play for the public (historical or otherwise) speaks to profound issues underpinning civics and citizenship

---

25 Bellis, above n 19; Willheim (2002), above n 22; Sharon Rodrick, 'Open Justice, the Media and Avenues of Access to Documents on the Court Record' [2006] *University of New South Wales Law Journal* 40.
26 *McCabe v British American Tobacco Australia Services Limited* [2002] VSC 150.
27 Australian Law Reform Commission, *Australia's Federal Record: A Review of Archives Act 1983*, Report No 85 (1998); Australian Law Reform Commission, *For Your Information: Australian Privacy Law and Practice*, Report No 108 (2008); New South Wales Attorney-General's Department, *Review of the Policy of Access to Court Information*, Discussion Paper (2006).
28 Chris McLeod, 'Reporting the courts' (2006) 15(2) *Australian Press Council News* 10.
29 *Grollo v Palmer* (1995) 184 CLR 348.
30 JJ Spigelman, 'Seen to be Done: The Principle of Open Justice' (2000) 74 *Australian Law Journal* 290.
31 Beverley McLachlin, 'Courts, Transparency and Public Confidence—To the Better Administration of Justice' (2003) 8(1) *Deakin Law Review* 1.
32 See, for example, *Habib v Commonwealth of Australia (No 2)* (2009) 175 FCR 350.
33 Willheim (2002), above n 22.
34 Rodrick, above n 25, 90.
35 *McCabe* [2002] VSC 150, [19].

INTRODUCTION

in our own time. As civil law scholar Hazel Genn has explained, 'for civil justice to perform its public role—to cast its shadow—adjudication and public promulgation of decisions are critical'.[36]

An Institutional, Interdisciplinary Method

In addressing these problems, our project placed at the centre of its inquiry the unique institutional role of the Federal Court of Australia and how it is distinct from other bodies that produce and curate comparable records of rich national significance. We were, in short, interested in the Federal Court as a legal institution: how it developed (as a matter of jurisprudence and history) and how it now operates and exists in relationship not only with the people it serves, but also with other institutions that share responsibilities for civic organisation and experience in Australia, and over time. This institutional approach had a unique starting point. As an interdisciplinary team, with expertise in citizenship and public law doctrine and jurisprudence (Kim Rubenstein); empirical court-based and historical archival research (Ann Genovese); and evidence law and documentary theory (Trish Luker), it seemed to us that to consider the role and duties of 'a court as archive' necessitated scrutiny of the Federal Court's own administrative practices, rather than the rich seam of litigation materials the court also holds that are more usually the subject of scholarly and public inquiry.

Our central contention has been that through viewing the operational decisions taken by the court, over time, it is possible to learn a great deal more about its past, present and future priorities. These priorities pertain to file management and record-keeping practices, as well as how the court has imagined itself and its relationship to the public, including how it grapples with the challenges of a what 'an archive' currently signifies in a settler colony like Australia.

To do this, we examined internal operational documents of the court housed at its registries, and documents about the court's relationship with other branches of government and agencies housed at the National Archives of Australia (NAA). We did this to understand, and be able to tell a story about, how administrative decisions have been taken over time about what materials should be retained, how they are stored, how they

---

36   Hazel Genn, *Judging Civil Justice* (Cambridge University Press, 2010) 21.

are organised and classified, and whether, how and by whom they can or should now be made accessible to broader society. We report on some of our findings in our respective chapters in this collection.

In undertaking this empirical archival work, there was a puzzle to piece together about which internal (and litigation) records are not currently available, to ask where they are held and why, and whether they have been subject to archival practices. We were reminded why scholars need more than official records to analyse and tell stories about their experience of institutions. In the case of the Federal Court of Australia, there are very few biographies, memoirs, public opinion pieces, scholarly articles or contemporary histories yet written that address the court as a national institution (in the ways that our project seeks to do) that we could draw on and that might help us contextualise these documentary traces and omissions. In addition, although there are farewell speeches by judges in open access, and also interviews undertaken with judges on the occasion of their retirement, for the most part, these form part of the court's own internal archive and are not available for public disclosure.[37] Further, and surprisingly for an institution that is only 40 years old, there are no records, beyond the files, of how court administrators or officers understood and experienced their duties, and perceived the court's responsibilities: whether to the immediate question of our research (record management) or to what the records signified and carried, and for whom. What we noticed in undertaking our own archival research was an absence of oral histories about the Federal Court as an institution that mediates the relations between Australian people and their law. This has meant that to undertake our project aims adequately, we had to create sources of our own. We undertook oral histories with court officers rather than judges for the simple reason that these lives lived with law are generally under-represented in scholarly conceptualisations of court histories, or in any archive broadly conceived.[38] In conducting these interviews, we perceived

---

37 The exceptions to this are Michael Black, 'The Federal Court of Australia: The First 30 Years—A Survey on the Occasion of Two Anniversaries' (2007) 31(3) *Melbourne University Law Review* 1017; and Susan Kenny, 'Federal Courts and Australian National Identity' (2015) 38(3) *Melbourne University Law Review* 996.

38 These interviews are unique in an Australian setting. While county and state courts in the United States appear to publish recorded interviews with court officers on a range of issues, it is not a practice common to Australian courts. The Federal Court has started to undertake oral histories with some of its retiring judges; these are on file with the court, but are not open to the public at this time. Some of the women who have been judges in the Federal Court of Australia have been interviewed in another ARC project for the National Library of Australia's oral history collection. See Kim Rubenstein, *Australian Women Lawyers as Active Citizens* (November 2016) <http://www.womenaustralia.info/lawyers>.

them clearly as oral histories, where our interview subjects' life experience and professional experience could be considered in relationship to each other and, once recorded, could become a 'significant part of our collective public memory'.[39] The interviews we conducted have been included in this collection.

The Court as Archive Collection

In February 2016, we convened the Court as Archive Symposium to provide an opportunity to report on our research findings up to that point and to engage in roundtable discussions with scholars, archivists, judges and administrators of courts and tribunals who share intellectual and administrative concerns in their own work and practices.[40] Participants were invited because of their important contributions to the field. These included senior members of the judiciary, court and public administration from Australia and Canada: the Hon Michael Black AC QC, former Chief Justice of the Federal Court of Australia; Warwick Soden OAM, Principal Registrar and Chief Executive Officer, Federal Court of Australia; Ian Irving, then Native Title Registrar, Federal Court of Australia; Barbara Kincaid, General Counsel, Supreme Court of Canada; and Ernst Willheim, Visiting Fellow at ANU, who had headed several policy and professional divisions in the Australian Attorney-General's Department. The concerns and perspectives of key archival and research institutions were addressed by Anne Lyons, Assistant Director-General, NAA; Dr Pamela McGrath, then Research Director, National Native Title Tribunal; Grace Koch, previous Director of Research, Australian Institute of Aboriginal and Torres Strait Islander Studies; and Mr Michael Piggott, a former Senior Archivist at the NAA with extensive experience in major archives and library institutions. Scholarly contributors joined us from the fields of law, jurisprudence, archival theory and history, and are represented by their chapters in this collection and discussed in more detail below. On the day, we were also joined by Katherine Biber (Law, University of Technology Sydney), Emma Cunliffe (Law, University of

---

39   Kim Rubenstein, '"Alive in the Telling": Trailblazing Women Lawyers' Lives, Lived with Law' (2016) 20 *Law Text Culture* 66, 70.
40   The Court as Archive Symposium, ANU College of Law, The Australian National University, 17 February 2016.

British Columbia) and Shaun McVeigh (Melbourne Law School), whose presentations were not developed for this collection, but whose work has been a valuable input to our thinking.[41]

The symposium was closely convened to provide productive engagement with the themes of the Court as Archive Project. We asked participants to consider specific questions in relation to three key areas around which the symposium was structured, as a way of focusing attention on the particular and unique issues relevant to our research. These themes were intended to draw together consideration of diverse institutional, legal and scholarly responsibilities around how courts and their records can also be understood as archives of national, and transnational, significance. The collection draws its arrangement from these themes, discussed below.

Public Law and Citizenship

The collection opens with the theme of public law and citizenship, linking court records to public law principles. This theme raises questions about the role of Chapter III courts and whether this can be extended to deepen our understanding of their function as guardians and producers of the civic experience, as well as the expectations of the Australian litigants who come before them. In 'Court Records, Archives and Citizenship', Kim Rubenstein (with Andrew Henderson) illustrates the importance of the Federal Court's records as an archival resource by exploring its role within a broader context where it contributes to understandings of citizenship. As a superior court of record, the Federal Court performs a fundamentally important role within Australia's democratic system. It has served as a site for the disputation, negotiation and resolution of issues important to Australian society. It does so in the context of a constitutional system affirming the principle of the separation of powers and the rule of law as a means of preserving and enforcing the rights of individuals and navigating the boundaries of the powers of the state. In that context, its records, gathered both through the internal workings of the court and through the cases that come before it, contain a narrative shaping our contemporary understanding of the rights of the individual and the role of the state. It is this relationship that is central to a conception of Australian citizenship. Citizenship in Australia, as described by Kim Rubenstein

---

41 Other participants who did not present papers on the day include Hollie Kerwin (who did develop a paper subsequently for this collection) and James Stellios, an expert on Chapter III of the *Australian Constitution*.

through her broader scholarship,[42] and in this chapter, represents an understanding of the changing balance between the power of the state (including its responsibilities and duties to its citizenry) and the citizen's rights in relation to the state. Given that the Federal Court hears matters that reflect on and are central to that relationship, through contestation around federal laws that regulate and determine that relationship, the importance of its records in that narrative is key. Yet the preservation of and access to the Federal Court's records continue to be seen through the lens of traditional understandings of the management of litigation.

The ability of individuals to access records of court proceedings is the subject of Ernst Willheim's contribution, 'Aspects of Citizen Access to Court Archives'. Willheim, a former senior lawyer in the Australian Attorney-General's Department, has unique legal and administrative insight into the consideration of court records as they exist in relationship to the principles of the separation of powers and open justice. In this chapter, he argues that the insistence on preventing access to records of proceedings is at odds both with the appearance of judicial independence and the implied freedom of political communication. In doing so, he provides a number of examples where maladministration in government may be concealed by the rigid application of existing controls of access to affidavit evidence and submissions.

In 'When the Carnival is Over: The Case for Reform of Access to Royal Commission Records', public lawyers Hollie Kerwin and Maya Narayan investigate the unique role and status of royal commissions as archives. As executive bodies, royal commissions may be characterised as public record-keeping institutions. However, their central function of receiving evidence, often coerced, raises important questions about the appropriateness of public access to their records, notwithstanding their distinctive characterisation as public events intended to facilitate truth-telling. Kerwin and Narayan argue that considering the royal commission as an archive raises risks, opportunities and imperatives for continued remembrance of significant public issues, critical engagement with state archives, as well as unpacking the royal commission as an instrument of government. The authors propose a *sui generis* regime for the management of and access to royal commission records involving a cooperative scheme between the Commonwealth and the states, supported by

---

42   See Kim Rubenstein, *Australian Citizenship Law* (Thomson Reuters, 2nd ed, 2017).

referrals of legislative power from the states. They remind and encourage policymakers to transcend the complex institutional identity of the royal commission, rather than accepting it as an organising principle to provide greater certainty around the management of archival material, and to set a benchmark for community expectations of records management during, and after, the life of a royal commission.

Histories and Jurisprudence of Australia

The second section of the book turns attention to the limits and possibilities of courts as archives from the vantage point of scholarly practice and production. Here, Ann Genovese, Susan Priest and Narrelle Morris, all Australian historians who are also legal scholars, consider what it means to publicise and attend to the records of courts, to write about how those records tell stories about the relationships between Australians and their law. They each consider distinct archives and institutions and the vulnerabilities of these institutions' records and materials. Reading their papers together enables consideration of broader questions about the conduct and establishment of legal institutions and jurisdictions in an under-theorised and under-researched aspect of the 20th century in Australia. The section also offers insight into how Australian historians of jurisprudence and law reflect on questions of temporality, method and duty in their own archival and narrative practices, often in response to the nature of materials preserved and available to tell the story.

In 'A Matter of Records: The Federal Court, The National Archives and "The National Estate" in the 1970s', Ann Genovese uses materials drawn from the Court as Archive Project to give a short history of the institutional provenance of the Federal Court, the NAA and their relationship to each other. Despite the Federal Court being officially exempt from the *Archives Act*, which established the NAA, both were conceived as consciously modern 'Australian' institutions and shared a material concern with records that drew them into association. In telling this story, Genovese offers one of the only histories of the Federal Court's establishment, written from archives and by a historian. In doing so, she also offers a side note about method and practice. She demonstrates and exemplifies that the records necessary to write modern histories of jurisprudence are precarious, contingent and require our attention, offering a particular view of writing histories. Genovese contends that fragmentation in the way the documents are kept itself requires careful documentation and opens the historiographical conversation about the forms and nature of sources and records adequate to represent our past for the present.

Susan Priest locates her narrative and methodological inquiries in the High Court of Australia in its earliest years. In 'Framing the Archives as Evidence: A Study of Correspondence Documenting the Place of Australia's Original High Court in a New Commonwealth Polity', Priest examines the archives of written communications that lead the original justices of the High Court, Chief Justice Samuel Griffith and Justices Edmund Barton and Richard O'Connor, in May 1905, to adjourn proceedings and famously 'go on strike'. She examines the official correspondence—namely, formal court and departmental letters—as well as the personal correspondence of the court at the time. For Priest, the personal nature of correspondence in the High Court's archival collection is a rich source of detailed information not only about historical events, but also about the individuals involved. Alongside the historical narrative, Priest is also offering a careful consideration of her methods, and her relationship as a historian to the materiality of the available archive, through the questions that arise when 'reading other people's mail'.

The 'national interest' has been a constant factor and idea in the state's creation and preservation of records, as well as how it controls those same records to guard the 'security' of its citizens.[43] In 'Accessing the Archives of the Australian War Crimes Trials after World War II', Narrelle Morris explores the creation and management of the extensive records of Australian war crimes trials conducted after World War II. Through short vignettes that describe the shifting relationships between Australia and Japan, as much as those between the institutions of the Australian Government, Morris demonstrates that despite the 'public' nature of Australian war crimes proceedings, they were later classified as confidential national records (not court records), and of such international political consequence that they had to be 'zealously protected' until our own times. In exploring the histories of archival access and international relationships, Morris, like Genovese and Priest, also offers insights into her own duties and practices as a historian. She shows how 'protectionism as

---

43 The control of access to those records is central to the recent Federal Court decision of *Hocking* [2018] FCA 340 in assessing the request for early access to the letters between the Governor-General, Sir John Kerr and the Queen around the dismissal by the Governor-General of the Prime Minister, Gough Whitlam.

confidentiality' operated to tell a history running parallel to the expected narrative of the trials themselves. Morris demonstrates how this has had 'an indelible effect on knowledge', and it is only now that we can see in this tale of archival refusal how Australia may still have some way to go in coming to terms with what it means to recognise that a complex national past, in which government is an actor, 'should be everyone's property', as Morris quotes former Attorney-General Kep Enderby from 1975.

Administration of Legal Records: Duties and Recommendations

In the final section of the book, we return to our project's research objectives. We do so by drawing into the discussion the practices of archival use and production, public law and public value and meaning, with accounts of how legal records are administered. Central to this section is the description of, and commentary on, the problems of modern legal institutions in coming to terms with their public role as 'an archive'. As a whole, this section asks the questions: How might we reconcile, as a matter of policy, practice and theory, the current tensions and future problems that occur in relation to legal records as archival material, especially in settler colonial states? And, can we think between different public institutions, and in different jurisdictions, to address these questions responsively? The chapters take two different approaches to address these questions. The first is directly institutional: the oral history interviews we conducted as part of our research, including an interview with Warwick Soden, the current, and only the second, CEO (previously Principal Registrar) of the Federal Court of Australia; and a joint interview with Louise Anderson (the first) and Ian Irving (the second) Native Title Registrars at the Federal Court. We chose to interview Ian and Louise together to draw out the collaborative role they played in centring the archival responsibility for the court in the late 1990s, and also to examine their shared (but different) experiences in undertaking these roles. Read together, the interviews demonstrate the centrality of procedural and institutional reforms at the Federal Court in its recent history. These reforms relate to practice directions and trial management as much as the reconsideration of the formal agreements between agencies regarding custodianship and preservation of court records. The interviews also clearly give an account of how a court record is not only legally determined, but also creates and maintains the conduct of law that lies beneath each matter the court must determine. In addition, the interviews also contribute to the history of the Federal Court more generally, giving insight into topics such as the transition to administrative independence from the executive arm of government, and the introduction of a native title jurisdiction. In different ways, we see what the legal professional conduct of an official life looks like, and the differences in time, location and gender in how those roles have been created and executed.

Therefore, court archives, in any form, are clearly not an impersonal or dehumanised collection of data but tell real stories about real people. Acknowledgement of what legal records carry, particularly in native title matters, has implications for litigants. However, as noted in the interview with Louise Anderson and Ian Irving, in a different way, it also has particular implications for those court officials charged with responsibility to institutionally care for the records. In 'Providing Public Access to Native Title Records: Balancing the Risks Against the Benefits', Pamela McGrath asks similar questions from her experience as an anthropologist who has worked in the field alongside Indigenous claimants and in her role as Research Director at the Native Title Tribunal. McGrath discusses some of the ethical concerns associated with the extensive archive of litigation materials and research reports produced for native title determinations in Australia. She argues that the potential significance and value of these collections far exceeds their original function as records of litigation, mediation and evidence gathering. Although there are some compelling reasons for making these records publicly available, there are many challenges around doing so. The chapter summarises, describes and complicates these from the perspective of a tribunal (rather than a court). McGrath argues that a seemingly incommensurable array of legal, cultural and ethical obligations around privacy and cultural authority are complicated by an overarching imperative to provide transparent justice. However, she concludes that the development of any future access policy for the Native Title Tribunal must recognise that 'a fundamental intention of the [*Native Title Act 1993* (Cth)] is to provide for the advancement and protection of Aboriginal and Torres Strait Islander peoples, and to progress the process of reconciliation among all Australians'. As such, McGrath reminds, and we agree, that it is 'incumbent on those of us who are responsible for developing policy to put those interests and relationships at the centre of all decisions about the fate of native title records'.

In 'Archiving Revolution: Historical Records Management in the Massachusetts Courts', Andrew Henderson provides a comparative assessment of the treatment of court records as valuable social and cultural records of the pre- and post-revolutionary United States by superior courts in Massachusetts. Massachusetts' superior courts hold colonial records of civil and criminal proceedings as far back as the 17th century. The sheer volume of paper records, and the haphazard manner in which they had been collected and preserved, meant that Massachusetts courts were confronted with a challenging question about the application of resources for ongoing preservation and retention. Through a careful process of inspection and sampling, Massachusetts superior courts have sought to preserve a representative sample of almost 300 years of records. Although the Federal Court does not face the same substantial volume of materials, the experience of the Massachusetts courts illuminates some important considerations when determining a policy for the management of nationally significant records.

In 'Sentencing Acts: Appraisal of Court Records in Canada and Australia', Trish Luker considers the role of courts as archives through an examination of approaches to appraisal and disposal of court records. Identifying a number of disputes over the preservation and destruction of records from legal inquiries and court processes from the Australian and Canadian contexts, she argues that these disputes highlight questions about responsibilities in relation to preservation, curation, storage and access to records. While legal principles and obligations are necessary and important requirements for courts' approaches to decisions about appraisal and disposal of records, Luker argues that courts can benefit from approaches reflected in contemporary archival theory, which recognises appraisal choices as political and ethical.

Finally, we conclude the book with a memorandum written for the Federal Court, with advice on a process for the selection of significant matters for its records authority regarding its archival responsibilities. The advice is the culmination of our empirical work and thinking on the basis of the research conducted for the project. We include it in the collection, as a postscript, and in its form as a memorandum, as an official response from us as academic researchers to those charged with the responsibilities of administration of the significant files of the Federal Court into the future.

INTRODUCTION

The Court as Archive: Future Directions

As we finalise this book for publication, it is remarkable to reflect on the 11 years that have passed since the CIPL symposium that ignited the project. That decade represents significant developments in scholarship around 'the archive', which we have been able to engage with, contribute to and draw upon to extend and grapple with our central research questions. Indeed, as we review the final proofs, judicial attention to the interpretation of the *Archives Act* itself has been of public interest through Jenny Hocking's application to the Federal Court to review the decision of the NAA to refuse early access to what has been described as the 'palace letters'.[44] Throughout this project, with the benefit of the ARC grant, we have conducted extensive research with the support of our capable research assistants throughout the process, Peter Moore and Andrew Henderson. We have created an extensive database that has informed our approach and we have developed a protocol for the Federal Court's consideration. This protocol reflects a methodology that recognises the relationship between records; the archive and the public it reflects; and the citizenry who benefit from understanding what it represents, both individually and institutionally, to the Australian community.

The research conducted for the Court as Archive Project has enabled us to interpret and clarify the institutional purpose and civic responsibilities of Australian superior courts of record through an analysis of their archival role. Therefore, this collection reflects and responds to our interest in the citizenship principles informing Australia's evolution as a democratic society through the empirically based qualitative analysis of the Federal Court's own archival practices. It has enabled us to engage with the question of how superior courts of record can address the demands of the Australian people who come before it.

In that sense, this book represents a significant moment, for it is the first time since its establishment in 1976 that the unique role of the Federal Court has been chosen for analysis as a site of production of significant national archives. In our view, this is the first step towards producing an institutional history of the Federal Court, which we believe needs further analysis to demonstrate how its constitutional role, and the way this

---

44   See *Hocking* [2018] FCA 340; and Michaela Whitbourn, 'Federal Court deals blow to early release of Palace Papers' *Sydney Morning Herald* (online), 16 March 2018 <https://www.smh.com.au/politics/federal/federal-court-deals-blow-to-early-release-of-palace-papers-20180316-p4z4r3.html>.

has been interpreted by those responsible for its operations, reveals and complicates our thinking about the state and its relationship and duties to citizens.

Indeed, the content in our extensive database created from this research will be a rich resource on which to draw to inform future oral histories that should be undertaken, together with further research on the significance of Federal Court as an institution. It is research that will benefit from bringing multiple perspectives to bear on important civic projects that help Australia identify and come to terms with its own citizenship—its own institutional story, as a nation, grappling with its past, enlivened in doing so by focusing on the meanings attributed to, and use of, the court as an archive.

In conclusion, it is important to consider that as the papers for this book were being finalised and brought to completion in 2017, the Federal Court itself marked its 40th anniversary. This is a telling reminder that the questions we collectively engaged with in *The Court as Archive* are ongoing. Indeed, the issues relevant to our present inquiries will themselves become of archival value. The material gathered in the Court as Archive Project, and the conversations with collaborators represented in this book, will also enable future researchers to assess and analyse how, from 2008 to 2019, we conceived of our own roles as active research citizens, committed to understanding the relationships between people and their institutions, in the past, present and for the future.

Part 1—Public Law and Citizenship

1

Court Records, Archives and Citizenship

Kim Rubenstein and Andrew Henderson

Introduction

The Federal Court of Australia performs a fundamentally important role within Australia's democratic system. Since its commencement in 1977, it has served as a site for the disputation, negotiation and resolution of issues centrally important to Australian society. It does so in the context of a constitutional system affirming the separation of powers and the rule of law, as well as providing individuals an avenue to preserve and enforce their rights, and navigate the boundaries of the powers of the state. As a 'court of record', the records of its proceedings constitute a permanent and incontrovertible record of those events. In that context, its records, gathered both through the internal workings of the court and through the cases that come before it, contain a narrative shaping our contemporary understanding of the rights of the individual and the role of the state. In many ways, this is a record of the evolution of Australian citizenship.

Although originally invested with a similar jurisdiction to the High Court,[1] over those 40 years, the Federal Court has experienced successive reforms to its jurisdiction in a diverse array of legal frameworks, including

---

1 *Judiciary Act 1903* (Cth) s 39B.

the review of government action;[2] access to government information;[3] the regulation of corporations;[4] the control of personal information;[5] Indigenous ownership of land;[6] migration;[7] and national security.[8] This has seen the Federal Court accumulate a significant jurisdiction concerning important aspects of those disputations, negotiations and resolutions of issues central to the evolution of the Australian community.

However, despite those transformations in the Federal Court itself and the important position it holds in our democratic system, accessing its records remains bound by traditional ideas of court files. Unlike bureaucratic and administrative records of government, access to which has been uniformly administered by the National Archives of Australia (NAA) under the *Archives Act 1983* (Cth) ('*Archives Act*'), the application of the doctrine of separation of powers embodied within the *Australian Constitution* has meant that the management of Commonwealth courts' records of proceedings are administered by the courts themselves.[9] Therefore, access to records of proceedings is inconsistent between the executive and legislative arms of government on the one hand, and the judiciary on the other.

Current access arrangements for the public, at least for court records over 20 years old, are also somewhat inconsistent. Although records of proceedings are not subject to the *Archives Act*,[10] it does not mean that some of the materials that might currently be unavailable from the Federal Court are in fact unavailable from NAA. Within the records held by NAA exists agencies' own records of litigation, including affidavits, copies of

---

2   *Administrative Decisions (Judicial Review) Act 1977* (Cth) ('*Administrative Decisions (Judicial Review) Act*').
3   *Freedom of Information Act 1982* (Cth).
4   Michael Whincop, 'The National Scheme for Corporations and the Referral of Powers: A Sceptical View' (2001) 12(4) *Public Law Review* 263; Cheryl Saunders, 'A New Direction for Intergovernmental Arrangements' (2001) 12(1) *Public Law Review* 274.
5   *Privacy Act 1988* (Cth).
6   *Native Title Act 1993* (Cth) ('*Native Title Act*').
7   Sigrid Baringhorst, 'Policies of Backlash: Recent Shifts in Australian Migration Policy' (2004) 6(2) *Journal of Comparative Policy Analysis: Research and Practice* 131.
8   George Williams, 'A Decade of Australian anti-Terror Laws' (2011) 35 *Melbourne University Law Review* 1136; Paul Fairall and Wendy Lacey, 'Preventative Detention and Control Orders under Federal Law: The Case for a Bill of Rights' (2007) 31 *Melbourne University Law Review* 1072.
9   *Archives Act* s 19.
10 Ibid.

exhibits and submissions that would be unavailable from the Federal Court.[11] Nevertheless, this material is presumptively publicly available under the *Archives Act*. The reason for the inconsistency is not clear.

This inconsistency sits uncomfortably with ideas about open justice and does not sufficiently take into account the Federal Court's role in Australia's democratic framework beyond its role in determining disputes between the parties before it. The current approach of the Federal Court to its records, to its 'archive', we argue, represents and perpetuates the position of citizens as unequal 'subjects' and limits access to this rich and unique set of materials. It also limits society's capacity to better describe and understand its own history of how citizenship has been shaped in Australia, both broadly and through the Federal Court's work.

The Federal Court and Australian Citizenship

As Justice Susan Kenny explains,[12] the origins of the Federal Court are often identified in the proceedings of the Australian Legal Convention in 1963. In a paper to the convention, Maurice Byers and Paul Toose argued for the creation of a new 'federal court'. The new court would be inferior to the High Court of Australia but vested with jurisdiction to hear and determine matters both in its original and appellate jurisdiction arising under Commonwealth law.[13] In the convention proceedings that followed, the Commonwealth Solicitor-General announced that the Attorney-General, Garfield Barwick, had been given 'authority [by Cabinet] to design a new federal court'.[14] However, as research conducted by the Court as Archive Project demonstrates, the convention was neither the first nor the last word on the new court. The project's research also further reveals and affirms Justice Kenny's observations on the development of an 'Australian national identity' as a driver for the creation of the Federal Court.

---

11 See, for example, the records of proceedings in *Law v Repatriation Commission* (1980) 29 ALR 64 and *Repatriation Commission v Law* (1980) 31 ALR 140 contained in National Archives of Australia (NAA): A1209, 1980/558 PART 1 and NAA: A12930, 639.
12 Susan Kenny, 'Federal Courts and Australian National Identity' (2015) 38(3) *Melbourne University Law Review* 996; see also Michael Black, 'The Federal Court of Australia: The First 30 Years—A Survey on the Occasion of Two Anniversaries' (2007) 31 *Melbourne University Law Review* 1017.
13 Maurice Byers and Paul Toose, 'The Necessity for a New Federal Court (A Survey of the Federal Court System in Australia)' (1963) 36 *Australian Law Journal* 308.
14 Ibid 325.

Moreover, as Ann Genovese notes in her chapter in this collection, the first references to a new federal court appeared in 1959 in parliamentary debate on the territories and family law. Barwick had first proposed the establishment of a 'new federal court' to Cabinet in 1962, two months before the convention, noting that it was something that he had been working on 'for some time'.[15] Although the Solicitor-General's statement to the convention was expressed in unconditional terms, the Prime Minister's own department and the Cabinet were less enthusiastic. The breadth of the new court's role led the Prime Minister's Department to note on the submission that it went 'too far, too soon' and instead recommended examination by a committee.[16] Barwick's Cabinet colleagues 'noted' (rather than agreed to) the submission and authorised the Attorney-General to prepare draft legislation on conditions, including that all Ministers reserved 'all rights to argue for *or against* the proposal' (emphasis added).[17]

Despite the laudatory announcement of the creation of a new court, at least within legal circles, the progress developing legislation to establish the new court following its first appearance in Cabinet was fitful. The proposal was prone to ongoing revision, particularly around the establishment of a 'big court' (superseding other Commonwealth courts and sitting continuously in capital cities) or a 'small court' (a 'peripatetic' court with a much smaller jurisdiction)[18] and competing priorities.[19] With successive general elections, responsibility for advancing the proposal also transferred between five Attorneys-General and a series of public servants, some of whom pressed enthusiastically for the creation of a new court,[20]

---

15   The Federal Judicature—Proposed New Court—Submission 461, Minute 581, NAA: A5819, VOLUME 12/AGENDUM 461. Interestingly, Byers and Toose, who would subsequently advocate for the new court at the Convention that followed, appear to have provided advice to Barwick in preparing his Cabinet Submission; see NAA: A432, 1961/2132 Part 1.
16   NAA: A5619, C430.
17   NAA: A5819, VOLUME 12/AGENDUM 461. Barwick appears to have argued later that he had never agreed to those conditions (see NAA: A4940, C3706). In an article published after the Cabinet decision in the *Federal Law Review*, Barwick maintained that the new court should assume responsibility for industrial relations and bankruptcy, contrary to Cabinet's 'authority'; see Garfield Barwick, 'The Australian Judicial System: The Proposed New Federal Superior Court' (1964) 1(1) *Federal Law Review* 1. Barwick's interpretation of the Cabinet decision might also explain the question mark in the margin of a departmental memorandum to the Attorney-General repeating the condition (see HT Bennett, 'Federal Superior Court: General Observations', NAA: A432, 1961/2132 Part 1).
18   For a discussion of the comparative elements of a 'big court' and a 'small court' model, see Bennett, above n 17 and Barwick, above n 17.
19   See, for example, Commonwealth, *Parliamentary Debates*, House of Representatives, 29 October 1964, 2642 (William Snedden, Attorney-General) and 'Extract from Minutes of Meeting of Executive of the Law Council of Australia, Canberra, March 1965', NAA: A432, 1961/2132 Part 1.
20   See, for example, Letter from Attorney-General to Minister for Housing, Health and Immigration, 2 January 1969, NAA: A432; 1961/2132 Part 8.

while others recommended its abandonment.[21] The withdrawal of support for a new court by its original architect, Garfield Barwick, now Chief Justice of the High Court, also hung heavily over the proposal's success.[22]

However, these skirmishes over the form of the new court, and the on-and-off nature of its development, conceal the development of the consistent line of argument running through all discussions about the motivations for its establishment: the development of a more coherent body of 'Australian' (rather than state-based) jurisprudence driven by the formation of a national identity. For example, in their presentation to the convention, Byers and Toose noted that:

> There is no longer a strong State sentiment amongst members of the public. Two World Wars, the financial crisis of the depression, uniform tax and Australia becoming a fully independent nation with its own ambassadors &c [sic] and a member of the United Nations have all helped to make citizens regard themselves as Australians rather than as belonging to any particular State.[23]

Barwick was more prosaic but nevertheless clear in his argument for a new court to administer the 'distinctive and separate character' of Commonwealth law. He also saw the new court's role as indirectly developing an Australian jurisprudence by taking on part of the workload of the High Court, which then would be able to 'concentrate on, and adequately perform, [its] primary responsibilities as interpreter of the *Constitution* and ultimate national court of appeal'.[24] A similar argument was made by then Solicitor-General Anthony Mason in his briefing to Attorney-General Nigel Bowen some three years later[25] and, ultimately, by Attorney-General Ellicott in his submission to Cabinet[26] and the House[27] on the eventual introduction of what would become the *Federal Court Act 1976* (Cth) ('*Federal Court Act*').

---

21 'The Federal Judicature: Proposed Commonwealth Superior Court', Submission no. 366, NAA: A5869, 366.
22 References to the withdrawal of Barwick's support for a new court is recorded at various points throughout archived materials and eventually makes its way to Cabinet (see, for example, ibid and the collected materials in NAA: A432, 1961/2132 Part 9). However, the authors were never able to find a copy of the letter itself.
23 Byers and Toose, above n 13, 313.
24 Barwick, above n 17, 9.
25 See, for example, Anthony Mason, 'A New Federal Court', 10 January 1967, NAA: A432, 1961/2132 Part 5.
26 'Federal Causes and Appeals Court: Transfer of High Court Jurisdiction to State Courts', Submission no 303, NAA: A10756, LC445 PART 1.
27 Commonwealth, *Parliamentary Debates*, House of Representatives, 21 October 1976, 2213 (Robert Ellicott, Attorney-General).

Evolution of Australian Citizenship

The description above reminds us that the Federal Court, in fulfilling its constitutional role, was intended to play a significant part in implementing basic concepts of national identity and citizenship in a democratic society. Moreover, the Federal Court is one of the democratic theatres in which the individual engages, disputes and negotiates with the executive arm of government, often referred to as the state.

Thinking in these terms takes us back to the core concept of the 'rule of law' in a democratic society—that those who exercise power on behalf of the state are governed by the rule of law in the same way that the individual is bound by law.[28] In that sense, there is an equality to the relationship in that both the state and the individual are governed by the law. This concept is also relevant to the way Australian citizenship as a status is different to the former 'British subject' status. The evolution from being a 'subject' to being a 'citizen' in Australia involves Australia's changing relationship with the United Kingdom (UK) *and* the changing conception of the proper exercise of power of the state in relation to its citizens.

In 1901, when propertied, white, male Australians—those bestowed with formal, active voting rights—came together to write the *Constitution*, there was a democratic element to its formation. The participants were elected directly to the constitutional conventions established to draft the *Australian Constitution*, rather than drawing from the existing representative colonial parliaments. For that reason, those conventions were known as the 'People's convention'.[29] That women and Indigenous Australians were not part of the people underlines an imbalance of power from the nation's inception.[30]

This is not to discount the voice of the women who were campaigning for the vote and who, as active citizens, ensured that s 41 of the *Constitution* guaranteed that those who already had the right to vote in the colonies would be able to vote in a new Commonwealth of Australia's federal

---

28 A commitment to the rule of law is also seen by the court in the privative clause cases including *Plaintiff S157/2002 v Commonwealth* (2003) 211 CLR 476.

29 The full records of these Conventions have now been scanned and are available online, see <https://www.aph.gov.au/About_Parliament/Senate/Powers_practice_n_procedures/Records_of_the_Australasian_Federal_Conventions_of_the_1890s>.

30 See Deborah Cass and Kim Rubenstein, 'Representation/s of Women in the Australian Constitutional System' (1995) 3(48) *Adelaide Law Review* 3.

elections.³¹ This included Indigenous and white women in South Australia who had the vote at that time and, by the time of federation, white women in Western Australia, too. Indigenous South Australian women would later lose their right to vote when the *Commonwealth Electoral Act 1902* (Cth), which introduced the franchise for women in federal elections, specifically excluded Indigenous people.³² The beliefs around people's equality, or lack thereof, influenced the balance of power within society at that time. Indeed, it was not until 1962 that Indigenous Australians' right to vote was passed into the *Commonwealth Electoral Act 1918* (Cth).³³

Formal citizenship status, which Indigenous Australians had by their birth in Australia,³⁴ as did women, did not mean they had substantive citizenship rights.³⁵ The 1967 referendum did not correct formal citizenship, which Indigenous Australians held, but, importantly, as the Uluru Statement from the Heart identified,³⁶ led to them being counted.³⁷ Indeed, formal legal membership status in 1901 was not Australian citizenship, which did not exist at that time, but rather was British subject status. A significant aspect of identity that influenced the compact of federal membership in Australia in 1901 was that the white male drafters saw themselves as British subjects, and not as Australian citizens. They did not seek to break their ties with empire at federation. In creating an Australian Commonwealth, they were establishing a compact that refigured the exercise of power in the Australian territory of the Empire between a central governing body (a federal government) and the continuing colonies (the states). Among other things, the male framers wanted to bolster their collective power to exclude immigrants (including non-white British subjects) and to create a uniformity of approach to questions of interstate trade.³⁸

---

31 Section 41 states: 'No adult person who has or acquires a right to vote at elections for the more numerous House of the Parliament of a State shall, while the right continues, be prevented by any law of the Commonwealth from voting at elections for either House of the Parliament of the Commonwealth'.
32 For an explanation of s 41 and the involvement of the South Australian women's role in its evolution, see Elisa Arcioni and Kim Rubenstein, '*R v Pearson; Ex parte Sipka* [1983] HCA 6: Feminism and the Franchise' in Francesca Bartlett, Trish Luker and Rosemary Hunter (eds), *Australian Feminist Judgments: Righting and Rewriting Law* (Hart Publishing, 2014) 55.
33 See Kim Rubenstein, *Australian Citizenship Law* (Thomson Reuters, 2nd ed, 2017) [2.220] and [6.190].
34 See discussion about citizenship by birth in ibid [3.50], [4.50], [4.70], [4.200], [4.250], [7.8].
35 Ibid [1.20].
36 See *Uluru Statement from the Heart* (26 May 2017) <https://www.referendumcouncil.org.au/sites/default/files/2017-05/Uluru_Statement_From_The_Heart_0.PDF>.
37 See some excellent material online about the 1967 Referendum at <https://www.nla.gov.au/research-guides/the-1967-referendum>.
38 See Helen Irving, 'To Constitute a Nation: A Cultural History of Australia's Constitution' in Anthony Blackshield and George Williams (eds), *Australian Constitutional Law and Theory, Commentary and Materials* (Cambridge University Press, 6th ed, 1999).

Ultimately, this led to a clear decision *not* to include a formal legal concept of Australian citizenship in the *Australian Constitution*.[39] All individuals born in Australia were British subjects by birth until the introduction of the *Australian Citizenship Act 1948* (Cth) on 26 January 1949.[40] When that Act came into effect, Australian citizenship status arose automatically by birth in Australia[41] and sat alongside the continuing British subject status. Australian citizens were both Australian citizens *and* British subjects until 1987.[42]

When British subject status was repealed, and Australians became solely Australian citizens in 1987, it represented an important shift. This was not only about a change around the relationship between Australia and the UK that had consequences for British subjects residing in Australia who were not Australian citizens,[43] but it reflected a change to Australian conceptions of sovereignty. It was also a time when the Australian executive acknowledged that no matter which country a person came from, they had equal access to applying for Australian citizenship.[44]

The earlier position of being a 'subject' in a colonial, monarchical setting represented an imbalance of power that underpins British subject status compared to Australian citizenship. Being a British subject was at its core a relationship between the Crown and the subject where the individual was *subjected* to the power of the Crown or the state. This was not only in the sense that any form of power (whether called the Crown or the executive) has a 'subject' to which the power extends, but also because the Crown was entitled, by its own divine foundations, to control the subject. This lies in British subject status's feudal origins, where the concepts of allegiance were tied up, as Peter Spiro explains:

---

39   See Kim Rubenstein, 'Citizenship and the Constitutional Convention Debates: A Mere Legal Inference' (1997) 25(2) *Federal Law Review* 295.
40   When first introduced, it was called the *Nationality and Citizenship Act 1948* (Cth) and was renamed the *Australian Citizenship Act 1948* (Cth) in 1973. See Rubenstein, above n 33, [4.130].
41   There are various ways to become an Australian citizen: by birth, descent and naturalisation (now known as conferral). See Rubenstein, above n 33, [4.200].
42   See the discussions about British subject status in ibid [3.120], [4.140], [4.170], [4.180] and [4.190].
43   This included British subjects being able to be deported under the *Migration Act 1958* (Cth). See also Kim Rubenstein and Niamh Lenagh Maguire, 'Citizenship Law' in Ian Freckleton and Hugh Selby (eds), *Appealing to the Future: Michael Kirby and His Legacy* (Thomson Reuters, 2009) 105.
44   See Rubenstein, above n 33, [4.190].

> In a medieval world, [where] individuals were identified not so much by primitive national affiliations as by personal allegiances tied to natural law. The notion of personal allegiances persisted as Europe divided into distinct territorial units, each ruled by an individual sovereign. So conceived, early models of nationality and citizenship worked from the putatively personal relationship between the individual and the sovereign.[45]

The Crown could ultimately determine who it chose to protect and upon whom to bestow its benevolence. This translated into the common law identifying all people born within the Crown's dominions as being subject to the Crown's power and benevolence. This was the result of the relationship in feudalism between the individual and the soil upon which she lived.[46] In terms of the subject–sovereign relationship, *jus soli* was justified on the grounds that the child was upon birth indebted to the King for her protection.[47] While subjects gained some benefits from that relationship (although not uniformly, as Indigenous and Chinese Australians' and women's experiences affirm),[48] there was a fundamental inequality in the relationship.

Becoming solely Australian citizens signified, linguistically, a move away from that foundational inequality. While Australia still had a Queen as Head of State, she became the Queen of Australia, and this move away from British subject status also changed the concept of power between the executive branch of government—those governing and making the law—and the people—those *subject* to the law. Citizenship, as opposed to 'subjectivity', philosophically and legally represents an *equality* between those exercising power and those subject to that power. In Australia, this also represented a move with parallels in timing to becoming a multicultural society. From that time on, all individuals, whether part of the Commonwealth or not, would have equal access to citizenship, compared to the earlier preference for British (white) subjects.

These changes are integral to the development of a democratic understanding of citizenship. It parallels a commitment to the principle that those exercising power are *subject to the law* in the same way that the citizenry is *subject to the law*. All citizens—those governing and those

---

45   See Peter Spiro, 'Dual Nationality and the Meaning of Citizenship' (1997) 46 *Emory Law Journal* 1411, 1419.
46   Ibid, citing WE Hall, *International Law* (Clarendon Press, 7th ed, 1917), 234.
47   Ibid, citing William Blackstone, *Commentaries on the Laws of England* (Clarendon Press, 1768) vol 1, 369–70.
48   See Peter Prince, *Aliens in their Own Land* (PhD thesis, The Australian National University, 2015).

being governed—are formally equal before the law. While the story of Indigenous citizenship, even at that point, highlighted some of the flaws in translating this theory to practice, the move to Australian citizenship over British subject status was the first step towards a democratic concept of Australian citizenship.

This change also built upon the growth of the application of administrative law principles in Australia with the 'new' administrative law framework introduced in the 1970s.[49] Those changes, including the introduction of freedom of information laws, the office of the Ombudsman, the creation of Administrative Appeals Tribunals and codified judicial review processes, all articulated and implemented clear controls on the exercise of executive power. Individual citizens could challenge government exercises of power, primarily in the Federal Court of Australia, and this administrative law foundation amplified this newer understanding of Australian citizenship. Just as the concept of the rule of law emphasises that those who exercise power are 'subject to the law', so too was the *sole status* of citizenship central to democratic understandings of citizenship and the fact that those citizens who were exercising power, the executive branch of government, were also 'subject to the law'.

It is within these 'matters', where individuals seek to challenge the exercise of executive power in the Federal Court, that we see a significant story of Australian citizenship.

The Federal Court as an Archive

The intent and history of the Federal Court is inherently linked to a narrative of national identity and is, therefore, not only a repository of legal procedure, but also an important legal, social, cultural and historical archive.

In practical terms, the traditional focus placed on the work of superior courts, like the Federal Court, is generally on their end product: judgments, orders and reasons. For the litigants, judgment represents the end the litigation, the consequence of which may be significant. The making of orders under the *Administrative Decisions (Judicial Review) Act*

---

[49] See Peter Cane, Leighton McDonald and Kristen Rundle, *Principles of Administrative Law* (Oxford University Press, 3rd ed, 2018).

may represent protection from unlawful executive action. The making of orders under the *Native Title Act* may represent the recognition of deeply held spiritual and cultural connections to the land. For the legal profession in a common law system such as Australia's, judgment might represent a statement of what the law is, with an eye to appeal if the statement is perceived to be wrong. For the public who do not generally see courts in action, judgments provide the opportunity to critically assess the performance of the courts and judges in terms of timeliness or even the extent to which they are 'in touch' with the community.[50]

For the High Court, the determination of a dispute between two or more parties is the fundamental purpose of a Commonwealth court established under Chapter III of the *Constitution*. The High Court's jurisdiction is circumscribed by s 75 of the *Constitution*. A 'matter' must 'involve some right or privilege or protection given by law or the prevention, redress or punishment of some act inhibited by law'.[51] In its narrowest sense, the resolution of the dispute involves 'attaching a definite legal consequence to a definite, detailed state of facts'.[52]

However, in common law systems reliant on precedent as both a body of law and a tool of statutory interpretation, the effects of judicial decision-making are not bound in space or time, but may be felt well beyond individual disputes. The resolution of a dispute and the publication of reasons may have a far-reaching effect in defining a community and its relationship with the state.[53] The application of a body of law derived from principles and precedent provides continuity, consistency and certainty in individuals' relationships with one another and with the state.[54] A decision may also reach back in time to either affirm or reject previous interpretations of the law or redefine legal and personal relationships.[55] In a broader sense, courts play an important role in

---

50 Murray Gleeson, 'Out of Touch or Out of Reach?' (2006) 7 *The Judicial Review* 241, 241. The concept is not a new one. See, for example, the remarks of the Hon Samuel Griffith on the first sitting of the High Court reported in 'The High Court: Opening Ceremony, Distinguished Gathering', *The Argus* (Melbourne), 7 October 1903, 9 <http://nla.gov.au/nla.news-page333047>.
51 In *Re Judiciary and Navigation Acts* (1921) 29 CLR 257, 266.
52 Ruggero Aldisert, 'The Role of the Courts in Contemporary Society' (1977) 38(3) *University of Pittsburgh Law Review* 438, 439.
53 Anthony Mason, 'The Use and Abuse of Precedent' (1988) 4 *Australian Bar Review* 93. See also traditional ideas of the common law representing common custom and usage in Rupert Cross and JW Harris, *Precedent in English Law* (Clarendon Press, 1991), 36–7.
54 Mason, above n 53. See also *Mirehouse v Rennell* (1833) 1 Cl & F 527, 546.
55 Oscar G Chase, '"Supreme" Courts and the Imagination of the Real' (2015) 518 *New York University Public Law and Legal Theory Working Papers* 14.

affirming the community's understanding of ideas of identity, belonging, citizenship and rights. Through their reasons for decision, courts reinforce the acceptance of certain ideas while rejecting or disapproving of others.[56]

Traditional ideas about archives saw their contents as embodying a form of impartial 'truth' or 'evidence' derived from ideas about providence.[57] Postmodern critiques of this traditional construction have argued that the selection, retention and preservation of records in state-run archival institutions means that a particular view of the state is created and preserved.[58] There is a strong parallel in this thinking between archives and reasons for decision. As a pronouncement of an impartial decision-maker whose decisions are enforced by the state, reasons represent a state-sanctioned account of the parties' relationship. As the product of an adversarial system, reasons are perceived to incorporate the distilled 'truth' of the matter. As a matter of providence, the pedigree of reasons is arguably impeccable. From a postmodern perspective, as a court established by Commonwealth legislation, the Federal Court's decisions are explicitly endowed with state-sanctioned significance. Whereas archival institutions might be seen to exercise a type of 'soft' power in terms of defining the community, the precedential value of judicial decision-making means that courts are expected to engage actively in defining acceptable behaviour.[59]

So why not stop there and accept the extent of the Federal Court's archives as currently understood? Shouldn't its orders and reasons for decisions meet the needs of all their potential users, including historical researchers? We argue that they represent the *end point* in litigation. Although the reasons for decision may provide a summary of the evidence and the proceedings at trial, they are just a summary. The summary is limited to only those facts that have been 'ascertained' by the court and identified as legally significant.[60] In effect, the reasons present a narrow set of facts viewed through a particular lens of relevance and legal principle and rendered for a particular purpose.[61]

---

56   Ibid.
57   Francis X Blouin Jr and William G Rosenberg, *Processing the Past: Contesting Authority in History and the Archives* (Oxford University Press, 2011) 232; Brien Brothman, 'Afterglow: Conceptions of Record and Evidence in Archival Discourse' (2002) 2 *Archival Science* 311.
58   Joan Schwartz and Terry Cook, 'Archives, Records and Power: The Making of Modern Memory' (2002) 2 *Archival Science* 1; Blouin Jr and Rosenberg, above n 57, 151.
59   J Willard Hurst, 'Legal Elements in United States History' in Donald Fleming and Bernard Bailyn (eds), *Perspectives in American History* (Little Brown Books, 1971) vol 2, 3.
60   Michael McHugh, 'Judicial Method' (1999) 73 *Australian Law Journal* 37, 37.
61   Clifford Geertz, *Local Knowledge: Further Essays in Interpretive Anthropology* (Basic Books, 2008) 173.

A reliance on reasons alone is the study of precedent that is often referred to as 'lawyers' history'.[62] To the extent that the decision reflects or affects the wider community, it tells only part of the story. Materials presented by the parties provide both the canvas and the frame for the decision. They provide the foundation for the decision and describe the broader context within which the decision is made. It is here that court records arguably hold more value to the researcher as a companion, or even contradictor, to state-run archives. As noted above, postmodern critiques of archives argue that to the extent archival institutions are created by, and contain records of, the state, they give primacy to a representation of the community constructed by the state and exclude contradictory voices.[63] In the context of the individual's relationship with the state, it might exclude or explicitly devalue or discredit voices of protest.

Within the court's own records, contradictory voices are not just heard but are explicitly required. The evidence and other materials submitted to the court are representative of the voices of those who submitted them. They do not contain just one version of a series of events but may contain two or more or multiple stories told in different ways and from different perspectives. Statements of claim and collected evidence describe the litigants' relationship and, to the extent that the eventual decision will affect that relationship in the future, their hopes or expectations of what it should be. Within these documentary accounts are cultural and social assumptions—both explicit and implicit—that provide insight into those relationships.[64] Perhaps even more crucially, the requirement in Commonwealth courts of a 'matter' means that these are snapshots of those assumptions in conflict and contested ideas about what is acceptable. A more complete archive begins to explain 'not only what went on in the law's formal processes, but what were the full actual effects that law and the life environing the law had on each other'.[65]

---

62   Kinvin Wroth, 'Documents of the Colonial Conflict: Part I—Sources for the Legal History of the American Revolution' (1976) 69 *Law Librarians Journal* 277, 277.
63   Brothman, above n 57; Blouin Jr and Rosenberg, above n 57; Jacques Derrida, *Archive Fever: A Freudian Impression* (Eric Prenowitz trans, University of Chicago Press, 1996); Nancy Cochran, Andrew Gordon and Merton Krause, 'Proactive Records: Reflections on the Village Watchman' (1980) 2(1) *Science Communication* 5; Ciaran B Trace, 'What is Recorded is Never Simply "What Happened": Record Keeping in Modern Organizational Culture' (2002) 2 *Archival Science* 137. See also s 2A of the *Archives Act* and the definition of 'archival resources of the Commonwealth'.
64   Michael Hindus, Theodore Hammett and Barbara Hobson, *The Files of the Massachusetts Superior Court, 1859–1959: An Analysis and a Plan for Action* (GK Hall & Company, 1979) 3.
65   Hurst, above n 59, 3.

The Federal Court's collected materials, therefore, allow the researcher to move beyond 'lawyers' history' and state-focused constructs of community. The voices of litigants, while advocates in their own cause, are inherently authentic and in that sense true to themselves. In our understanding of an individual's relationship with the state and with each other, in an understanding of this story of Australian citizenship, those records provide a time capsule of the assumptions, ideas and the conflicts between the state and its citizenry. To the extent that the law also reaches both forward and backward, these firsthand accounts also serve to explain how current relationships have evolved.

This concept of superior courts as archives is further strengthened by the historical development of the concept of 'courts of record'— ongoing, permanent and inconvertible records of the disputes that come before them.

Public Access to the Courts and Court Records

At its establishment, the Federal Court was created as a 'superior court of record'.[66] The concept of 'courts of record' is inherently linked with the origins of an Anglo-Australian legal system and defines the status of a court within a legal hierarchy. However, what constitutes 'the record', and the manner in which it is to be kept, remains largely undefined. It is determined by context.[67] In the best traditions of the common law, what is 'the record' for the purposes of public access has therefore been determined by tradition and practice adopted as precedent. The Federal Court, as with other courts, has adopted a role as custodian and curator of records confined to traditional ideas of access.

The practice of courts creating and maintaining records of proceedings developed in or about the 13th century.[68] Until that time, records of what had happened before the justices were largely oral. Over time, what were originally referred to as rolls developed from notes to aid memory to more

---

66 *Federal Court of Australia Act 1976* (Cth) s 5.
67 For example, see the discussion of what constitutes an inferior court's record for the purposes of a writ of certiorari in *Craig v South Australia* (1995) 184 CLR 163.
68 SE Thorne, 'Courts of Record and Sir Edward Coke' (1937) 2(1) *The University of Toronto Law Journal* 24, 28.

complete records containing detailed statements of what happened in proceedings. According to some accounts of the development of English courts, those holding records therefore become 'courts of record' and different from those that did not.[69] From this relatively simply distinction, courts of record have accumulated further distinguishing characteristics, including the power to fine, imprison and punish contempt.[70] In Australia, questions about whether a court is one 'of record' have generally been resolved by the legislation establishing it.[71]

The history of proposals to establish what is now the Federal Court is generally silent on its status, other than it was always intended to be 'superior'.[72] However, it is implicit throughout the development of proposals for the Federal Court over the following decade that it should at least have the status equivalent to a superior court, or the state supreme courts, suggesting that it was always intended to be a court 'of record'.

What is the Record?

While a court's status may be clear, what constitutes its 'record', particularly for superior courts, remains vague. Decisions about the content of 'the record' are largely confined to administrative law and focus on the records of inferior courts, the content of which is to be determined by the court on an application for review[73] or by reference to the legislation establishing the court or tribunal.[74]

While not determinative, these definitions set a logical minimum content for the record. As the High Court notes, it provides an account of how the matter came before the court, the contentions of the parties and the orders made—the basic information necessary to record the dispute between the parties and its resolution. In that sense, it remains tied to

---

69 Ibid 35. Interestingly, Thorne goes on to discuss the distinction argued for by Sir Edward Coke that only courts of record can fine and imprison and finds that there is no authority for the connection other than common lawyers' desire to 'cripple' rival courts that kept no record.
70 Enid Campbell, 'Inferior and Superior Courts of Record' (1997) 6 *Journal of Judicial Administration* 249, 254. For a comprehensive history of the development of these other distinctions, see also Thorne, above n 68.
71 Campbell, above n 70, 257.
72 NAA: A432, 1961/2132 Part 1.
73 *Craig v South Australia* (1995) 184 CLR 163, 182 quoting *Hockey v Yelland* (1984) 157 CLR 124, 143; see also *Kirk v Industrial Court of New South Wales* (2010) 239 CLR 531, 576 and the discussion there of the Privy Council's similar conclusion in *R v Nat Bell Liquors* [1922] 2 AC 128.
74 *Kirk* (2010) 239 CLR 531, 578.

the historical purposes of the maintenance of a record, both as an aid to memory of how proceedings had been disposed and as a summary for the purposes of superior courts' supervision.[75] The advent of court registries and standard forms has arguably extended the idea of the record to include the documents filed with the registry.[76]

This idea of records reflects a traditional procedural and precedential understanding of how or why those records are important. However, it tells us very little about their character and ignores the larger context within which written records developed. That context reveals their significance and begins to describe how issues about their access and retention might be approached.

Perpetual Memorial, Incontrovertible Evidence and Status

While the practice of keeping records began as an aid to justices,[77] their evolution as detailed accounts of proceedings endowed them with a sense of permanence. Holdsworth, in his history of English law, refers to courts of record as being courts whose 'proceedings are enrolled in parchment for a *perpetual* memory and testimony' (emphasis added).[78] The nature of the record as being perpetual was echoed by Lord Denning 20 years later,[79] and by the High Court,[80] which defined the records of a court with a similar sense of permanence as being the proceedings 'preserved in [the court's] archives'.[81]

In addition to permanence, court records were considered incontestable as to their contents. Oral records of proceedings in the King's courts were considered incontrovertible and not open to question.[82] With the development of written records of proceedings, the written form was

---

75 The High Court's own discussion of the 'the record' in *Kirk* in fact begins with a reference to the role of the King's Bench in the 18th century; *Kirk* (2010) 239 CLR 531, 568.
76 *Baldwin & Francis Ltd and Patents Appeal Tribunal* [1959] AC 663, 688.
77 Thorne, above n 68.
78 William Searle Holdsworth, *A History of English Law* (Methuen & Co., 1924) vol 5, 157.
79 *Baldwin & Francis Ltd and Patents Appeal Tribunal* [1959] AC 663, 688.
80 *Lane v Morrison* (2009) 239 CLR 230.
81 Ibid 243.
82 Thorne, above n 68.

similarly incontrovertible. Further proof of the content of the record was neither required[83] nor accepted:[84] a position that has been enshrined in the *Evidence Act 1995* (Cth).[85]

Taken together, these two principles—an incontrovertible record to be held in perpetuity—makes courts' records more than a procedural catalogue. They speak directly to both the status of the record itself and its custodian. For example, on the establishment of the failed Australian Military Court (AMC), the Commonwealth Government inserted amendments to the bill making the AMC 'a court of record'. Arguments to make the AMC a 'court of record' had been opposed by the Department of Defence on the basis that it was unnecessary and that the bill already provided for the new AMC to keep records.[86] However, submissions on the bill recommended that regardless of whether the bill already provided for the powers of a 'court of record', the AMC should be explicitly created as one in recognition of its powers, its status and its authority.[87] On the introduction of the amendment, the government noted that the amendment 'further enhance[d] the status of the AMC'.[88]

Open Justice

While it is one thing to argue that a court's record of proceedings constitutes a permanent archive of proceedings, why should those records be available to the public? The origins of 'the record' are found in aids to the court, rather than the outside world. However, to argue that the 'the record' is a private or an exclusive collection ignores other elements of the administration of courts. In particular, the position that the conduct of proceedings is transparent and open to all (subject to limited conditions) as a fundamental guarantee of the fairness of those proceedings.

---

83 Ibid; Gaillard Lapsley, 'The Court, Record and Roll of the County in the Thirteenth Century' (1935) 51 *Law Quarterly Review* 299, 319.
84 See LexisNexis, *Halsbury's Laws of Australia*, (online at 25 January 2019) 195 Evidence, '3 Special Modes of Proof' [195–2310].
85 *Evidence Act 1995* (Cth), s 157 (proof of civil proceedings) and s 178 (proof of criminal proceedings).
86 Department of Defence, Answers to Questions Raised to Senate References Committee on Foreign Affairs, Defence and Trade, Parliament of Australia, Inquiry into provisions of the Defence Legislation Amendment Bill 2006, 9 October 2006, 6.
87 Len Roberts-Smith, Submission No. P3 to the Senate References Committee on Foreign Affairs, Defence and Trade, Parliament of Australia, Inquiry into Provisions of the Defence Legislation Amendment Bill 2006, 19 September 2006, [9].
88 Supplementary Explanatory Memorandum, Defence Legislation Amendment Bill 2006 (Cth), [13].

The commitment to courts operating in public is most immediately recognisable in the traditional adage that 'justice should not only be done, but should manifestly and undoubtedly be seen to be done'.[89] The origins of the idea are not clear, either arising out of the practices of early courts,[90] a corollary of courts being public events[91] or 'more or less accidental' as a necessary part of criminal jury trials.[92] However, since at least the 17th century,[93] it has been accepted and entrenched in English law. It is also now seen to be closely tied to the principles of a fair trial, judicial impartiality, judicial independence and the maintenance of public confidence in the courts.[94]

As Ernst Willheim outlines in his chapter in this collection, the concept of 'open justice' is acknowledged in Australia and internationally as a fundamental element of the judicial process, consistently acknowledged in both precedent and extrajudicially by members of the High Court.

The judicial and academic discussion of open justice has mainly constructed the concept around direct, unmediated access to courts in person. However, this 'face-to-face model' of courts' relationship with the community is inconsistent with current practice, is outdated and increasingly problematic. With the advent of more extensive media and more universally consistent levels of literacy, it has been argued that the traditional model of the public visiting the courts to see justice 'being done' is outmoded.[95]

---

89 This statement comes from *R v Sussex Justices; Ex parte McCarthy* [1924] 1 KB 256, 259.
90 *Raybos Australia Pty Ltd & Anor v Jones* (1985) 2 NSWLR 47, 51, citing P Wright, 'The Open Court: The Hallmark of Judicial Proceedings' (1947) 25 *Canadian Bar Review* 721.
91 Garth Nettheim, 'The Principle of Open Justice' (1984–86) 8 *University of Tasmania Law Review* 25, 26.
92 Ibid, citing Max Radin, 'The Right to a Public Trial' (1931–1932) 6 *Temple Law Quarterly* 381, 382. A similar observation is made by Chief Justice Burger in *Richmond Newspapers Inc v Virginia*, 448 US 555, 565 (1980), who, in turn, attributes it to William Holdsworth, *A History of English Law* (Little Brown Books, 3rd ed, 1938) vol 10.
93 In *Raybos* (1985) 2 NSWLR 47, Kirby P identifies references to public trials as early as 1649, while Nettheim, above n 91, 27 refers to Sir Edward Coke's *Institutes of the Laws of England* published in 1642.
94 *Hogan v Hinch* (2011) 243 CLR 506, 530.
95 Helen Gamble and Richard Mohr, 'Courts and Communities: Tensions and Accommodations' in Richard Mohr and Sandra Lloyd (eds), *Delivering with Diversity* (University of Wollongong, 1996), 7; Patrick Keyzer, 'What the Courts and the Media Can Do to Improve the Standard of Media Reporting of the Work of the Courts' (1999) 1 *University of Technology Sydney Law Review* 150, 152.

Assuming for the moment that the public can attend proceedings, what is it that they are likely to hear? As has been discussed by Willheim,[96] and others,[97] legal proceedings in the Federal Court are now largely conducted by the exchange of written evidence, materials and submissions, almost all of which are unavailable to the public. To the extent that the principle of 'open justice' is based on the assumption that all, or a large part of, the material available to the court would be read aloud in open court, it refers to practices that are now largely defunct. Byrne J in *McCabe v British American Tobacco Australia Services Limited*[98] summarised the development of civil litigation since the 1980s as:

> The ensuing two decades of civil commercial litigation have witnessed the progress of this trend in the interests of increased efficiency in the trial process. The modern trial judge is confronted with substantial court books, often in electronic form, volumes of witness statements, written outlines of counsel's openings and final addresses, chronologies and photocopies of cases relied upon, most of which are to be read out of court and which, for the most part, are merely alluded to at trial. This serves to make the curial and adjudicative process less and less comprehensible to the person in the public gallery.[99]

The emphasis on greater efficiency in litigation has been further reinforced in the Federal Court with the introduction of amendments intended to 'bring about a cultural change in the conduct of litigation'.[100] Since 2010, the procedures applying to civil litigation must be consistent with an 'overarching purpose' of facilitating 'the just resolution of disputes according to law as quickly, inexpensively and efficiently as possible'.[101] Amendments have also been introduced requiring the parties to take 'reasonable steps' to attempt to resolve the dispute before initiating proceedings.[102]

---

96 Ernst Willheim, 'Are Our Courts Truly Open?' (2002) 13 *Public Law Review* 191.
97 Sharon Rodrick, 'Open Justice, the Media and Avenues of Access to Documents on the Court Record' (2006) 29(3) *UNSW Law Journal* 90.
98 *McCabe v British American Tobacco Australia Services Limited* [2002] VSC 150.
99 Ibid [19].
100 Explanatory Memorandum, Access to Justice (Civil Litigation Reforms) Amendment Bill 2009 (Cth), 3.
101 *Federal Court of Australia Act*, s 37M. This includes an obligation on the parties to conduct litigation in accordance with the 'overarching purpose' (see s 37N). See also *Cement Australia Pty Ltd v Australian Competition and Consumer Commission* (2010) 187 FCR 261 for a discussion of the interpretation of the provision.
102 *Civil Dispute Resolution Act 2011* (Cth), ss 6 and 7.

These measures seeking to reduce the cost of litigation, or avoid it completely, are valuable and significant in improving access to justice. However, allied to these changes is also the active encouragement of the parties and the Federal Court to attempt to resolve issues informally or through processes that are not available to the public.[103] Even for members of the public who do seek access to written materials, there is the additional burden of cost. Inspection and copying of accessible materials attract a fee,[104] while parties, the public and the media must order transcripts from an external provider and pay a fee.[105]

Conclusion: Access and Citizenship

Restrictions on access to courts' unique store of materials reflect on all aspects of Australian citizenship: as a legal term, as a frame for thinking about the relationship between the citizen and the state, and as a way of encouraging active citizenship. This chapter has explained how our thinking about courts' archives is related to, and influenced by, the evolution of citizenship in Australia historically, from federation to the growing jurisdiction of the Federal Court of Australia. Restrictions on access to documents impacts on Australian citizenship as well as on a general understanding of the rule of law and open justice as modern expectations of the justice system.

Maintaining a narrower view of 'the archive' perpetuates a system of inequality between the citizen and the state that is now out of date. In the present context, the state determines what the citizen can see based on old ideas about courts, their proceedings and their records. It also restricts access based on a practical fiction that the public can, at any time, turn up and witness proceedings.

Given the evolving jurisdiction of the Federal Court, and changing ideas about restrictions on access based on its function as a court, maintaining a traditional view of the Federal Court's record ignores its role evolving in parallel as an archive. The Federal Court's role as a site for disputation,

---

103 See, for example, Federal Court of Australia, *Practice Note CM 1: Case Management and the Individual Docket System,* 1 August 2011; Law Council of Australia and Federal Court of Australia, *Case Management Handbook* (Law Council of Australia, 2014).
104 *Federal Court and Federal Circuit Court Regulation 2012* (Cth), Schedule 1, Part 1, Item 123.
105 Federal Court of Australia, *Access to Transcript* (n.d.) Federal Court of Australia <www.fedcourt.gov.au/services/access-to-files-and-transcripts/transcript>.

negotiation and resolution about rights, particularly those around the power of the executive and the role of the state, means that its records speak directly to the evolution of Australian society. The different perspectives and the process by which the state (in the broadest sense) decides what those rights and roles are, in the growing jurisdiction of the Federal Court of Australia, ultimately confirms it is part of the evolution of Australian citizenship. The citizenry must, therefore, be in a position to access materials that inform that national identity, consistent with a change in status from 'subjects' to equal 'citizens'.

2

Aspects of Citizen Access to Court Archives

Ernst Willheim

Introduction

The openness of judicial proceedings is a fundamental constitutional and common law principle. It ensures that citizens and the media can come in to the courtroom and observe and report on the administration of justice. In 2015, the Federal Court won a National Archives of Australia award for digital excellence for its implementation of electronic court files. In accepting the award, the Principal Registrar and Chief Executive of the Federal Court said:

> Court records provide a snapshot of Australia's evolving social and legal history. A digital version of them will ensure their long-term preservation so future generations can understand the legal questions and concerns of the day and the Court's role in the Australian community.[1]

The public availability of court records as a means of reinforcing the Federal Court's role arose in discussion in *Grollo v Palmer*.[2] *Grollo* was a challenge to legislation authorising 'eligible judges'[3] to issue warrants for

---

1 Warwick Soden, 'Federal Court Wins National Archives Award' (Media Release, 4 May 2015).
2 *Grollo v Palmer* (1995) 184 CLR 348.
3 A person who is a judge of a court created by the Parliament (*Telecommunications (Interception) Act 1979* (Cth) s 6D).

phone tapping on the grounds that the function was incompatible with judicial office. The warrants were issued *ex parte* and in secret. No records were kept in the court's registry. Justice McHugh dissented from other members of the High Court on the incompatibility issue and made this powerful observation on the importance of open justice in the Federal Court:

> Open justice is the hallmark of the common law system of justice and is an essential characteristic of the exercise of federal judicial power. Participation in secret, ex parte, administrative procedures by those who hold federal judicial office contravenes the spirit of the requirement that justice in the federal courts should be open; it weakens the perception that the federal courts are independent of the federal government and its agencies. Much of the litigation in the Federal Court is between the ordinary citizen and the federal government and its agencies. The maintenance of public confidence in the independence and impartiality of the Federal Court judges in hearing disputes between the citizen and the government and its agencies is contingent upon the public perception that the judges of the federal courts are impartial and entirely independent of the executive arm of government. That public perception must be diminished when the judges of the Federal Court are involved in secret, ex parte administrative procedure.[4]

What both the Principal Registrar and Justice McHugh emphasise is the importance of open justice as an essential characteristic of federal judicial power.

Openness was identified as an important feature of the common law in early classical English writings. Hale, Blackstone and Bentham all attached importance to oral evidence, submissions and rulings in open court.[5] In this respect, the common law is in sharp contrast with the secret practices of the ecclesiastical courts, and the investigative and inquisitorial processes of the civil law system.

---

4   *Grollo* (1995) 184 CLR 348, 379–80.
5   Matthew Hale, *The History of the Common Law of England* (University of Chicago Press, 3rd ed, 1971) 163–4; William Blackstone, *Commentaries on the Law of England* (Strahan & Woodfall, 11th ed, 1791) vol 3, 372–4; Jeremy Bentham, *Draft for the Organisation of Judicial Establishments Compared with that of the National Assembly, with a Commentary on the Same, Works of Jeremy Bentham* (William Tait, 1843) vol 4, 305, 316–7; Ernst Willheim, 'Are Our Courts Truly Open?' (2002) 13 *Public Law Review* 191.

The snapshot to which the Federal Court's Chief Executive refers is taken with a narrow lens, with much of the subject-matter obscured from view. The Federal Court, by its practices and rules, appears to be seeking to shield some of its most important records from public scrutiny. Far from assisting researchers to understand the legal and factual questions raised in its proceedings, the Federal Court appears to be seeking to obstruct genuine research. The policy considerations that lie behind the Federal Court's practices and rules are unclear. This chapter argues that the relevant provisions of the court's rules may be of uncertain constitutional validity.

The chapter also draws a distinction between records of judicial proceedings and records relating to the internal administration of the Federal Court. In relation to records of court administration, *prima facie* they should be subject to the same sorts of access provisions as the records of the executive government.

Openness

Successive decisions in England and Australia have confirmed openness as an essential feature of the common law judicial system.[6]

In *Scott v Scott*,[7] a House of Lords decision, Lord Shaw emphasised 'publicity in the administration of justice' as 'one of the surest guarantees of our liberties'.[8] He went on to criticise 'encroachments by way of judicial procedures in such a way as to impair the rights, safety and freedom of the citizen and the open administration of the law'.[9] Those remarks are especially apposite. It is through 'encroachments by way of judicial procedures' adopted by the Federal Court in the interests of efficiency that open administration of the law is impaired. Arguably, the principles so eloquently espoused by Justice McHugh are regularly breached.

---

6   *Scott v Scott* (1913) AC 417, 476, 478: *Dickason v Dickason* (1913) 17 CLR 50, 51; *Russell v Russell* (1976) 134 CLR 495, 520 and 532; *Grollo* (1995) 184 CLR 348, 379–80.
7   *Scott* (1913) AC 417.
8   Ibid 476.
9   Ibid 478.

In *Dickason v Dickason*,[10] in a short but succinct judgment, Acting Chief Justice Barton wrote, 'one of the normal attributes of a court is publicity, that is, the admission of the public to attend the proceedings'.[11]

In *Russell v Russell*,[12] the High Court held invalid section 97 of the *Family Law Act 1975* (Cth) requiring proceedings under that Act to be heard in closed court. Referring to the openness rule, Justice Gibbs wrote: '[t]his rule has the virtue that the proceedings of every court are fully exposed to public and professional scrutiny and criticism, without which abuses may flourish undetected'.[13] He continued:

> the public administration of justice tends to maintain confidence in the integrity and independence of the courts. The fact that courts of law are held openly and not in secret is an essential aspect of their character. It distinguishes their activities from those of administrative officials, for 'publicity is the authentic hall-mark of judicial as distinct from administrative procedure'.[14]

In *John Fairfax Publications Pty Ltd v District Court of NSW*,[15] Chief Justice Spigelman said:

> It is well established that the principle of open justice is one of the most fundamental aspects of the system of justice in Australia. The conduct of proceedings in public is an essential quality of an Australian court of justice. There is no inherent power of the Court to exclude the public.[16]

Of course, the openness principle is not absolute. In *Hogan v Hinch*,[17] a case concerning orders prohibiting publication of names of convicted sex offenders, Chief Justice French said:

> It has long been accepted at common law that the application of the open justice principle may be limited ... where it is necessary to secure the proper administration of justice. In a proceeding involving a secret technical process, a public hearing of evidence of the secret process could 'cause an entire destruction of the whole matter in dispute'. Similar considerations

---

10   *Dickason* (1913) 17 CLR 50.
11   Ibid 51. The other members of the court concurred.
12   *Russell* (1976) 134 CLR 495.
13   Ibid 495.
14   Ibid 520, citing *McPherson v McPherson* [1936] AC 177, 200.
15   *John Fairfax Publications Pty Ltd v District Court of NSW* (2004) 61 NSWLR 344.
16   Ibid [18]. See also James Spigelman, 'The Principle of Open Justice: A Comparative Perspective' (2006) 29 *University of New South Wales Law Journal* 147.
17   *Hogan v Hinch* (2011) 243 CLR 506.

inform restrictions on the disclosure in open court of evidence in an action for injunctive relief against an anticipated breach of confidence. In the prosecution of a blackmailer, the name of the blackmailer's victim, called as a prosecution witness, may be suppressed because of the 'keen public interest in getting blackmailers convicted and sentenced' and the difficulties that may be encountered in getting complainants to come forward 'unless they are given this kind of protection'. So too, in particular circumstances, may the name of a police informant or the identity of an undercover police officer. The categories of case are not closed, although they will not lightly be extended.[18]

Openness in judicial proceedings is well established in common law systems. More recently, it has been incorporated in international human rights instruments. Article 14 of the *International Covenant on Civil and Political Rights* and Article 6 of the *European Convention for the Protection of Human Rights and Fundamental Freedoms* establish an entitlement to 'a fair and public hearing by an independent and impartial tribunal established by law'.[19]

The importance of openness is not confined to protection of the rights of the parties. By exposing the judicial process to public scrutiny, courts are publicly accountable. Openness is a prerequisite for public confidence in the integrity of the judicial system. Practices to the contrary, sometimes adopted in the interests of administrative efficiency, breach the openness principle and may well be unconstitutional.

Chief Justice French has referred to public adjudication, or adherence to the open court principle, as one of the essential and defining features of courts.[20] He went on to observe that the defining characteristics of courts are of constitutional significance and emphasised the need to maintain the distinctiveness of the public function of courts as the third branch of government and the special character of public adjudication.

---

18   *Hogan* (2011) 243 CLR 506, 531–2. The references in the passage have been omitted.
19   *Universal Declaration of Human Rights*, GA Res 217A (III), UN GAOR, 3rd session, 183 plen mtg, UN Doc A/810 (10 December 1948), art 10; *International Covenant on Civil and Political Rights,* opened for signature 16 December 1966, 999 UNTS 171 (entered into force 23 March 1976), art 14 and 38; *Convention for the Protection of Human Rights and Fundamental Freedoms* ('*European Convention on Human Rights*'), opened for signature 4 November 1950, 213 UNTS 221 (entered into force 3 September 1953), art 6. The *European Convention on Human Rights* omits the word 'competent', included in the ICCPR.
20   Robert French, 'Essential and Defining Characteristics of Courts in an Age of Institutional Change' (Speech delivered at Supreme and Federal Court Judges Conference, Adelaide, 21 January 2013).

Openness and Court Records

Most of the principles relating to open justice were developed in the context of physical access to the courtroom. In an article provocatively titled 'Are Our Courts Truly Open?', [21] I explained, with particular reference to the High Court and the Federal Court, that in light of modern procedures adopted by most superior courts—written pleadings, requirements for written submissions to which counsel and judges refer but that are not read out in open court, and evidence on affidavit 'taken as read'[22] but not in fact read out orally—cases are determined on the basis of material not freely available to the public.

For example, the Federal Court's *Central Practice Note* explains that written submissions are now a 'useful way of shortening addresses'.[23] The 'usual orders' now made by the Federal Court at the first directions hearing of a case often include orders that evidence in chief be by way of affidavit and that deponents to affidavits be called for cross-examination only by leave. It follows that issues of fact are determined by reference to evidence that is not publicly available.

The openness principle is, of course, fundamental to public confidence in the judiciary—but it is not so confined. Witnesses are also exposed to public scrutiny. Few would dispute that the expectation of public scrutiny, including scrutiny by the media, can constitute an important deterrent to false evidence. As Blackstone wrote, 'a witness may frequently depose that in private which he will be ashamed to testify in a public and solemn tribunal'.[24] In consequence of procedures adopted in the interests of efficiency, public scrutiny and public understanding of the judicial process is inhibited. It is difficult to argue that court processes now fully comply with the openness principle.[25]

---

21 Willheim, above n 5.
22 That is, admitted into evidence. I do not contend that affidavits that are filed but not admitted into evidence should be publicly available.
23 Federal Court of Australia, *Central Practice Note: National Court Framework and Case Management (CPN–1)* 25 October 2016 <http://www.fedcourt.gov.au/law-and-practice/practice-documents/practice-notes/cpn-1>.
24 Blackstone, above n 5.
25 In the case of the High Court, written submissions are now available on the court's website.

When the openness principle was developed, the emphasis was indeed on physical access to the courtroom. Nowadays, physical access remains important but most of us rely on the media to report what is happening in the courts. The ability of the media to provide a proper report of court proceedings is, therefore, an important aspect of the principle of open justice.[26] Where a newspaper reporter is seeking to prepare an article on a Federal Court proceeding, if a written submission is read out in full or an affidavit is read out in full, the reporter is able to report on them. However, where the case is heard on the basis of written submissions and affidavits that are, in the contemporary jargon, 'taken as read' but not read out in fact and not publicly available, can the reporter prepare a meaningful account of the case for her or his newspaper? Open justice requires the opportunity for the media to publish fair and accurate reports of submissions and of evidence. The same considerations apply to researchers and commentators. An academic commentator seeking to analyse a case may wish to analyse the written submissions by the parties and the evidence as well as the actual judgment. Critical scrutiny may well involve analysis of whether, and to what extent, a judgment appropriately reflects the submissions and the evidence. For example, a researcher with an interest in public administration or corporate fraud may have a special interest in the evidence in cases falling within the field of interest. It is very much in this context that access to the court's records, to the written submissions and to the affidavits that have been 'taken as read', but not in fact read out in open court, is crucial. In the absence of any specific orders made by the court in relation to sensitive documents, those records should be treated as public records open to the public to inspect and copy. The same principles that apply to the public's right of access to the physical courtroom should apply to access to the court's records of the proceedings. In the modern world, where few have the opportunity to attend the court and most of us rely on media reports of court proceedings, access to the court's records is of greater practical importance than physical access to the courtroom itself.

Many Australians learn more about the law through watching American television and American films. For example, in the American film *Spotlight*, a *Boston Globe* reporter walks into a court registry and asks to see a court file. When the clerk refuses the request, the reporter runs upstairs, walks into the chambers of a judge and is able to obtain access to the court file. In the film, the file turns out to include damning evidence that a Cardinal had been aware of sexual abuse of a child by a priest.

---

26 *Hogan* (2011) 243 CLR 506, 532; *John Fairfax & Sons Ltd* (1986) 5 NSWLR 465, 476–7.

In Australia, we cannot storm into a judge's chambers in the manner that appears to be possible in the United States. But can we obtain access to court records on matters of public interest? Could an Australian academic researcher or investigative reporter obtain access to submissions and evidence in Federal Court proceedings? In the broader community, there would be a general presumption that, just as judicial proceedings are open, so the records of those proceedings will also be open. In particular, submissions and evidence[27] should be freely available to the public.

The Importance of Public Access

The Federal Court's Chief Executive correctly identified the importance of the court's records as providing 'a snapshot of Australia's evolving social and legal history'.[28] Records of commercial litigation relating to competition policy may include important evidence and submissions relating to economic and social conditions. Records of litigation relating to Indigenous heritage protection and native title may include significant anthropological and other historical material not available elsewhere. Records of challenges to government decisions may cast light on public administration. Therefore, court records are a rich resource relating to Australian society.

Some years ago, I was urged by some Aboriginal leaders to make a submission (as a private citizen) to a joint committee of the Commonwealth Parliament inquiring into the findings of the Committee on the Elimination of Racial Discrimination (CERD) that the *Native Title Amendment Act 1998* (Cth) was inconsistent with Australia's international legal obligations, in particular, the *Convention on the Elimination of All Forms of Racial Discrimination*.[29] One of the joint committee's key terms of reference was whether CERD's finding was 'sustainable on the basis of informed opinion'.[30] 'Informed opinion' was, therefore, critical to the inquiry by the joint committee.

---

27 Naturally, only evidence that has been admitted.
28 Soden, above n 1.
29 *International Convention on the Elimination of All Forms of Racial Discrimination*, opened for signature 21 December 1965, 660 UNTS 195 (entered into force 4 January 1969).
30 The full terms of reference are set out in the Commonwealth *16th Report: CERD and the Native Title Amendment Act 1998*, Parl Paper No 134/2000 (2000) iv.

Provisions of the Australian legislation criticised by CERD included those validating titles over pastoral leases that had been granted by state governments after the date of commencement of the *Native Title Act 1993* (Cth) ('*Native Title Act*') and before the High Court's subsequent decision in *Wik Peoples v Queensland*,[31] where the court held that pastoral leases did not necessarily extinguish native title. In light of the *Wik* decision, the validity of pastoral leases granted without compliance with the *Native Title Act* procedures was doubtful, hence the perceived need for validation of those leases—the 'bucketloads of extinguishment' provision. Validation of leases that had been granted without compliance with the *Native Title Act* and consequential extinguishment of native title was highly controversial.

What was the state of 'informed opinion'? How could 'informed opinion' be established?

In response to criticism of the legislation—criticism that in light of the known uncertainty of whether pastoral leases did in fact extinguish native title—and that the relevant state governments should have complied with the *Native Title Act* requirements, officials of the Attorney-General's Department submitted that, at the relevant time, the weight of legal opinion had supported the view that native title could no longer subsist on pastoral lease land.[32] On that view, there would have been no need to comply with the *Native Title Act* requirements.

Were the submissions of the officials soundly based?

Legal submissions made by the Commonwealth in proceedings in the Federal Court and the High Court, were, in my view, inconsistent with the evidence given by the departmental officers to the joint committee.[33] While the justification for the validation provisions was a matter for political judgment, in my view, the committee's consideration should have

---

31 *Wik Peoples v Queensland* (1996) 187 CLR 1.
32 Commonwealth Attorney-General's Department, Submission No CERD 24.
33 It was not appropriate for me to disclose to the joint committee that my own legal advice to the government had expressed the contrary view that pastoral leases did not necessarily extinguish native title. The advice was given at a time when I was a senior officer of the Commonwealth and counsel for the Attorney-General in the key Federal Court proceedings raising the question whether pastoral leases extinguish native title. I feel able to disclose the substance of my advice now. First, with the passage of time, it is now in the 'open' period; and second, the relevant Commonwealth Minister has agreed to me disclosing that I had advised that pastoral leases did not necessarily extinguish native title.

proceeded on a factually correct historical record. I sought to obtain for the joint committee the legal submissions made by the Commonwealth to the Federal Court and the High Court.

In the case of the High Court, there was no difficulty. A summary of the argument was reported in the *Commonwealth Law Reports*.[34] Copies of the Commonwealth's submissions were obtained from the High Court's registry upon payment of a modest fee and provided to the joint committee.

However, in the case of the Federal Court, the registry refused access, relying correctly on what was then Order 46 rule 6 of the *Federal Court Rules*. That rule prevented a person not a party to proceedings from inspecting a wide range of court documents, including affidavits and written submissions. I had a copy of the submissions made by counsel for the Attorney-General in the leading case and was able to provide a copy to the committee. I would have preferred to have provided the joint committee with a copy of the Commonwealth's submissions obtained from and authenticated by the Federal Court.

When I explained to the joint committee that the copy I was providing was from my personal records (as I was Counsel for the Commonwealth in the case), authenticity was not called into question. Five members of the joint committee rejected the evidence given on behalf of the government that the balance of legal opinion was that pastoral leases extinguished native title. They cited the Commonwealth's legal submissions to the High Court and the Federal Court. They concluded that these submissions to the High Court and the Federal Court demonstrated that the Commonwealth did not believe that the question of whether pastoral leases extinguished native title was settled.

Access by a private citizen to court records—in this case, access to submissions made on behalf of the executive government—was important to enable evidence subsequently given by officials of the executive government to a joint committee of the Commonwealth Parliament to be corrected. It was fortuitous that the citizen had a personal copy of the relevant submissions to the Federal Court. In other circumstances, the Federal Court rule would have inhibited consideration by a committee of the Australian Parliament of an important public issue.

---

34 *North Ganalanja Aboriginal Corporation v State of Queensland* (1996) 185 CLR 595, 602.

2. ASPECTS OF CITIZEN ACCESS TO COURT ARCHIVES

Further, as McHugh J pointed out in *Grollo v Palmer*,[35] one of the Federal Court's most important areas of jurisdiction concerns challenges to the lawfulness of administrative decisions of the executive government, generally by way of proceedings brought under the *Administrative Decisions (Judicial Review) Act 1977* (Cth) ('*Administrative Decisions (Judicial Review) Act*'). Access to court records is of particular importance in relation to Federal Court proceedings challenging decisions of the executive government. The court's practice, that evidence in chief is introduced by way of affidavit, has meant that issues of fact were determined by reference to evidence that was not publicly available. Judicial review of executive action was clothed in secrecy.

The *Federal Court Rules* were remade in 2011. Custody and inspection of documents is now dealt with in Division 2.4. Rule 2.32 enables a person who is not a party to inspect a range of documents in Federal Court proceedings. The list covers a number of formal documents such as an originating application, an address for service and a pleading. Significantly, the list does not include written submissions or affidavits. Rule 22.32(5) enables a person to apply to the court for leave to inspect a document that the person is not otherwise entitled to inspect.

Does the former O 46 r 6 or Division 2.4 of the current rules give effect to the worthy objectives articulated in the media statement by the Federal Court's Chief Executive?

Are those provisions consistent with the constitutional principles articulated by Justice McHugh?

Would the former or current rules be open to challenge on the basis that they breach the principle of open justice?

Does the opportunity to apply to the Federal Court for leave to inspect a document rectify possible constitutional invalidity?

In relation to key Federal Court records, such as submissions and affidavits, the rules in effect establish a presumption *against* access. While that presumption can be set aside by the court, the approach should be the very reverse: a presumptive right of access, which can be denied on appropriate grounds by order of the court.

---

35   *Grollo* (1995) 184 CLR 348.

There would appear to be no published explanation of the court's rule. The purpose of the rule, the policy considerations behind it, the reasons for a *prima-facie* exclusion of submissions and affidavit evidence from open access are not known. If the reason relates to cost, this could surely be addressed by imposition of an appropriate fee. In any event, in the digital age it should be possible to post submissions and affidavits admitted into evidence on the court's website.

The rules inhibit free access to basic details of Federal Court proceedings. That constraint on open justice may give rise to constitutional invalidity. The inability to freely access submissions and evidence may inhibit public understanding of litigation before the court and public debate concerning public policy issues arising in Federal Court litigation.

Proceedings under the *Administrative Decisions (Judicial Review) Act* are an obvious example of litigation that may give rise to questions of public concern. This Act enables individuals to challenge the lawfulness of administrative decisions made by officers of the executive government, including Ministers and senior officials. Submissions made on behalf of officials and the evidence given by officials may be critical. The public must be entitled to know the submissions and the evidence given by officials in defence of challenged decisions. Assume it becomes apparent during the hearing of a challenge to an administrative decision or from a reading of the judgment that serious impropriety is alleged, or is found to have taken place, on the part of an officer of the executive government. Allegations and findings of executive impropriety are matters of public interest and public debate. If, by reason of the court's rules, the written submissions made on behalf of the government defendant, or affidavits filed by the government defendant and 'taken as read' but not in fact read in open court, are not available, the inability to access these documents burdens or impairs the implied freedom of communication about the affairs of the executive government.

The High Court has recently confirmed that 'the implied freedom (of political communication) is essential to the maintenance of the system of representative and responsible government for which the Constitution provided'.[36] The public interest in fair reporting of court proceedings is not in dispute. If the public is not able to access what public officials have put to the court, if the media is not able to report on the submissions

---

36   *Brown v Tasmania* [2017] HCA 43, [88].

made on behalf of the executive and the evidence given by an officer of the executive, then the opportunity for political comment on the conduct of the executive is seriously impaired.

The first question in the analytical framework for determining whether a law contravenes the implied freedom of political communication[37] is whether the rules burden the implied freedom. This must be answered in the affirmative.

It is appropriate to interpose here that the implied freedom of political communication is usually seen as a constraint on the exercise of legislative and executive power.[38] That constraint may or may not apply to the exercise of judicial power. While the rule-making function is conferred on the court, the court is not exercising judicial power in the strict or narrow sense in the exercise of that function.

On the basis that the first arm of the constitutional test is established, further questions arise:[39] whether the purpose of the law or the burden on the implied freedom is justified or legitimate, in the sense that it is compatible with the maintenance of the constitutionally prescribed system of representative and responsible government, and whether the law is reasonably appropriate and adapted to advance that purpose in a manner compatible with the maintenance of the constitutionally prescribed system of government.

In implied freedom of political cases determined by the High Court, the court has been able to identify the purpose of the relevant legislation, and to analyse whether the burden is justified. However, in the case of the Federal Court's rules, there is a threshold difficulty. Neither the court itself nor the court's rules identify the purpose of the restriction. There is no obvious identifiable legitimate legislative purpose. Therefore, it is difficult to discern a case that the restriction is justified, legitimate and reasonably appropriate and adapted to advance a legitimate purpose.

---

37 *Lange v Australian Broadcasting Corporation* (1997) 189 CLR 520, 560; *Wotton v Queensland* (2012) 246 CLR 1; *McCloy v NSW* [2015] HCA 34. Slightly different frameworks were applied in *Brown* [2017] HCA 43, [90]–[104] (Kiefel CJ, Bell and Keane JJ), [156] (Gaegler J) and [271] (Keane J).
38 *Lange* (1997) 189 CLR 520, 560; *Hogan v Hinch* (2011) 243 CLR 506, 554; *Unions NSW* (2013) 252 CLR 530, 554; *Tajjour* (2104) 254 CLR 508, 558; *Brown* [2017] HCA 43, [90].
39 *Brown* [2017] HCA 43, [93], [96], [102], [104], [156] and [318]–[325].

Cost and administrative convenience would scarcely provide an appropriate justification. How can a burden on public access to the submissions and evidence put to the court by officers of the executive government in litigation challenging the decisions of the executive government be compatible with the maintenance of the constitutionally prescribed system of representative and responsible government? Simply put, there is no obvious justification. Where the answer to one or both of the further questions is 'no', a case for invalidity is made out.

A further question arises whether the opportunity to apply to the court for leave to inspect[40] cures the apparent invalidity. Why the rule is cast in this way, rather than in the form of open access subject to any specific orders, is not apparent. Is this an attempt to save the rule from potential invalidity? A question arises of whether potential invalidity arises from the rules themselves or from the manner of their exercise. I emphasise that the invalidity argument relates to impairment of political communication about the executive. To establish this argument, it is not necessary to establish that the implied freedom extends to communications about the judiciary. Of course, if Justice McHugh is, in effect, saying that openness is constitutionally entrenched,[41] it may not be necessary to rely on these additional arguments.

Sensitive Documents

Federal Court archives will obviously include a wide range of sensitive documents. Chief Justice French identified a range of circumstances where the application of the open justice principle may be limited.[42] Those circumstances related to sensitivity arising in the judicial process. The most common circumstances are likely to be in litigation involving Indigenous issues such as heritage protection and native title; commercial litigation; and litigation involving national security issues. Sensitivity can also arise in the internal administration of the court.

---

40 Rule 22.32(5).
41 *Grollo* (1995) 184 CLR 348, 379–80.
42 *Hogan* (2011) 243 CLR 506.

Examples from the Administration of Justice

For example, the unreported proceedings in *Western Australia v Minister for Aboriginal and Torres Strait Islander Affairs*[43] brought on at short notice arose out of a challenge by the State of Western Australia to the validity of declarations made by the Commonwealth Minister for Aboriginal and Torres Strait Islander Affairs under the *Aboriginal and Torres Strait Islander Heritage (Protection) Act 1984* (Cth) ('*Aboriginal and Torres Strait Islander Heritage (Protection) Act*'). The Minister's declarations related to a site claimed by the Yawuru people to be a traditional Aboriginal area associated with male initiation ceremonies.

In the course of giving discovery, the Minister disclosed a number of anthropological reports (referred to in the proceedings as the Sullivan Report) and affidavits provided to the Minister on condition that they not be reproduced or be seen by women or by uninitiated Aboriginal men. Late on Wednesday, 27 July 1994, the state made application to the Federal Court for orders requiring the production of the Sullivan Report to its counsel and solicitor (who were both women). I was briefed on 28 July and flew to Perth that evening. The matter was heard the next day. Justice Carr ordered that the Sullivan Report be produced for inspection by the state's counsel and solicitors save that only one of such persons should be female. In his reasons, he explained that the interests of justice required that at least one of the state's counsel and solicitor have access to the report. By excluding one of them, there should be no real prejudice to the applicant's case and the interests of the Yawuru people were protected to the fullest extent possible.

Similar issues arise in a wide variety of cases. In *Tickner v Chapman*,[44] another challenge to a declaration under the *Aboriginal and Torres Strait Islander Heritage (Protection) Act*, the Aboriginal women claimed gender-sensitive documents filed with the court related to a women's birthing site and should not be seen by men (these documents were labelled 'secret women's business' in the media). In the *Broome Crocodile Farm* case,[45] the gender-sensitive material related to a male initiation track.

---

43 The unreported decision of Carr J, 29 July 1994 cf the later different decision *Western Australia, Minister of Lands of Western Australia and Another v Minister of Aboriginal and Torres Strait Islander Affairs of the Commonwealth of Australia* [1995] FCA 1052.
44 (1995) 57 FCR 451.
45 *Minister for Aboriginal and Torres Strait Islander Affairs v State of Western Australia* (1996) 67 FCR 40.

These issues will undoubtedly also arise in native title cases.

Evidence in heritage protection and native title cases is a rich resource, especially in relation to Indigenous history and culture. Often, it is only when a sacred site comes under serious threat that intensive anthropological work is undertaken, and stories are recorded. Sometimes those stories are culturally sensitive. According to Aboriginal tradition, some stories may only be disclosed to elders, or to initiated men, or the stories may be gender-sensitive and must only be told to those of a particular gender. Obvious questions arise in relation to access to evidence that was given on conditions of confidentiality.

Other confidentiality issues can arise in other types of cases, such as those identified by Chief Justice French and now especially national security issues. In those cases, it is likely that the court will have issued appropriate orders during the hearing protecting the confidentiality of records. If, in the future, access to court records including submissions and evidence is opened up, it may be necessary for the parties in those matters to apply to the court for orders that relevant confidentiality orders extend as appropriate to the records, following the disposition of the proceedings and for the court to adopt appropriate procedures to ensure that relevant documents are appropriately identified and protected.

Examples from Internal Administration

The *Freedom of Information Act 1982* (Cth) and the *Privacy Act 1988* (Cth) apply to the Federal Court only in relation to matters 'of an administrative nature',[46] an expression that has been held to be 'incapable of precise definition'.[47] However, these Acts would not apply to functions that are 'truly ancillary to an adjudication by the court',[48] but would apply to, for example, employment records, contractors, travel expenses and property management.

---

46 *Freedom of Information Act*, s 5(1), *Privacy Act*, s 7(1)(b).
47 *Hamblin v Duffy* (1981) 34 ALR 333, 338–9; *Evans v Friemann* (1981) 35 ALR 428, 433.
48 *Kotsis v Kotsis* (1970) 122 CLR 69, 92.

Any large organisation will have the occasional administrative problem. The court, like any body funded by monies appropriated by the Parliament, is accountable for its expenditure. The Chief Justice is formally responsible for managing the administrative affairs of the court.[49] On a day-to-day basis, court administration is handled by the Registrar.[50]

But what sorts of files should be available to the public?

For example, what if furniture from a retiring Justice's chambers could not be found? Assuming the District Registrar opened a file on this matter, should that file be accessible?

What about details of Comcar usage by Justices that may appear unnecessarily high? A former Speaker of the Commonwealth Parliament found himself in a lot of trouble for using a Comcar to visit a Canberra district winery. Assuming the District Registrar opened a file on Comcar usage by a judge, should that file be accessible?

What about 'unusual' adjournments. An order to adjourn a matter is undoubtedly made in the exercise of the judicial function of the court—but the order may be controversial. Assume that a judge is required to sit in a remote but attractive location, for example, a tropical location in the middle of winter. Assume also that the judge's personal staff, who travel with him, are family members. The judge sits on a Monday morning but after hearing argument for only a few minutes and over objections from counsel adjourns to the following Monday. The judge and his staff remain in the remote location until the hearing the following Monday. Legal representatives make complaints to the Chief Justice and to the Attorney-General and court files and departmental files are created. The departmental file would be accessible under the normal rules. Should the court's file be accessible?

Other examples relate to spouse travel. Judges have entitlements to spouse travel. Assume that a judge is to hear a matter in another registry and the matter is scheduled for a lengthy hearing. The judge arranges to take their spouse in accordance with standard spouse travel entitlements. It becomes apparent that the parties are negotiating and that the parties are likely to announce a settlement on the first day of hearing. The judge had been looking forward to an extended stay in the other location and the spouse

---

49 *Federal Court of Australia Act 1976* (Cth), s 18A.
50 Ibid s 18B.

travels with the judge notwithstanding the anticipated settlement. It was necessary for the judge to travel. Should the spouse travel have been cancelled? Subsequently, the Chief Justice questions the appropriateness of the spouse travel and a court file is created.

Should court records relating to travel and accommodation costs incurred by a judge and a judge's spouse and their staff be publicly accessible? Would anyone ever want access to these sorts of records? A researcher preparing a biography of a judge may wish to access all records relating to the judge. A student of court administration may wish to identify difficulties and how they were handled—for example, whether they were handled by the Chief Justice or by the Chief Executive, and whether the Attorney-General or the Attorney-General's Department were involved. Any relevant records would have been Commonwealth records.

In relation to records in the possession of the Federal Court, the main provisions of the *Archives Act 1983* (Cth) ('*Archives Act*') would not apply. The *Archives Act* would presumably apply to records of the department itself.

Conclusion

The records of the Federal Court constitute a rich resource covering enormous fields of public interest, including Australia's economic and financial affairs, public administration and Indigenous issues. Many of those records are of great public and historical importance. In the same way as justice is administered in open court, so should the records of the court be open. Only in special circumstances—for example, where the court has made orders restricting access—should access be denied.

Insofar as the Federal Court's current rules restrict access to legal submissions and evidence, the rules should be reviewed.

The preferable approach would be to allow unrestricted access to both legal submissions and evidence unless orders have been made restricting access. Ideally, legal submissions should be available on the court's web site. Affidavit evidence should also be available after the evidence has been admitted.

Where confidentiality orders are made in the course of hearings, those orders should be expressed to extend to the relevant records of the proceedings in the court's archives. Registry procedures should ensure that records that are the subject of confidentiality orders are appropriately identified and protected.

If, contrary to this suggestion, the court prefers to maintain its current approach, the purpose of the restriction should be explained to ensure constitutional validity.

3

When the Carnival is Over: The Case for Reform of Access to Royal Commission Records

Hollie Kerwin and Maya Narayan[1]

Introduction

Royal commissions occupy a complex position within the three arms of Australian Government. As executive bodies, they may be more amenable to characterisation as public record-keeping institutions than Chapter III courts, but the royal commission's central function of receiving evidence, often coerced, raises similar questions as to the appropriateness of permitting public access to their records.

At the same time, the royal commission is a fundamentally public event. Paralleled only by electoral voting and judicial determination, the royal commission draws an exceptionally direct line between the citizen and government. It casts lines out into public space: inviting—and at times compelling—individual witnesses to tell their stories, and recording testimony, before speaking back to tell 'public truths' and propose legal and social change. In this process, royal commissions are heralded as

---

[1] The views expressed in this chapter are the authors' and do not in any way reflect those of their employers. The authors are grateful to Prue Gregory, Principal Lawyer, Knowmore, Dr Katie Wright, La Trobe University, and the National Archives of Australia for their assistance in the preparation of this chapter, and to Kerry Ford and Joel Townsend for their generous review of an earlier version of it.

singularly able to 'get at the truth',[2] and as a powerful instrument of governance that constructs and encourages public endorsement of certain, official knowledge, thereby also eliding or silencing other narratives.[3] Despite their public significance, the royal commission remains an under-researched institution, especially in respect of its function as archive.

In this chapter, we seek to encourage attention to the 'royal commission as archive'. Engagement with the royal commission as archive, we suggest, raises risks, opportunities and imperatives for the continued remembrance of significant public issues, for critical engagement with the state archive and for unpacking the royal commission as an instrument of government. We argue that the records of these unique organs of government inquiry and public power remain in an unstable legislative and governmental compromise.

In response, this chapter proposes a *sui generis* regime for management of and access to the records of these unique organs of government inquiry and public power.

The Royal Commission as Government Inquiry—A Complex Institutional Identity

Locating Royal Commissions in the Australian Constitutional Setting

The royal commission has been described as 'the most ancient and dignified' organ of government inquiry.[4] In many ways similar to a court, the royal commission has historically been defined by its power to compel individuals to give evidence and its capacity to make findings on broad matters of public and private importance, including misconduct, corruption, negligence and pressing legal and social issues. However, the royal commission is not a judicial entity. Formally an extension of the

---

2   Joyce Chia, 'Inquiring into Inquiries: The Review of the Royal Commissions Act' (2009) 94 *Reform* 49, 49.
3   Jeanine Purdy, 'Royal Commissions and Omissions' (1992) 17(1) *Alternative Law Journal* 32, 33; see also Hugh McDowall Clokie and J William Robinson, *Royal Commissions of Inquiry: The Significance of Investigations in British Politics* (1969, Octagon Books), 139–40 and 177; Gillian Cowlishaw, 'Inquiring into Aboriginal Deaths in Custody: The Limits of a Royal Commission' (2007) 7 *Journal of Indigenous Policy* 28, 31.
4   Clokie and Robinson, above n 3, 24–5.

executive arm of government, the royal commission's position outside Parliament and the judiciary reflects 'the constitutional struggles which have centered around the royal prerogative' and attempts to restrict royal action to certain, defined modes of legal procedure.[5]

Despite the royal commission's foundation in British legal history, the institution remains relevant, important and a major facet of Australian government. At the Commonwealth level, for example, 133 commissions have been established under the *Royal Commissions Act 1902* (Cth) since 1902.[6] These commissions have considered various matters of national importance throughout the 20th and 21st centuries, including the sites of the seat of the Commonwealth Government (1903); 'industrial troubles' on Melbourne wharfs (1919–20); the basic wage (1919–20); monetary and banking systems (1935–37); Aboriginal land rights (1973–34); and drug trafficking (1981–83).[7] More recently, the royal commission has been employed to investigate alleged corruption, complex crime and major institutional failures in the context of the 'HIH Insurance collapse' (2001–04), the Australian Wheat Board and the United Nations Oil for Food program (2005–06), the Home Insulation Program (2013–14), child sex abuse (2013–17) and the protection and detention of children in the Northern Territory (2016–17).[8]

Critically, despite the continued currency of the royal commission, there is no single or enduring institution known as '*the* royal commission'.[9] Rather, while it is possible to speak of a royal commission as an institution of government, individual royal commissions are enlivened by the Crown to conduct particular inquiries. Unlike other forms of executive inquiry

---

5   Ibid 25.
6   See Parliament of Australia, *Royal Commissions and Commissions of Inquiry* (2015) <http://www.aph.gov.au/About_Parliament/Parliamentary_Departments/Parliamentary_Library/Browse_by_Topic/law/royalcommissions#1977>.
7   Ibid.
8   Ibid.
9   Accepting that there remain rare, permanent, subject-specific royal commissions in British legal history. See, for example, the Royal Commission into Historical Manuscripts appointed under royal warrant in 1869 and continuing (with amendments to the warrant) as part of the United Kingdom National Archives. See further, National Archives, *Historical Manuscripts Commission Warrant* (n.d.) <http://www.nationalarchives.gov.uk/information-management/legislation/hmc-warrant/>.

carried out by government departments and law reform bodies, a royal commission ceases to exist when its particular inquiry concludes and the commission makes its report.[10]

Contemporary royal commissions continue to be created by the Governor-General or the Governors of the Australian states by issue of letters patent, a mechanism by which the Monarch has historically made commands or determined rights. The letters patent compel certain people—the commissioners—to make inquiries in relation to certain matters (the terms of reference). Unsurprisingly, given the royal commission's continued evolution in the age of statutes, each inquiry is now supported by detailed legislation in each of the Australian states, territories and at the Commonwealth level.[11]

Complicating the Picture

Despite their technical position within the executive, the royal commission does not resemble or neatly reflect the methods of any single arm of government.[12] As Clokie and Robinson have observed, royal commissions are a 'notable example of the wise combination of fact-finding and policy forming in the modern State'.[13] In one sense, each commission is effectively independent of the executive, given that it is not directed by it except as to its composition, timelines and terms of reference (which are, of course, not wholly without some effect on their operation).[14]

---

10   Leonard Arthur Hallet, *Royal Commissions and Boards of Inquiry* (Law Book Company, 1982) 1. We discuss the implications of the impermanence of a commission in connection with its archive, below.

11   Legislation is required to empower royal commissions to compel the production of evidence; however, many modern royal commissions statutes go beyond mere provision of such a power: see, *Royal Commission Act 1902* (Cth); *Royal Commissions Act 1923* (NSW); *Commissions of Inquiry Act 1950* (Qld); *Royal Commissions Act 1968* (WA); *Royal Commissions Act 1916* (SA); *Commission of Inquiry Act 1995* (Tas); *Royal Commissions Act 1991* (ACT); *Inquiries Act 2014* (Vic) and *Inquiries Act 1985* (NT).

12   Clokie and Robinson, above n 3, v, 2; see also Gregory J Inwood and Carolyn M Johns, 'Why Study Commissions of Inquiry' in Gregory J Inwood and Carolyn M Johns (eds), *Commissions of Inquiry and Policy Change: A Comparative Analysis* (Toronto Press, 2015) 3.

13   Clokie and Robinson, above n 3, v.

14   For example, as Dibelius has said of the British commissions, 'the statesman who nominates the commission can almost always determine the course that it is going to take, since he will have a pretty good knowledge beforehand of the minds of the experts whom he puts on it, while, of course, avoiding any appearance of "packing his team"', cited in Martin Bulmer, 'Introduction' in Martin Bulmer (ed), *Social Research and Royal Commissions* (Routledge, 2015) 3.

Further, royal commissions weave in and out of the space commonly occupied by the courts. In conducting their inquiries, royal commissions obtain evidence, issue subpoenas for production of documents and witnesses, cross-examine witnesses and determine conflicting matters of fact using legal method.[15] They sit in tribunals and courtrooms, often emulating the ceremonies of justice typically seen in those spaces, and are frequently presided over by members of the legal profession, including sitting judges.[16] As the joint judgment of the High Court reflected in the *Hindmarsh Island* case:[17]

> A judge who conducts a Royal Commission may have a close working connection with the Executive Government yet will be required to act judicially in finding facts and applying the law and will deliver a report according to the judge's own conscience without regard to the wishes or advice of the Executive Government except where those wishes or advice are given by way of submission for the judge's independent evaluation.

Similarly, while the findings of royal commissions are not binding, they have been elevated in government and academic discourse to the status of judicial precedent.[18] At the same time, the royal commission has been described as the 'ideal Senate' or as akin to Question Hour in the British Parliament.[19]

The Australian royal commission is also attended by the complexities of intergovernmental interaction and cooperative federalism. Fourteen joint commissions, commenced by separate letters patent issued by the Commonwealth and Australian states and territories have enabled major inquiries to occur in relation to subject matters extending across federal

---

15 As Cowlishaw writes in relation to the Royal Commission into Aboriginal Deaths in Custody, for example, 'the practices of the legal profession naturally dominated the proceedings ... Legal enquiry operates in terms of certain principles. "The truth" or "the facts" is supposed to emerge from the presentation of evidence and questioning of witnesses in an adversarial context'. See further, Cowlishaw, above n 3, 32–5.

16 See further, Fiona Wheeler 'Anomalous Occurrences in Unusual Circumstances? Towards a History of Extra-Judicial Activity by High Court Justices' (Speech delivered to the High Court of Australia Public Lecture Series, Canberra, High Court of Australia, 30 November 2011).

17 Which considered, among other things, the appointment of a Federal Court judge to conduct an inquiry under the *Aboriginal and Torres Strait Islander Heritage Protection Act 1984* (Cth); see *Wilson v Minister for Aboriginal & Torres Strait Islander Affairs* (1996) 189 CLR 1, 17. See further, Fiona Wheeler, 'The Use of Federal Judges to Discharge Executive Functions: The Justice Matthews Case' (1996) 11 *AIAL Forum* 1.

18 Hallet, above n 10, 4.

19 Clokie and Robinson, above n 3, 6–7.

and state spheres of power.[20] For example, the Royal Commission into Aboriginal Deaths in Custody (RCIADIC), the Royal Commission on Human Relationships (Human Relationships RC), the Royal Commission into the (organised crime) activities of the Federated Ship Painters and Dockers Union (Painters and Dockers RC) and the Royal Commission into Institutional Responses to Child Sexual Abuse (Child Abuse RC) are the products of letters patent issued by multiple Australian governments. We return to the archives of these important commissions in greater detail below.

While the royal commission may reflect a constitutional struggle to confine royal action to 'certain modes of procedure', this mode, we suggest, is multifaceted and spans the gamut of governmental action.

Social and Cultural Functions of Royal Commission Inquiries

The inquiries of royal commissions also have a complicated social and cultural function and identity. First, modern royal commissions are commonly elaborate public events. Their core processes are premised on active participation by citizens in political life and democracy, beyond obedience of laws (or the burden of sanctions for their breach) and electoral voting.

As Bulmer has described, 'making invitations to submit evidence; receiving written evidence; holding public hearings at which oral evidence is presented; and making visits of inspection relevant to their subject' lie at the heart of the royal commission's processes.[21] 'The public' are invited in, often literally by published invitations in newspapers and online. The spaces in which they sit are designed for public participation, as witnesses of the commission and in the public galleries. In this sense, royal commissions are sites for active citizenship[22] on issues of civil

---

20 Stephen Donaghue, *Royal Commissions and Permanent Commission of Inquiry* (Butterworths, 2001) 5.
21 Bulmer, above n 14, 2–3.
22 See further, Kim Rubenstein, *Australian Citizenship Law in Context* (Lawbook Co, 2002) ch 3; Barry Sullivan, 'FOIA and the First Amendment: Representative Democracy and the People's Elusive "Right to Know"' (2012) 72(1) *Maryland Law Review* 1, 24–6; TJ Cartwright, *Royal Commissions and Departmental Committees in Britain: A Case-Study in Institutional Adaptiveness and Public Participation in Government* (Hodder and Stoughton, 1975).

importance. As Elizabeth Evatt AC recently reflected in relation to the Human Relationships RC, in which she, Anne Deveson and Felix Arnott were appointed commissioners:

> The success of the royal commission was largely due to Anne's insistence that we take the inquiry out to the people. We did this by holding open hearings and meetings in many places throughout Australia in an attempt to hear the voices of as many Australians as we could. The resulting report is enriched by the words of the people who spoke to us.[23]

Second, royal commissions have very often established a direct line of communication to the public during the life of the inquiry, culminating in the publication of their final report. Since at least the early 2000s, most royal commissions have created large websites, which, during the period of the commission, variously provide access to live and archived streams of evidence, transcripts of proceedings, narratives of selected private evidence read by actors[24] and messages from the relevant commission asking for assistance. Previously, evidence of commissions has been broadcast or provided daily to media through briefing summaries.[25] Hearings have also been largely public events, at least until specific reforms enacted for the taking of private testimony regarding child sexual abuse. In the British historical context, edited serials of the transcripts of each day of evidence were published and distributed.[26] Further, in the context of the Child Abuse RC, a single copy of a book containing 'Messages to Australia' from a select number of survivors was published and deposited with the National Library of Australia when this royal commission concluded in December 2017.[27]

---

23 Elizabeth Evatt, cited in Wendy McCarthy, 'Anne Deveson, a warrior for thoughtful, social change', *Sydney Morning Herald* (online) 13 December 2016 <http://www.smh.com.au/comment/obituaries/anne-deveson-a-warrior-for-thoughtful-social-change-20161213-gt9wkr.html>.
24 See Royal Commission into Institutional Responses to Child Sexual Abuse, *Narratives* (n.d.) <https://www.childabuseroyalcommission.gov.au/narratives>.
25 Departmental Committee on the Procedure of Royal Commissions, *Report of the Departmental Committee on the Procedure of Royal Commissions* (The Stationery Office, 1910), [12].
26 See, for example, United Kingdom, Royal Commission on Public Records, *Minutes of Evidence* (House of Commons, 1912–13).
27 Royal Commission into Institutional Responses to Child Sexual Abuse, *Message to Australia* (n.d.) <https://www.childabuseroyalcommission.gov.au/message-australia>.

In this way, as sociologist Katie Wright argues, the effects of royal commissions may be 'multi-layered, as much social and cultural as they are political and practical'.[28] In her view, their inquiries:

> throw into sharp relief issues of major social concern: they are symbolic of an open and transparent society 'where the voices of the powerless are heard' and the powerful are held accountable, and importantly, they increasingly provide a cathartic function for victims/survivors and indeed for societies more broadly.[29]

In a related way, the capacities of a royal commission to reshape social norms are evident. For example, in relation to the Canadian Royal Commission on New Reproductive Technologies, Weir and Habib argue that:

> Some of the resulting statements defining women's interests, such as those made by Aboriginal women's organizations, were unprecedented anywhere. Hence, the process of participating in the Royal Commission also led to the dissemination of new dialogic positions. A state inquiry was thus the eliciting condition for the development of knowledge by a social movement about changes in scientific knowledge.[30]

At the same time, the royal commission is a powerful instrument of governance and knowledge production. While they may create opportunities for a multiplicity of views to be heard or for the interrogation of hostile witnesses, through their curated websites, daily press summaries, lines of inquiry and reporting, they also produce—from a vast mass of information—powerful narratives and official knowledge for public consumption and endorsement.[31] As Clokie and Robinson observed of the broadcasts of evidence made by royal commissions through the 1960s in Britain, the royal commission serves the 'great Benthamite principle of government, namely publicity', including drawing the public into government and consolidating public support for the legal outcomes of the commission.[32] Similarly, the commission

---

28   Katie Wright, 'Childhood, Public Inquiries and Late Modernity' in B West (ed), *Challenging Identities, Institutions and Communities, Refereed Conference Proceedings of the Australian Sociological Association Conference* (University of South Australia, 2014) 5.
29   Ibid 4.
30   Lorna Weir and Jasmin Habib, 'A Critical Feminist Analysis of the Final Report of the Royal Commission on New Reproductive Technologies' (1997) 52 (Spring) *Studies in Political Economy* 137, 148.
31   Charles J Hanser, *Guide to Decision: The Royal Commission* (Bedminster Press, 1965) ix.
32   Clokie and Robinson, above n 3, 139–40, 177.

has been described as promoting social control by government;[33] as an ideological crisis management strategy;[34] and as a tool in the resolution of public controversy and promotion of public consensus about key issues.[35]

It must also be accepted that in the process of eliciting and announcing public truths, some voices and narratives may not be heard, or indeed may be silenced, by royal commissions. Even in the context of the Canadian Reproductive Technologies Royal Commission referred to above, some forms of knowledge assumed an untouchable position. For example, Weir and Habib have illustrated the privileging of 'biomedical visions' of the body at the expense of understanding or hearing feminist voices in relation to the 'social and cultural changes associated with the government of human reproduction'.[36] By 'proceeding from a binary distinction between nature and culture', the commission elided any 'notion that expertise could in any way be constitutive of the body' and failed to:

> heed the warning in a number of feminist briefs to the royal commission, particularly those from Quebecois feminists, which broke the Commission's biomedical and legal framing of issues in order to argue that the discourse of new reproductive technologies is especially dangerous because it assimilates women's activity in having children with men's.[37]

Similar issues have arisen in the context of Australian royal commissions. As Purdy has forcefully argued in relation to the RCIADIC's findings:

> practices and rules of law combined to create a space in which legal discourse in the form of judgments and reports can be constructed. This space is created not only by the determination of who will be able to speak and what they will be allowed to say … but also who will be able and prepared to speak, and what they will be prepared to say.[38]

---

33 Hanser, above n 31, 160; see also, Geoffrey Lindell, 'British Tribunals of Inquiry: Legislative and Judicial Control of the Inquisitorial Process: Relevance to Australian Royal Commissions' in *Research Paper No 5* (Department of the Parliamentary Library, Australia, 15 April 2003) 6.
34 George Gilligan, 'Royal Commissions of Inquiry' (2002) 35(3) *Australian and New Zealand Journal of Criminology* 289, 289–90.
35 Scott Prasser, 'Royal Commissions and Public Inquiries: Scope and Uses' in Patrick Weller (ed), *Royal Commissions and the Making of Public Policy* (MacMillan Education, 1994) 6–8.
36 Weir and Habib, above n 30, 151.
37 Ibid 151.
38 Purdy, above n 3, 33.

As an employee of the RCIADIC, Cowlishaw, too, has described a coalescence of factors that resulted in circumstances where it 'rarely had direct evidence other than from police and prison wardens'.[39] As she argues:

> neither in the legal process, the scientific discourse of experts, nor in the welfare framework of the socially concerned was there much room for Aboriginal voices, and certainly a radically different framework of discussion could not be accommodated.[40]

Moreover, Cowlishaw demonstrates how, together, the commission's terms of reference and legal method privileged attention to a dogged but largely elusive pursuit of 'culprits' for the deaths of the particular people in question, at the expense of attention to subtler, more difficult social processes contributing to Aboriginal incarceration and deaths in custody. In the legal process, she writes, 'there is little room for recognising that a particular kind of account of events is being created, and another kind excluded'.[41] Rather, for example, while the RCIADIC 'sought out anyone who might be able to give evidence, perused police daybooks and worksheets, calculated times and distances, and examined fingerprints as in the most careful murder investigation',[42] swearing, for example, was erased from accounts of the interaction between police and Aboriginal people despite the centrality of abusive swearing to police–Aboriginal relations and, potentially, the incarceration of Aboriginal people.[43]

---

39 Cowlishaw, above n 3, 30.
40 Ibid 36. She describes insufficient funding to key Indigenous rights advocacy bodies that had been tasked to investigate issues underlying the deaths under inquiry, alienation of Aboriginal people from the commission's processes, a reluctance to give evidence by prisoners based on fear of reprisal and severe limitations on the utility of evidence given by prisoners in relation to historical deaths in circumstances where they had not been interviewed at the time of death. Amy McQuire argued, further, that the voices of Aboriginal women were 'completely drowned out'. See Amy McQuire, 'Black Women, And A Tale Of Two Commissions' *New Matilda* (online) 15 April 2016 < https://newmatilda.com/2016/04/15/a-tale-of-two-royal-commissions/>. The RCIADIC is not the only Australian royal commission in which legal processes have been applied to Aboriginal people's experiences with the effect of 'believing' and 'valuing' certain voices, nor in which the voices of certain Aboriginal people have been absent. See, in relation to the Hindmarsh Bridge (South Australian) Royal Commission, Joanna Bourke, 'Women's Business: Sex, Secrets and the Hindmarsh Island Affair' (1997) 20(2) *UNSW Law Journal* 333. See, in relation to royal commissions more broadly, Steve Hemming and Daryle Rigney, 'Decentring the New Protectors: Transforming Aboriginal Heritage in South Australia' in Emma Waterton and Steve Watson (eds), *Heritage and Community Engagement: Collaboration or Contestation?* (Routledge, 2013) 100–14. Hemming and Rigney write at 104 that 'Legislation, royal commissions, court cases and other legal spaces play an ongoing role in constructing and authenticating histories and stories of Indigenous culture. In this context, the colonial archive is both activated and reinvigorated, and new elements and interpretations are introduced'.
41 Cowlishaw, above n 3, 33.
42 Ibid 31.
43 Ibid 34.

Therefore, royal commissions are undeniably poised in a delicate relationship of trust between citizen and government.[44] While their letters patent compel the commissioners to inquire into certain matters and advise the Crown, the royal commission also powerfully recalibrates or affirms social norms, rearticulates or further embeds dominant discourses and amplifies or placates the anxieties of members of the community. As we argue below, the royal commission's social and cultural identity and effects compel attention to the archives of these complex bodies.

Royal Commission as Archive

As a result of their functions—both institutional and sociocultural—royal commissions hold vast archives of important historical material. However, unlike courts or government departments, once the royal commission ends, it ceases to exist. In practice (and at law), then, questions of access, care and responsibility in respect of its records leave the 'commission as inquiry' behind, to be answered, often incompletely, by agencies who take, or are left with, responsibility for the commission's archive.

There remains a dearth of attention to the practical and theoretical issues attending royal commission archives. Indeed, when the Australian Law Reform Commission considered the arrangements for royal commission records in 2007, it noted that it had 'received limited feedback from stakeholders regarding issues of access and use of documents or things collected by completed Royal Commissions or other public inquiries'.[45]

As we illustrate below, access, care and responsibility for these records are, often, adrift between multiple legislative regimes, which prejudices their public availability and promotion, as well as the integrity of the archive itself. However, before doing so, it is necessary to conceive of 'the royal commission as archive' and to identify the risks, stakes and imperatives for civil society, public accountability, transparency and governance posed by these volumes of material.

---

44 Dara M Price and Johanna J Smith, 'The Trust Continuum in the Information Age' (2011) 11 *Archival Science* 253, 266.
45 Australian Law Reform Commission, *Royal Commissions and Official Inquiries*, Discussion Paper No 75 (2007), [8.47].

The Royal Commission as Archive?

The documentary record of a royal commission cannot be conceived of as mere residue, pressed into obscurity by the primacy of the commission's final report and the fulfilment of its terms of reference. Rather, the royal commission's archive must be treated as a powerful and important product of government in its own right. While it may be correct that 'there seems to be little consensus as to what an archive is',[46] in describing the archives of the royal commission here, we seek to speak of the totality of material held by the institution before its cessation, including the transcripts of evidence, commissioner's notes, documents produced to, or seized by, an inquiry, investigative records and the administrative records of the commission regarding its own operation.[47] In this sense, as we discuss below, it is an archive—the 'official record' of the commission[48]—but also a body of material, which may have a life of its own after the commission's terms of reference are fulfilled. This is so in three key respects.

Royal Commission Archives as Key to Executing its Functions

First, the vast archives of royal commissions are a substantial product of the inquiry process. Inasmuch as the inquiry process may have invited or coerced individuals and institutions to provide it with information, it is the total record of its work, and not necessarily the report, that retains the information it has elicited. Clearly, in this way, the archive has 'obvious informational value'[49] and is integral to taking action on the basis of that information. For example, the Australian Law Reform Commission has highlighted the critical importance of royal commission records for law enforcement, implementing inquiry recommendations and advising on the administration of laws.[50] It is an archive in the sense described by Ridener as a 'place for the uncovering of records which are not duplicated in any other [single] place'.[51] The importance of the archive here is

---

46   Spieker Sven, *The Big Archive: Art from Bureaucracy* (MIT Press, 2008) 4.
47   Developing a conception of the archive in this way has been a central goal of the Court as Archive Project, undertaken by the editors of this text. Both authors acknowledge the work of the project in foregrounding attention to the archives of institutions in this way.
48   For further discussion of the multiple meanings of 'the archive' in connection with legal processes, see Katherine Biber and Trish Luker, 'Evidence and the Archive: Ethics, Aesthetics and Emotion' (2014) 40(1) *Australian Feminist Law Journal* 1, 5–11.
49   Price and Smith, above n 44.
50   Australian Law Reform Commission, above n 45, [8.47].
51   John Ridener, *From Polders to Postmodernism: A Concise History of Archival Theory* (Litwin Books, 2008) 4.

straightforward: it provides for direct action on the information gathered by the commission towards the purposes for which it was established. Similarly, especially in the case of commissions that have uncovered harm to individuals, the particular records of this evidence are vital for individuals who may seek to pursue civil or coronial proceedings.

As a body of evidence, too, the records created by the commission may arguably represent *the* key product of a royal commission's processes. As Price and Smith write of Canadian royal commissions (referring here to the Indian Specific Claims Commission [ISCC]):

> In light of the fact that the ISCC had no real legislative or adjudicative power, the records represent the key product of the process, and the most important means by which it could exert moral influence in society. The *raison d'etre* of the Inquiry becomes the collection, collation and preservation of a permanent, coherent body of evidence.[52]

Royal Commission Archives as an Accountability and Critique Mechanism

Second, prioritising and thinking consciously about the royal commission as archive is critical to allowing for critique of the commission's governmental, social and cultural functions. Given the delicate relationship of trust between the institution of the commission and the public outlined above, its records may form, at the very least, 'evidence that the government has [or has not] carried out its responsibilities to society'[53] and an 'audit trail', which may reveal 'evidence of negligence, malfeasance and missteps'.[54] In this sense, the archive is an accountability mechanism providing an 'official record' against which the technical strength and cogency of the commission's findings and recommendations may be assessed.[55]

---

52 Price and Smith, above n 44, 270.
53 Ibid 265.
54 Ibid 266.
55 The archive here may arguably provide a continued honouring of the active engagement sought by the commission as inquiry between 'active citizens' and government. For example, Barry Sullivan (citing James Madison) has argued that 'the right to know' is a fundamental tenet of a model of representative democracy, which expects engagement by citizens with the architecture of government. See Sullivan, above n 22, 35.

Moreover, as cultural theorists, archivists and (now) legal scholars[56] argue, the ability to interrogate the form and context of state archives, in addition to its content, provides opportunities for critical engagement with the power relations inherent in its production, and of state power. As Steedman has written, 'in its quiet folders and bundles is the neatest demonstration of how state power has operated, through ledgers and lists and indictments, and through what is missing from them'.[57]

In this context, we are concerned not just with the content of information acquired by the commission, but also with information *created* by it. This includes the records of its own administration, its operational decisions and evidence of the way it has curated its public presence and shaped its priorities. At a deeper level, it includes the totality of the record and what it may implicitly reveal about the commission as an instrument of governance; the construction and resolution of the issues under its remit; and the things it silences and privileges. In this sense, the archive is the site at which to read, for example, 'what can be said' before a commission[58] and what cannot, and the ways in which knowledge, semantics and the legal method may elevate certain evidence, or diminish or disempower others during its operation.[59] In addition, as Stoler makes clear, attention to the 'surplus production' of state archives—the marginalia, edits and footnotes, handwritten drafts and the contradiction between official and unofficial records—may open up new reflections on the psychic state of the empire.[60]

Importantly, the royal commission as archive is a site for disturbing, potentially, the 'coherence' of the official record and its intended 'moral influence' (as referred to by Price and Smith, cited above). It is an opportunity to critique the state and the commission, and to see more

---

56   See, for example, the emerging literature in relation to 'law's archive' captured in a special issue (2014) 40(1) *Australian Feminist Law Journal*.
57   Carolyn Steedman, *Dust: The Archive and Cultural History* (Manchester University Press, 2001) 68.
58   As van Rijswijk writes, for Foucault, the archive is not just 'that whole mass of texts that belong to a single discursive [in this case legal formation]', but should also be thought of as the 'law of what can be said, the system that governs the appearance of statements'; see Honni van Rijswijk, 'Archiving the Northern Territory Intervention in Law and in the Literary Counter-Imaginary' (2014) 40(1) *Australian Feminist Law Journal* 117, 119.
59   Rebecca Monson, 'Unsettled Explorations of Law's Archives: The Allure and Anxiety of Solomon Islands' Court Records' (2014) 40(1) *Australian Feminist Law Journal* 35, 39.
60   Ann Laura Stoler, 'Colonial Archives and the Arts of Governance' (2002) 2 *Archival Science* 87; Ann Laura Stoler, *Along the Archival Grain: Epistemic Anxieties and Colonial Common Sense* (Princeton University Press, 2009) 41.

clearly the interaction between those who govern and are governed. It is a place to read what is missing (eg, the omission of swearing from the accounts of police–state interaction, witnessed by Cowlishaw during the RCIADIC) and, potentially,[61] to uncover traces of alternative narratives.

Royal Commission Archives as Social, Public Memory

Third, the collected records of royal commissions are undeniably significant repositories of public memory. In collecting together previously untold life stories, investigations of institutional actions, narratives of the interaction between the state and its citizens, corruption, corporate failures and other matters of national importance, the records of royal commissions provide a 'vital aspect of the social memory of modern societies'.[62] In particular, in the minutiae of the documents created during an inquiry, the royal commission archive is a record not just of public decisions and the formation of public policy, but also of 'information about how public laws and regulations and public institutions affect individual citizens in various aspects of their lives'.[63] For example, as Cowlishaw observed of the public material she viewed during the conduct of the RCIADIC (and which is now, as we discuss below, subject to a complex legislative access scheme), 'the vast array of files reveals the levels of monitoring and surveillance, which Aboriginals [sic] have been subjected to, and attests to the fact that they have not been authorised to produce their own accounts of their experiences'.[64]

---

61 Accepting that there are strong critiques of an uncritical approach of 'going back to the archives' to 'produce a more correct account'. See further, Victoria Brown 'Explorations in Feminist Historiography: Rhetoric, Affect and "What Really Happened" in Feminism's Recent Past' (2014) 7(2) *Subjectivity* 210, 212.
62 Inge Bundsgaard, 'The Question of Access: The Right to Social Memory versus the Right to Social Oblivion' in Francis X Blouin Jr and William G Rosenberg (eds), *Archives, Documentation, and Institutions of Social Memory* (University of Michigan Press, 2006) 114.
63 Blouin Jr and Rosenberg, above n 62, 114.
64 Cowlishaw, above n 3, 33; see also, for example, the use of inquiry transcripts (in this case, a parliamentary inquiry, rather than a royal commission) in the 'Minutes of Evidence Project', which aimed to 'spark … conversations about history and structural justice through the professional performance of transcripts of evidence given before the 1881 Victorian Parliamentary Coranderrk Inquiry'. See further, Minutes of Evidence Project, *Performance: We Will Show the Country* (n.d.) <http://www.minutesofevidence.com.au/performance/>.

Dislocation, Absence and Complexity in Locating and Accessing the Commission as Archive

The existing scheme for managing the records of royal commissions does not understand these records as a single archival resource and relies heavily on ad hoc executive action—be it ministerial direction, ministerial approval to 'special access' or intergovernmental agreement—to supply the content of custody and access arrangements. As we suggest below, this dislocated regulatory approach undermines both the integrity of the royal commission archive and the capacity of the royal commission to fulfil its functions and create meaningful public records.

The legislative difficulty in regulating records of royal commissions (whether of single or joint jurisdictional character) is in part a product of the unique nature of royal commissions as entities. Although an executive entity during the term of an inquiry, a royal commission ceases to exist in law once the period provided for in its establishing letters patent lapses (without being extended by issue of subsequent or amending letters patent). Thus, given absent specific legislative provision, complex questions can arise as to the ownership of royal commission records once a commission ends.

Joint Commonwealth and State/Territory Royal Commissions

The complexities attending access to royal commission records in this respect are most acute in the context of joint royal commissions. Such commissions are the necessary institutional structure where the Commonwealth seeks to inquire into matters that wholly or partly fall outside the scope of Commonwealth legislative power.[65] They may also be the preferred institutional structure—though one strictly unnecessary, as a matter of constitutional power—where the governments of more than one Australian jurisdiction seek to inquire into a subject matter within Commonwealth legislative power, but in which the states have some interest. To enable joint royal commissions to coercively obtain

---

65 Within the terms of s 51 of the *Australian Constitution*.

information and documents across territorial boundaries, the relevant inquiring institution is typically conferred with evidence-gathering powers under the statutes of each participating jurisdiction.[66]

In the context of these royal commissions, where material is received and produced during the course of an inquiry, records within the archive may be of multifaceted jurisdictional character. Is a document produced under summons issued in reliance on more than one coercive power (ie, under legislation of more than one participating jurisdiction)[67] a document of the jurisdiction in which it was produced, a document of the jurisdiction in which the summons was served or a document of both state and federal character? Similarly, is a document produced by a commission sitting as a state and federal commission a state, Commonwealth or state *and* Commonwealth document?

The existing legal apparatus to meet such complexity is presently also multifaceted and, we argue, unresolved. As we detail below, further complexity attends the custody and access to records of joint royal commissions, but also commissions commenced by a single government.

Custody, Possession and Use of Commonwealth and Joint Commonwealth and State/Territory Royal Commission Records

Although each Australian jurisdiction has enacted legislation providing for the exercise of coercive powers by joint royal commissions, these legislative schemes operate incompletely in their treatment of records produced by such inquiries once the relevant inquiry ends. Only the *Inquiries Act 2014* (Vic) makes express provision for the treatment of records of state

---

66   *Royal Commissions Act 1923* (NSW), s 8; *Commissions of Inquiry Act 1950* (Qld), s 5; *Royal Commissions Act 1917* (SA), s 10; *Commissions of Inquiry Act 1995* (Tas), s 22; *Inquiries Act 2014* (Vic), s 17 (read with s 7); *Royal Commissions Act 1968* (WA), s 9; read with ss 2 and 7AA of the *Royal Commissions Act 1902* (Cth).
67   See, for example, *Re Winneke; ex Parte Gallagher* (1982) 152 CLR 211, concerning a summons issued in reliance on the *Royal Commissions Act 1902* (Cth) and the *Evidence Act 1958* (Vic) (which, at that time, governed the powers exercisable by state commissions). The question of how documents were produced in response to a summons with dual jurisdictional character was not answered by the High Court.

commissions to which that Act applies.[68] Other state jurisdictions merely treat royal commission records as any other document of an executive body, subject to state public archives legislation, but not differentiated in their treatment (for custody, possession, use and access purposes).[69]

This characterisation becomes important when considering the application of the archives provisions of the *Royal Commissions Act 1902* (Cth) and the *Archives Act 1983* (Cth) ('*Archives Act*'). Overlaying the idiosyncratic state royal commissions regimes, the *Royal Commissions Act 1902* (Cth) and *Archives Act* make specific provision, albeit incompletely, for the treatment of the records of joint royal commissions.

Section 9(2) of the *Royal Commissions Act 1902* (Cth) provides for the making of regulations for the custody in which some or all of the records of a Commonwealth royal commission[70] are to be kept. Such regulations may also provide for the purposes for which relevant records may and must not be used,[71] as well as the circumstances in which a custodian[72] of royal commission records must give possession of, or access to, those records to other persons or bodies.[73]

Section 9(3) prescribes the persons and bodies who may be given custody of royal commission records by regulations made under s 9(2). All of the prescribed custodians are Commonwealth institutions, save for two: state Attorneys-General and state law enforcement bodies. That the Act provides for state custodians of royal commission records is relevant to the discussion below of the access regime prescribed by the *Archives Act*. This is because where regulations are made for the purposes of s 9(2) of

---

68 The *Commissions of Inquiry Act 1950* (Qld) does empower the commissioner of a relevant inquiry to make directions as to the custody of records while a commission is on foot, but is otherwise silent on what is to happen once a commission ends: s 19B(2).
69 See, for example, *State Records Act 1998* (NSW), s 3(1)(i) (definition of 'public office'), which includes a 'Royal Commission or Commission of Inquiry'; and s 7(4A), which provides, relevantly, that the records of a public office that has ceased to exist, and which was a royal commission or commission of inquiry, are to be subject to the control of the Cabinet Office. See also the various record-keeping obligations of 'public offices', as defined: *State Records Act*, ss 11–15, 21–25 and 26–36A.
70 See s 1B(1) definition of 'Royal Commission'.
71 Section 9(2)(b), (e); see also s 9(6), (7).
72 Section 9(3) prescribes the persons and bodies who may be given custody of records by regulations made under s 9(2).
73 Section 9(2)(c), (d).

the *Royal Commissions Act 1902* (Cth), the *Archives Act* has effect as if a direction to the same effect were in force under s 22(3) of that Act.[74] In any event, it is worth noting that regulations for the purposes of s 9(2) have only been made in the context of two previous commissions.[75]

The *Archives Act* extensively prescribes the circumstances in which a 'Commonwealth record' is to be dealt with and accessed.[76] A 'Commonwealth record' is defined as a record that is either the 'property of the Commonwealth or of a Commonwealth institution' or a record that is deemed to be a Commonwealth record by operation of s 22.[77] Royal commission records fall outside the ordinary definition of 'Commonwealth record', given that there is no legal entity in possession of relevant records once a commission ends. However, s 22(2) of the *Archives Act* deems records kept by a royal commission (defined, relevantly, as a Commonwealth royal commission)[78] to be 'Commonwealth records' for the purposes of the Act and provides that the Commonwealth is entitled to the possession of such records once they are no longer required for the purposes of a commission.

Section 22(3) requires that deemed Commonwealth records be kept in such custody as the relevant responsible Commonwealth Minister directs and the National Archives of Australia (NAA) is not entitled to the 'care' of such records except in accordance with such a direction.[79] As the Australian Law Reform Commission has observed, the effect of s 22(3) is that there is no legal requirement for records of royal commissions to be

---

74 Section 9(5).
75 The Royal Commission into Trade Union Governance and Corruption and the Oil-for-Food Inquiry: *Royal Commissions Regulations 2001* (Cth), regs 8 and 9. A separate regulatory regime was enacted to provide for the transfer of certain records of the HIH Royal Commission (which was not a joint commission) to the Australian Securities and Investment Commission: *HIH Royal Commission (Transfer of Records) Act 2003* (Cth); *HIH Royal Commission (Transfer of Records) Regulations 2003* (Cth).
76 Pt V, divs 3 and 4.
77 *Archives Act*, s 3(1). The definition excludes certain presently irrelevant material.
78 Being the records kept by a royal commission commenced or completed before or after the commencement of Part V of the *Archives Act*, s 22(1).
79 Section 22(3).

transferred to the NAA.[80] The authors suggest that this lack of obligation to transfer royal commission records to the NAA, coupled with the potential in the existing legislative context for the records of a royal commission to be in the custody or possession of multiple Commonwealth and state agencies, undermines the integrity of such records as archival resources. This problem is exacerbated by the complex regime governing access to the records of joint royal commissions, considered further below.

Access to Royal Commission Records — Commonwealth and Joint Commonwealth and State/Territory

Royal commission records to which the *Archives Act* applies are subject to the ordinary open access periods prescribed by that Act,[81] save in the case of certain records relating to 'private sessions' of the Child Abuse RC.[82] It is important to consider the practical implications of this statement. First, the import of this rule is that many of a royal commission's records that were public during the life of the commission (eg, public submissions, transcripts of public hearings and other material hosted on the commission website, if it is not maintained online) cease to be public before the open access period is reached. Except in the case of Cabinet notebooks or recordings containing Census information, the open access period commences 31 years after the date the document was created. Second, in order to be subject to the *Archives Act* and the open access period, a record must be a Commonwealth record: a status that is by no means clear in relation to the records of joint royal commissions.

---

80   Australian Law Reform Commission, *Making Inquiries: A New Statutory Framework*, Report No 111 (2009), [8.47–8.48] ('*Making Inquiries*'). Section 27 of the *Archives Act* prescribes a time frame for transfer of certain 'Commonwealth records' to the NAA; however, that provision is unlikely to apply to royal commission records. Section 27 only applies to a record that is in the custody of a Commonwealth institution other than the NAA (s 27(1)(a)) and that has been determined to be part of the archival resources of the Commonwealth under s 3C (s 27(1)(b)). It would seem to subvert the clear legislative intention of s 22 (namely, that royal commission records be dealt with under a regime separate to that applying to ordinary Commonwealth records) if the Director-General could make a direction under s 3C that, of its own force, had the effect of bringing royal commission records within the operation of s 27 and, thus, circumventing the operation of s 22 (which, critically, provides that the responsible Minister is the *only* decision-maker who can determine that royal commission records be transferred to the NAA). In our view, this regime is very likely to engage the principle in *Anthony Horden & Sons Ltd v Amalgamated Clothing and Allied Trades Union of Australia* (1932) 47 CLR 1, 7. In any event, s 27 would not apply to records of joint royal commissions, given that the provision only applies to Commonwealth records (that meet the requirements of s 27(a) and (b)).
81   *Archives Act*, pt V and definition of 'open access period' (s 3(1)(c) and (7)).
82   *Royal Commissions Act 1902* (Cth), s 6OM.

Records that are in the open access period and in the care of the NAA or the custody of a Commonwealth institution (and which are not otherwise exempt)[83] are required to be made publicly available. Any non-publication direction given by a royal commission in respect of such records (necessarily during the life of a commission) ceases to apply once the records enter the open access period.[84]

Access to royal commission records may be provided under the *Freedom of Information Act 1982* (Cth), subject to the limitations of that Act; however, this may only occur while the relevant record is not in the open access period.[85] Access may also be provided outside of the open access period where 'special access' is granted by the responsible Minister, in accordance with arrangements approved by the Prime Minister.[86] However, 'special access' may only be granted in respect of royal commission records deemed to be Commonwealth records by operation s 22 of the *Archives Act*.

In the context of joint commissions, a greater impediment to access is s 22(6), which provides that the deeming and custody provisions of s 22(2) and (3) only apply to joint royal commissions to the extent determined by agreement between the Commonwealth and the relevant participating state(s). Neither the *Archives Act* nor the *Royal Commissions Act 1902* (Cth) supply the content to arrangements made by the Commonwealth and the states for the purposes of s 22(6) and such arrangements are not required to be tabled in Parliament, gazetted or otherwise published publicly. Practice also suggests that such arrangements may not be finalised until a royal commission is approaching its effluxion date or may not be made at all.

Before turning to consider difficulties of access in practice, one further point of note is that records of Commonwealth royal commissions that are in the custody of a state custodian (ie, a state Attorney-General or a state law enforcement agency) would seem not to be subject to the access obligations in the *Archives Act* and may not be subject to the access obligations contained in state public records legislation.[87] As will be

---

83 As to which, see ss 29, 33 and 35.
84 *Archives Act*, s 22(4).
85 *Freedom of Information Act 1982* (Cth), ss 12(1) and 13(3).
86 *Archives Act*, s 56(1).
87 For example, records received by the Attorney-General of Victoria or Victoria Police would seem not to meet the definition of 'public record' for the purposes of the *Public Records Act 1973* (Vic): see the s 2(1) definitions of 'public record' (para (a)), 'public officer' and 'public office'.

suggested later, legislative gaps of this sort would best be addressed by a cooperative legislative scheme, supported by referrals of power from the states to the Commonwealth.

Record Movements and the Difficulties of Access in Practice

Although royal commission records *may* be transferred to the NAA, the existing legislative scheme does not prescribe a time frame for such transfer.[88] The absence of such a requirement, combined with the existing scheme's reliance on executive action, gives rise to the real possibility that a commission may end without clear requirements for record management having been in place during the course of its inquiry. In an immediate sense, this creates a risk of records being be disposed of or collated ineffectively by the commission (and subsequent custodians). In the longer term, failure to have arrangements in place for the treatment of records before a relevant inquiry ends leaves those records in an ambiguous legal state, productive of accessibility issues for citizens and administrative burden for participating governments.

Thus, royal commission records often exist in an indeterminate state of partial regulation, formally subject to the *Archives Act*, but not to substantive arrangements of the kinds contemplated by that Act.

Contact with the NAA and with researchers and practitioners attempting to engage with the work of royal commissions reveals the practical impediments created by such complexities.

Locating the Archive in the Regulatory Penumbra

The NAA estimates that there are over 100 royal commissions affected by issues arising from the application of ss 22(3) and (6) of the *Archives Act*. This includes commissions where no direction under s 22(3) was given before the commission ended and joint commissions, of which there are several, for which there are no arrangements in place for the purposes of s 22(6).[89] The vast majority of these commissions have long since ended.

---

88 Australian Law Reform Commission, *Making Inquiries*, at [8.48]. Please see n 80 for the authors' analysis of the relevant provision of the *Archives Act*.
89 Interview with the staff of the National Archives of Australia (4 September 2017).

Because the existing scheme does not proscribe the division of collections of royal commission records, when a royal commission ends, its records have often been divided and dispersed. In this respect, the report of the Australian Law Reform Commission Inquiry into Royal Commissions, *Making Inquiries: A New Statutory Framework*, noted that, as a matter of practice, records concerning the administration of royal commissions (such as internal correspondence) have been transferred to the Attorney-General's Department, while substantive records (such as transcripts, evidence and submissions) have been transferred to the Department of the Prime Minister and Cabinet.[90] Further, because there is no existing legislative mechanism for automatic transfer of records to the NAA and the *Archives Act* does not otherwise specify a time frame within which records should be transferred to the NAA,[91] the existing scheme creates the potential for records to remain indefinitely with a custodial department (be it the Attorney-General's Department or the Department of the Prime Minister and Cabinet).

In the case of commissions for which no s 22(3) direction is given, or no s 22(6) arrangement is agreed, there may be no formal mechanism by which the NAA can grant access to such records.[92] In the case of commissions for which there are no s 22(6) arrangements in place, the records of those commissions (at least on one argument) may not necessarily be Commonwealth records at all. More broadly, because s 22(6) agreements subject certain records to the legislation of one jurisdiction,[93] unless an agreement is in place, it may be unclear whether Commonwealth or state legislation properly governs such records. While original records are generally not split across states, in the case of one or two joint commissions, the NAA may hold copies of publicly available material, while a state holds the original documents.[94] Of course, this will not necessarily mean that an individual's access is straightforward without a s 22(6) arrangement being in place. It appears, too, that some material relating to a royal commission may have been deposited by the Commissioner himself (Frank Costigan QC) with his personal papers at the State Library of Victoria.[95]

---

90 *Making Inquiries* [8.48]; see n 80 for the authors' analysis of the relevant provisions of the *Archives Act*.
91 Ibid.
92 Interview with the staff of National Archives of Australia (4 September 2017).
93 Ibid.
94 Ibid.
95 Francis Xavier Costigan, *Papers of Francis Costigan* (1968–2009), State Library of Victoria <http://search.slv.vic.gov.au/MAIN:Everything:SLV_VOYAGER2442558>.

While the NAA endeavours to facilitate access to material of royal commissions affected by ss 22(3) and (6) issues, the NAA has not been able to give access to some of these records.[96] In the NAA's view, this is a consequence of the inconsistent application of the existing legislative scheme.[97]

Websites recording the work of royal commissions are also not uniformly dealt with. Some are preserved and hosted by the Attorney-General's Department for an indeterminate period of time, although they are generally not preserved in any permanent sense.[98] Material on commission websites may or may not be selected by the National Library of Australia to go to the PANDORA Archive[99] or to the Australian Government Web Archive.[100] However, difficulties abound around how such material, particularly audio and video files, is harvested and may be particularly acute in the context of content-heavy websites, such as royal commission sites.[101] For example, in its *Statement of Preservation Intent on Selective Web Harvesting*, the National Library acknowledges the limits of web archiving, including that 'the way in which the content is collected and displayed may mean that there is significant limitation on the presentation of the archived artefact as an authentic record of the publisher's original date'.[102]

Section 22(3) and the Human Relationships RC

The Human Relationships RC was a joint commission established by the Whitlam Government in 1973 to 'inquire into and report upon the family, social, educational, legal and sexual aspects of male and female relationships, so far as those matters are relevant to the powers and functions of the Australian Parliament and Government, including powers and functions in relation to the Territories', and to give particular emphasis to

---

96 Interview with the staff of National Archives of Australia (4 September 2017).
97 Ibid.
98 *Making Inquiries*, [8.48]. Contrary to the Australian Law Reform Commission's view, websites that it considered 'safe' are no longer accessible and have not been re-archived elsewhere.
99 A web archive established by the National Library of Australia, which is now maintained by the National Library of Australia and 10 other Australian libraries. At least some records of the Royal Commission into HIH Insurance were dealt with in this manner.
100 An initiative of the National Library of Australia, designed to complement the PANDORA Archive.
101 National Library of Australia, *Statement of Preservation Intent on Selective Web Harvesting* (1 March 2013) <https://www.nla.gov.au/content/preservation-intent-selective-web-harvesting>; see also Paul Koerbin, *Report on the Crawl and Harvest of the Whole Australian Web Domain Undertaken during June and July 2005* (10 October 2005), National Library of Australia, <http://pandora.nla.gov.au/documents/domain_harvest_report_public.pdf>.
102 National Library of Australia, above n 101.

various matters associated with responsible parenting.¹⁰³ A controversial commission, which was ended abruptly following Whitlam's dismissal, the commission's records were transferred to the NAA without a direction under s 22(3) having been made.¹⁰⁴ In the absence of a s 22(3) direction, the Department of the Prime Minister and Cabinet remains responsible today for determining how access to the records of that commission is given.¹⁰⁵ The basis for such access would appear to be the 'special access' mechanism in s 56(1) of the *Archives Act*, the parameters of which are otherwise not prescribed by the Act.

It took sociology researcher Dr Katie Wright over a year to gain access to records of the Human Relationships RC. This was eventually granted as 'special access', although only on the condition that the NAA would be required to examine each record before the material could be used for research.¹⁰⁶ In obtaining this permission, the researcher was advised that, although the records of the Human Relationships RC are in the open access period and that several records have already been examined for public access (as well as made digitally available on the NAA's website), most of the records are yet to be examined for the purposes of determining whether access to them can be granted.¹⁰⁷

Section 22(6) and the Child Abuse RC

The Child Abuse RC, a joint commission of all Australian jurisdictions, concluded its inquiry in December 2017, and is currently the site of contestation and ambiguity with respect to its records. Questions of access are of particular importance to participants in this inquiry, many of whom are survivors of abuse with a direct and profound interest in the commission's work.¹⁰⁸

---

103 Australia, Royal Commission on Human Relationships, *Final Report* (1977), Volume 1, xi.
104 Interview with Dr Katie Wright, La Trobe University (20 January 2017).
105 Ibid.
106 Ibid.
107 Ibid.
108 The Child Abuse RC's own final report noted that easily accessible, high-quality records and record-keeping practices have particular significance for survivors of child sexual abuse: Child Abuse RC, *Final Report: Volume 8, Recordkeeping and Information Sharing*, 38–40. Justice Coate, writing about her role as a Commissioner of the Child Abuse RC, has also directly detailed the significance of records generally to care leavers and survivors of abuse. See Jennifer Coate, 'Perspectives on Records and Archives: An Update from the Royal Commission' (2017) 45(3) *Archives and Manuscripts* 237.

Knowmore, which is a specialist community legal centre that was established to assist survivors of child sexual abuse to engage with the commission's inquiry, anticipates that issues concerning access to the commission's record will, in two respects, be of immediate practical significance for survivors of abuse.[109] First, access to commission records (particularly transcripts of public hearings) will be important for holding institutions accountable for evidence given to the commission; that is, for verifying that their conduct in response to allegations of abuse is consistent with representations made to the commission about such responses.[110] Second, access to recordings of private sessions[111] will be a significant tool for avoiding retraumatising survivors when legal representatives take instructions for the purposes of preparing civil claims or claims under the Commonwealth redress scheme.[112]

Despite discussions between the commission, government and stakeholders in the commission's work that occurred prior to the commission ending, uncertainty remains as to whether, and, if so, how, survivors will be able to access such material now that the commission has ended. For example, it seems likely that the commission's website will remain accessible, although it is unclear whether a systems' administrator will be employed to maintain that material and to ensure that the website's links remain active.[113] Moreover, prior to the commission ending, no formal arrangements, including for the purposes of s 22(6), had been agreed and no provisions had been put in place for the transfer of records to the NAA or for access to records more generally.[114]

---

109 Interview with Prue Gregory, Principal Lawyer, Knowmore (29 September 2017).
110 Ibid.
111 In this respect, the Child Abuse RC was the first Commonwealth commission to be empowered by legislation to receive information from witnesses in private session. Amendments made to the *Royal Commissions Act 1902* (Cth) by the *Royal Commissions Amendment Act 2013* (Cth) made specific provision for how information given at a private session is to be held and used: *Royal Commissions Act 1902* (Cth), pt 4, div 2.
112 *National Redress Scheme for Institutional Child Sexual Abuse Act 2018* (Cth); see also Royal Commission into Institutional Responses to Child Sexual Abuse, *Redress and Civil Litigation Report* (2015), <https://www.dss.gov.au/families-and-children/programs-services/children/commonwealth-redress-scheme-for-survivors-of-institutional-child-sexual-abuse>.
113 Interview with Prue Gregory, Principal Lawyer, Knowmore (29 September 2017).
114 At the time of writing, the Child Abuse RC's website states only that inquiries concerning access to records should be directed to the Commonwealth Attorney-General's Department.

The *Royal Commissions Act 1902* (Cth) itself also creates access impediments. Relevantly, that Act prescribes that, for the purposes of the *Archives Act*, records that contain information obtained at a private session or that relate to a private session, and which identify a natural person who appeared at a private session, enter the open access period only 99 years after the relevant record came into existence.[115] Knowmore already anticipates that it will be important for survivors of abuse to have access to private session material well before the end of the 99-year closed access period.[116] Survivors may have an interest in accessing both the recording of a private session in which they gave information to the commission and in otherwise knowing what is contained in their private session file.[117] With respect to the former category of material, in practice, no transcripts of private sessions are available.[118] Rather, a survivor or their representative has previously been able to seek access to the audio recording of a private session by giving several months' notice to the commission.[119] Access to such records has been closely supervised by the commission and has typically been provided on the condition that no notes are made of comments made by commissioners, or commission officers, during these sessions.[120] However, the last date by which requests could be made for access to private session recordings was the end of September 2017, and it remains unclear where these recordings will be held now that the commission has ended.[121] With respect to original documents given to the commission during a private session, it was anticipated that the commission would attempt to return such documents to the relevant survivor before its inquiry ended.[122] However, if it was unable to do so in time, such documents will likely be destroyed.[123]

---

115 *Royal Commissions Act 1902* (Cth), s 6OM.
116 Interview with Prue Gregory, Principal Lawyer, Knowmore (29 September 2017).
117 Ibid.
118 Ibid.
119 Ibid.
120 Ibid.
121 Ibid.
122 Ibid.
123 Ibid.

When the Carnival is Over: The Case for Reform

Beyond Institutional Identity as an Organising Principle

The Australian Law Reform Commission has noted that the utility of royal commissions 'depends in large part upon the extent to which their findings and recommendations are able to be acted upon and the uses to which their records may subsequently be put'.[124] Gaps in records management—such as those created by royal commissions ending without s 22(3) directions and/or s 22(6) arrangements in place—thus, inevitably undermine the practical value of the work of such commissions.

The regulatory deficiencies identified above are a consequence of the central premise of the existing legislative scheme; namely, that the complex institutional identity of royal commissions, particularly joint royal commissions, should in some way govern how records are dealt with once the relevant inquiry comes to an end. On the one hand, s 22(3) reflects a view of the royal commission as an executive entity. It betrays an assumption that there may be a department or agency of government better placed than the NAA to manage the care and custody of certain royal commission records (whether by reason of the nature or provenance of the records or the nature of the inquiry during which the records were produced). On the other hand, s 22(6) reflects a view of the royal commission as jurisdictionally bounded, reserving as it does a capacity for states and territories to exert control over the records of their own commissions.

These conceptions of the commission—as executive decision-maker with immutably jurisdictional character—admit of the potential for multiple archival authorities to become responsible for the documentary fruits of a commission's labour. The involvement of multiple archival authorities in turn creates risks to the integrity of the archive at multiple stages of the archival journey: from appraisal and acquisition to description and access. As Cook notes, concepts such as *respect des fonds*, original order and provenance serve to ensure that records are preserved 'as evidence of

---

124 Australian Law Reform Commission, above n 45, [8.4].

the functional-structural context and actions that caused their creation'.[125] A dislocated approach to archives management also undermines the capacity of the royal commission to provide opportunity for critique of its findings and, as we suggested, has broad implications for its functions as a body of evidence, a repository of social, public memory and a tangible product of a non-binding inquiry.

Towards Cooperative Centralisation

In light of the complexities discussed above, the authors suggest that reform is necessary to facilitate greater public access to the content of the archive, and, in turn, greater critical understanding of the silences and priorities in its creation. Good archival practice also assists investigative processes[126] and is central to ensuring that royal commissions are able to perform their roles as 'recognizable and repeatable components of a successful and reliable democratic civil society'.[127]

Pursuit of a general intergovernmental agreement, providing certain minimum standards for arrangements between the Commonwealth and a state (or states) for the purposes of s 22(6) of the *Archives Act*, could provide greater certainty around management of archival material and set a benchmark for community expectations of records management during, and after, the life of a commission. A general agreement of this type might provide for the types of documents that, in all cases, will go to the NAA, and for the custody in which those documents will be held once a commission ends.

However, relying on non-legislative means to provide for care, custody, use and access arrangements would not bind future governments in the establishment of new royal commissions. Nor would it address the serious legislative deficiencies arising from the interaction of the *Royal Commissions Act 1902* (Cth), the *Archives Act* and state commissions

---

125 Terry Cook, 'Evidence, Memory, Identity, and Community: Four shifting archival paradigms' (2013) 13 *Archival Science* 95, 100.
126 Considering the relevance of archival practice to judicial inquiry, Barrera defines good archival practice as including identification of the institutional context in which documents have been produced, accurate archival descriptions and use of electronic resources: Giulia Barrera, 'Of Condors and Judges: Archival Musings over a Judicial Investigation' (2009) 9 *Archival Science* 203, 212.
127 Price and Smith, above n 44, 266.

and public records legislation. In the context of joint royal commissions, reliance on ad hoc executive action to fill gaps in legislative prescription is particularly problematic.

At the best of times, intergovernmental cooperation can be fraught, piecemeal and dependent on the political will of the government of the day. In the context of commissions concerning issues of public trust or government accountability, it might be exceptionally difficult to disabuse participating jurisdictions of their possessive tendencies towards documents produced in, or by the governments of, each jurisdiction. So much can perhaps be inferred from the number of concluded joint commissions for which there are still no s 22(6) arrangements in place. Equally, legislative reform, particularly cooperative reform—that is, with the participation of more than one Australian jurisdiction—would require longer term commitment by participating jurisdictions and deeper intergovernmental cooperation, often at the highest levels of government.

Acknowledging these challenges, a cooperative scheme, supported by referrals of legislative power from the states, for the purposes of s 51(xxxvii) of the *Constitution*, offers the most effective means of achieving archival reform applicable to royal commissions. This might involve the Commonwealth Parliament being referred, to the extent necessary, the power to legislate with respect to the subject matter of royal commission records.[128] Although the features of such a scheme are beyond the scope of this chapter, it bears repeating that any proposed model for archival reform would need to transcend the complex institutional identity of the royal commission, rather than accept it as an organising principle.

---

128 The Commonwealth would already have legislative power with respect to the records of Commonwealth royal commissions, but a referral may be necessary to empower the Commonwealth to legislate in respect of records of joint commissions that could be characterised as state documents. For an example of this approach, see the terms of the referrals supporting the *Corporations Act 2001* (Cth): *Corporations (Commonwealth Powers) Act 2001* (NSW) s 4; *Corporations (Commonwealth Powers) Act 2001* (Qld) s 4; Corporations *(Commonwealth Powers) Act 2001* (SA) s 4; *Corporations (Commonwealth Powers) Act 2001* (Tas) s 5; *Corporations (Commonwealth Powers) Act 2001* (Vic) s 4; *Corporations (Commonwealth Powers) Act 2001* (WA) s 4.

Part 2—Histories and Jurisprudence of Australia

4

A Matter of Records: The Federal Court, The National Archives and 'The National Estate' in the 1970s

Ann Genovese

Introduction

Australian scholars of law and history have duties to the places and institutions in which we practice our activities, to show adequately the conduct of the encounters between laws, and the histories of lives that have experienced those laws. This includes being conscious of the diverse range of records and sources that are needed to tell these law stories (the institutional to the unofficial; film to interview; diary to case law; legislation to memoir). It also means being conscious of the diversity of styles and genres of writing (reports, chronicle and fragments as much as articles, reviews and scholarly monographs) that are required to shape those records into narrations and dissertations that make visible the traditions and innovations of 'an Australian jurisprudence'.[1] For Australian historians of law of the 20th century, the matter of records is something we have perhaps experienced in unique ways to our colleagues

---

1   This contention underpins much of my current work; see, for example, Ann Genovese, 'About Libraries: A Jurisographer's Notes on Lives Lived with Law (in London and Sydney)' (2016) 20 *Law Text Culture* 32; Ann Genovese, 'Introduction: Australian Critical Decisions: Remembering the Koowarta and Tasmanian Dam Cases' in Ann Genovese (ed), *Australian Critical Decisions: Remembering the Koowarta and Tasmanian Dam Case* (Routledge, 2017) 1.

whose concerns lie primarily in interpreting earlier periods. For a start, Australian historians of the 20th century not only need to work with documents that are comparative, but must also undertake the basis of the comparison by prioritising the records produced by Australian institutions whose formation and arguments are themselves often the subject of our attention. This raises some obvious problems. The most pressing is how to account for the fraught ways the relationship between records, institutions and national histories has been experienced, particularly by Indigenous peoples in settler colonies.[2] The second is how the complex questions of complicity and authority that lie between documents of state and the articulation of national visions and nightmares are addressed by each generation of scholars. It is worth noting that although experiencing a reinvigorated critical turn in the sun for legal theorists and historians alike,[3] this particular questioning of archives is not a new historiographical problem.[4] As Hegel famously noted, 'it is the state that first presents a subject-matter that is not only *adapted* to the prose of History but involves the production of such History in the very progress of its own being'.[5]

In light of these concerns, it is perhaps incumbent on historians of Australian law and state of the 20th century, writing their immediate past as it edges into frame, to worry overtly about what historiographer and theorist Hayden White has called 'the preconditions of the kind of interests in the past which informed historical consciousness and the pragmatic basis for the production and preservation of the kind of records

---

2   Antoinette Burton (ed), *Archive Stories: Facts, Fictions, and the Writing of History* (Duke University Press, 2005); Ann Laura Stoler, *Along the Archival Grain: Epistemic Anxieties and Colonial Common sense* (Princeton University Press, 2009).
3   For leading examples across the scholarly and disciplinary spectrum, see Jacques Derrida, *Archive Fever: A Freudian Impression* (University of Chicago Press, 1996); Carolyn Steedman, *Dust: The Archive and Cultural History* (Rutgers University Press, 2002); Matthew S Hull, *Government of Paper: The Materiality of Bureaucracy in Urban Pakistan* (University of California Press, 2012), doi.org/10.1525/california/9780520272149.001.0001; Arlette Farge, *The Allure of the Archives* (Yale University Press, 2013); Francis X Blouin Jr and William G Rosenberg, *Processing the Past: Contesting Authority in History and the Archives* (Oxford University Press, 2011); Cornelia Vismann, *Files: Law and Media Technology* (Stanford University Press, 2008). For the particularity for legal administration in a different sense, see Bruno la Tour, *The Making of Law: An Ethnography of the Conseil D'Etat* (Polity Press, 2010).
4   For a classic historian's account, see Fritz Stern, 'Introduction' and Jules Michelet, 'History as National Epic' in Fritz Stern (ed), *The Varieties of History: from Voltaire to the Present* (Meridian Books, 6th ed, 1960) 1 and 108.
5   Georg Hegel, *The Philosophy of History* (Dover Publications, 1956), cited in Hayden White, 'The Question of Narrative in Contemporary Historical Theory' (1984) 23 *History and Theory* 1, 4.

that made historical enquiry possible'.⁶ This includes worrying about the changing relationships in the 20th century between administrative practices, archival science, historiographical reflexivity and concepts of public accountability, and how these underpin our theoretical questions and reshape the possibilities of our empirical practices. For those of us who are historians of the late 20th century rather than the federation or mid-century period, this also includes the specific technical difficulty of working in the gloaming: between a distinct administrative paper past that is unencumbered by copyright, privacy and living memory (and also now often digitised newspaper records or case law or cabinet documents free of the 30-year rule); and a present and future where records are digitally born.⁷

I have been worrying about these questions, the records we keep (and those we do not) and how I might personally undertake my duties to address them, in a range of projects for some time. But I have been doing so in deliberate and direct fashion regarding the Court as Archive, the subject of this collection and the name of the project I have been undertaking with Kim Rubenstein and Trish Luker. A key concern in this project has been to consider the nature and responsibilities of courts to past records and future histories. Part of our purpose is very practical: to think alongside the Federal Court of Australia about how, as an institution of law, they might also function as an archival repository, although that goes beyond, and potentially complicates, their status as courts of record.⁸ The other part of our purpose is to flesh out the implications of what it means to recognise that a modern court like the Federal Court (which was established in 1976 and commenced its institutional life in 1977) carries records of meaning to a diverse public that tell stories of experiences of law and people in a particular time, and over time, as well as shape our law and our experience of life lived in Australia now. This includes how we take responsibility for the relationships between Anglo-Australian law and people and Indigenous Australian laws and peoples.⁹

---

6   Ibid 3.
7   See, for example, Blouin Jr and Rosenberg, above n 3, 13–33.
8   That superior courts have duties as courts of record is a matter of history and of common and constitutional law; see *Kirk Group Holdings Pty Ltd v WorkCover Authority of New South Wales* (2010) 239 CLR 531 and *Craig v South Australia* (1994) 184 CLR 163. They also have a range of different duties to the people and state because of the nature of court record more broadly defined, as noted in the Introduction to this volume.
9   This question has a long history in itself: Henrietta Fourmile, 'Who Owns the Past? Aborigines as Captives of the Archives' (1989) 13 *Aboriginal History* 1; Henrietta Fourmile, 'The Need for an Independent National Inquiry into State Collections of Aboriginal and Torres Strait Islander Cultural Heritage' (1992)

In this chapter, I want to add some particularity to our project's purposes in the context of my own body of work and methodological activities. As a historian of modern Australian jurisprudence, the practical activity of my work involves two things that I aim to join that act as a point of orientation and organisation. One, as already noted, is a duty of historians to demonstrate, and remind, that history writing is intimately related through sources and records to the practices of institutions and institutional life—archives broadly conceived—and is always a contested relationship. The other is a duty of jurisprudence—to contemplate, and elucidate, how people in time and place relate to their law—and this relationship is mediated, not always happily, by the procedure and purpose of institutions.

What this means in terms of my own practice, the doing or writing of histories of jurisprudence (or *jurisography*, as I have called it),[10] suggests a particular relationship with, and responsibility for, records. This is not identical in every project, but in the Court as Archive Project has involved my taking responsibility for institutional experience that complements and underscores the technical questions of archival practice, the problems of public law and court administration, and the changing nature of the political community that mark what it means to consider the court as archive.

In this chapter, I will endeavour to demonstrate these interrelated duties to records in two different forms of historical writing. The first is narration: to tell a small slice of the institutional provenance of the Federal Court and the National Archives of Australia (NAA). Both were established as consciously modern 'Australian' institutions at a particular moment in time and shared material concern—records—that drew them

---

1 *Aboriginal Law Bulletin* 3; Martin Nakata and Marcia Langton, *Australian Indigenous Knowledge and Libraries* (Australian Academic & Research Libraries for the Australian Library and Information Association, 2005); Terri Janke, *Our Culture our Future: Report on Australian Indigenous Cultural and Intellectual Property Rights* (Australian Institute of Aboriginal and Torres Strait Islander Studies, 1998); Lynette Russell, 'Indigenous Records and Archives: Mutual Obligations and Building Trust' (2006) 34(1) *Archives and Manuscripts* 32; Livia Iacovino and Trust and Technology Project, *Exposure Draft Position Statement: Human Rights, Indigenous Communities in Australia and the Archives* (Monash University, 2009); Tahu Kukutai and John Taylor, *Indigenous Data Sovereignty: Toward an Agenda*, CAEPR Research Monograph No 38, (ANU Press, 2016), doi.org/10.22459/CAEPR38.11.2016; Darren Jorgensen and Ian McLean (eds), *Indigenous Archives: the Making and Unmaking of Australian Art*, (UWA Press, 2017); see also UN General Assembly, *United Nations Declaration on the Rights of Indigenous Peoples: Resolution adopted by the General Assembly*, 2 October 2007, A/RES/61/295, arts 3, 4, 7 and 8; *Charter of Human Rights and Responsibilities Act 2006* (Vic) s 19.
10   Jurisography is a practice and term devised in collaboration with Shaun McVeigh and Peter Rush; see Ann Genovese and Shaun McVeigh, 'Nineteen Eighty Three: A Jurisographic Report on *Commonwealth v Tasmania*' (2015) 24 *Griffith Law Review* 68; Ann Genovese, Shaun McVeigh and Peter Rush, 'Lives Lived with Law: An Introduction' (2016) 20 *Law Text Culture* 1.

into association. The other is to offer a commentary on the provenance, location and status of the records that should be available to tell that story through my own methodological adventures in undertaking the project.

To address the Court as Archive in these ways—as jurisographer, rather than theorist or legal policy advisor—I also want to suggest, by way of brief conclusion, that the sum of my experience in undertaking the project offers a particular view of writing histories: that fragmentation in the way the documents are kept itself requires careful documentation; and that such fragmentation opens the historiographical conversation about the forms and nature of sources and records adequate to represent our past for the present.

The National Estate (A Narrative)

How the period of Australian renaissance from the late 1950s to the late 1980s has been described and recorded is diverse. Both in style and form, as well as the terms of dispute of its political legacies.[11] But there is consensus in what the 1970s in particular represented, and it is useful to consider what those best trained to review and make sense of events in the context of politics—historians—wrote of the period, while also living through it. Manning Clark, for example, expansively described in his *Short History* that during this period, 'Australians … liberated themselves from the fate of being second rate Europeans'.[12] Russell Ward was more pointed. Before abruptly ending *A Nation for a Continent* with a cliff-hanger (the Dismissal in 1975), he argued that although:

> basic cultural and material ties with Britain remained strong, Australia adopted a more critical and self-reliant attitude. After the UK's entry into the European Economic Community on 1 January 1973 it was hardly possible to do anything else. The words 'British Subject' disappeared from Australian passports and 'Advance Australia Fair' replaced 'God Save the Queen'.[13]

---

11   As examples, see now famous contemporaneous accounts of the times, written across disciplines: Donald Horne, *The Lucky Country* (Penguin Books, 3rd ed, 1971); Manning Clark, *A Short History of Australia* (Penguin Books, 4th ed, 1995); Bernard Smith, *The Antipodean Manifesto: Essays in Art and History* (Oxford University Press, 1976); see also biographies and histories that address the period, written from the perspective of our own time: Frank Bongiornio, *The Eighties: The Decade that Transformed Australia* (Black Inc., 2015); Jenny Hocking, *Gough Whitlam: The Definitive Biography* (Miegunyah Press, 2014).
12   Clark, above n 11, 351.
13   Russell Braddock Ward, *A Nation for a Continent: The History of Australia, 1901–1975* (Heinemann, 1977) 403–4.

What interests me in the context of the Court as Archive Project is how this orientation away from Britain and towards an articulation of an independent and self-confident Australia manifested itself in a range of state-generated national projects (from art galleries to the Australian Film Institute, childcare to conservation), but had a particular institutional focus for the law. On a purely qualitative basis, this resulted in a proliferation of law and legal institutions—the artefact of a growing and diversifying population with changing desires and requirements—and a slow encroachment of federal power over states with a concomitant development of federal jurisdictions that required more, and more responsive, legislation.[14] What is a harder-to-pin-down story (but the one I want to show) is how the idea of the 'Australian Nation' as a law story is not only about accounting for Acts, but carries a jurisprudence of public relationship, public accountability and, less overtly, public record. To sketch, rather than give a detailed accounts of the establishment of the Federal Court or the NAA in those terms (noting that aspects of both the Federal Court and NAA's establishment histories are already written by key participants),[15] I want to discuss three reports that link that story together: the Committee of Inquiry into the National Estate ('Hope Report');[16] the Report into the Development of the National Archives ('Lamb Report');[17] and the Commonwealth Administrative Review Committee Report ('Kerr Report').[18]

Although the Kerr Committee was established by the Gorton Government in 1968, the commissioning of specialist commissions and inquires, their rate and number, was a marked technique of the Whitlam Government after 1972. Whitlam expressly noted the development in his 1973 Robert Garran Lecture 'The Role of the Australian Public Service'.[19]

---

14   This is clearly evidenced in an example of direct relevance to this essay: Michael Black, 'The Federal Court of Australia: The First 30 Years — A Survey on the Occasion of Two Anniversaries' (2007) 31(3) *Melbourne University Law Review* 1017.
15   Susan Kenny, 'Federal Courts and Australian National Identity' (2015) 38(3) *Melbourne University Law Review* 996; Sue McKemmish and Michael Piggott (eds), *The Records Continuum: Ian Maclean and Australian Archives First Fifty Years* (Ancora, 1994); Black, above n 14.
16   Australia, Committee of Inquiry into the National Estate, *Report of the National Estate: Report of the Committee of Inquiry into the National Estate* (Australian Government Publishing Service, 1974) ('Hope Report').
17   W Kaye Lamb, *Development of the National Archives* (Australian Government Publishing Service, 1973) ('Lamb Report').
18   Commonwealth, *Commonwealth Administrative Review Committee Report 1971*, Parl Paper No 144 (1971) ('Kerr Report').
19   EG Whitlam, 'The Role of the Australian Public Service', (Speech at the Sir Robert Garran Memorial Oration, Canberra, 12 November 1973).

4. A MATTER OF RECORDS

In this address to (perhaps) unsettled officers of the Commonwealth encountering Labor after 23 years of coalition government, Prime Minister Whitlam was careful to reassure that Westminster traditions remained an unshakeable foundation to responsible government. However, Whitlam was also unabashed in opening a conversation about the changing status and political demands of the Australian people towards the end of the 20th century and the need to modernise government policy, law and institutional action in response. He stated:

> All governments are expected to make changes and deliver benefits with a precision and promptitude never before expected or experienced in history. When a new government comes in after so long an absence, those demands, those pressures are accelerated and intensified.[20]

Whitlam's broad theme was 'greater participation in the affairs of Government by concerned people in the community'.[21] As he explained, 'we want Australian people to know the facts, to know the needs, to know the choices before them. This is really at the heart of what has been called "open government"'.[22] For Whitlam, this involved two broadly defined programs. One program was about the accountability to the public of the business of government itself. This included proposed legislative schemes such as the yet-to-arrive freedom of information legislation 'to provide greater information to the public' and to 'clarify the rules relating to access to official records and facilitate such access'.[23] It also included a related national scheme to store those records at a national archive, rather than a Commonwealth repository of state documents *per se*, which was to also 'greatly improve the service that the public gets when they want to consult some of the more ancient records'.[24]

The other program was about how these, and other national projects, might best be achieved to bring about 'immediate action' on 'a wide range of issues'.[25] This involved the establishment of 'no less than continuing bodies to assist us achieve our policies',[26] and drawing into

---

20 Ibid 1.
21 Ibid 7.
22 Ibid.
23 Ibid.
24 Ibid. It is important to note that there, of course, existed a repository of administrative files and records before this time, but these did not yet have the same status as public records as exist in the NAA; see Lamb, above n 17; McKemmish and Piggot, above n 15.
25 Whitlam, above n 19, 3.
26 Ibid.

policy formation a range of experienced Australians from the business, law and community sectors, who did not sit within the traditional structure of government.[27] The importance of these task forces, inquiries, committees and commissions; who sat on them; their powers to hear and receive submissions and undertake social and factual investigations; and the recommendations of their reports, was to provide 'a key channel of communication between Parliament and the people'.[28] As Whitlam noted, 'a real contribution is made to public administration and to the development of policies [and institutions] acceptable to the community'.[29]

Of these bodies, it is the aptly named Hope Committee (named after its Chair, Justice Robert Hope of the New South Wales Supreme Court)[30] that offers the underpinning example of how aspirations about the government's relationship with the Australian public was broadly conceived and how these bodies were concretely given shape. Although the concept of the national estate had United Kingdom (UK) precedents,[31] it was the example of the Kennedy Administration in the United States that Whitlam (and other senior Australian Labor Party figures, like Tom Uren and Moss Cass) chose to emulate and apply to the Australian experience. The aim was to preserve the past for the future by maintaining 'intergenerational equity' and 'to bequeath our full national estate to our heirs'.[32] The rhetorical term entered Australian political conversation in the 1960s as a way to capture government action and public commitment to preservation of the natural and built environments.[33] The purpose of the Hope Committee, convened in 1973,[34] was to recommend ways

---

27 Ibid 5.
28 Ibid 7.
29 Ibid.
30 The committee also included Milo Dunphy, Judith Wright, Len Webb, Keith Valance and Judith Brine; it, thus, had 'several prominent conservationists' in its ranks; see Sharon Veale and Robert Freestone, 'The Things We Wanted to Keep: The Commonwealth and the National Estate 1969–1974' (2012) 24 *Historic Environment* 12, 16.
31 Ibid 12, citing the work of British architect Clough Williams-Ellis, the Hobhouse Committee and the 1949 *National Parks and Countryside Act* as UK precursors.
32 Ibid 12, citing Whitlam's open acknowledgment of American President John F Kennedy's influence in adoption of the rhetoric and political commitments.
33 As the Hope Report noted, what they sought to protect and preserve were sites and objects 'of such aesthetic, historical, scientific, social, cultural, ecological or other special value to the nation or any part of it, including a region or locality, that they should be conserved, managed and presented for the benefit of the community as a whole'; above n 16, 334.
34 One of the Hope Report's key terms of reference was to determine 'the role which the Australian Government could play in the preservation and enhancement of the National Estate'. Hope's view was that the Commonwealth 'could and should give a lead to the whole of Australia'; above n 16, 27; Veale and Freestone, above n 30, 16.

'to conserve and present' and 'bring under direct Government control' objects and places of 'such aesthetic, historical, scientific, social, cultural, ecological or other special value to the nation', and to do so for 'the benefit of the community as a whole'.[35] This was, it is important to note, a commitment shared by the Coalition Opposition. As Senator Alan Missen argued in support of the Australian Heritage Commission Bill in 1975, the aim of the Hope Inquiry was to show how 'the Government can give a practical lead. People of a later generation will either bemoan the fact that we have destroyed things which should have been preserved, or they will be grateful to us for those things we have retained'.[36]

The Hope Report recommended, among other things, establishing a system of national parks;[37] promoting sites and buildings for World Heritage status;[38] protecting and taking responsibility for 'significant Aboriginal sites' (this was 'not only for the benefit of Aboriginals themselves and of the world's cultural heritage but for the sake of the national conscience');[39] establishing university research and teaching priorities on 'conservation and protection of built and national environments';[40] and establishing a Heritage Commission and National Trust.[41] The Hope Report also, significantly for my purposes, understood cultural property and its institutions (such as museums and libraries) as central components and representations of this national estate, and was explicit that the artefacts and records these institutions held were essential for government to preserve and manage.[42] The Hope Report noted expressly that 'the new initiative by the Australian Government in establishing a national archives system will help to ensure the preservation of archival resources'.[43]

---

35 Hope Report, above n 16, 334.
36 Commonwealth, *Parliamentary Debates*, Senate, 5 June 1975, 2361 (Alan Missen). Senator Missen also noted (2360): 'Therefore there is one thing that comes from the Report and the creation of this Commission and that is we are recognizing at last the wide range, the very much wider view that we have now of the heritage that should be preserved'.
37 Hope Report, above n 16, 337.
38 Ibid 339.
39 Ibid 340 and continues: 'It is past time that the Australian Government accepted the full responsibility laid on it by the people at the 1967 referendum'.
40 Ibid 347.
41 Ibid.
42 Ibid 341–2.
43 Ibid 342. Note, too, Missen's comments, *Parliamentary Debates* above n 36, 2362: 'One of the jobs found probably in all other States is the important job of preserving the archives of the community. These are often kept in conditions of great danger from fire and decay. If this were to happen, part of our history would disappear because we were not farsighted. In that one area in which I was doing some work, I believe that the position has not improved greatly. There is obviously a great need for the restoration and preservation of this part of our National Estate'.

The 'new initiative' to which the Hope Report referred was the subject of a different inquiry on a smaller and more specialised scale. In June 1973, the Special Minister of State, Don Willesee, had commissioned W Kaye Lamb to 'visit Australia for six weeks to advise on the development of a charter, and necessary legislation, for a National Archives'.[44] Lamb was the Dominion Archivist—the title of the National Archivist of Canada—and had been educated in British Columbia and at the London School of Economics, completing a PhD with Harold Laski.[45] Clearly understood in the Commonwealth world as a man capable of building national institutions, W Kaye Lamb 'earned wide recognition for turning the Canadian National Archives system into a highly successful institution at the service of the Canadian people'.[46]

During his six weeks in Australia, Lamb visited all established state archives and public records offices, including university archives.[47] Lamb's Report, at the conclusion of his tour, unsurprisingly recommended that the then Commonwealth Archive Office was capable of being 'developed into a fully-fledged National Archives of Australia',[48] with its own building, permanent staffing and its own specialist headquarters in Canberra.[49] The Lamb Report stated that the function of such a national archive was 'to assume custody, ownership and control of the records of permanent value that will form the permanent official archives of government of Australia and to make available for research those that can be released for use by the public'.[50] This gave the proposed framing of the NAA a particular set of responsibilities. For example, Lamb recommended that it was the NAA who should, as might be expected, have authority to guide and control the final disposition of records. But the NAA should work with government departments and agencies cooperatively on which of their records should be acquired for permanent preservation,[51] and what

---

44   Lamb Report, above n 17, 1.
45   *William Kaye Lamb*, The Canadian Encyclopedia (24 July 2015) <http://www.thecanadian encyclopedia.com/en/article/william-kaye-lamb/>.
46   Lamb Report, above n 17, 1. This a worthy topic for another paper: the relationship between thinking of the state and the public in the 20th century in terms of different official duties, and the transmission of ideas by those who perform those duties, across the Commonwealth.
47   Ibid 1–2.
48   Ibid 1.
49   Ibid 13.
50   Ibid 9. The Report also stated: 'The heart and centre of any system must be a strong national archives … its success as a national institution will depend upon the extent to which its influence is felt and its services are provided outside its own walls and outside Canberra': ibid 29.
51   The Report stated that it was important to make clear to agencies that there is a difference between 'housekeeping' and 'operational' records, the latter being preserved: ibid 7–8.

restrictions might apply to classes of those documents in terms of public access.[52] However, the Lamb Report also argued that official government records should, by the 1970s, be subject to greater scrutiny by, and availability to, the general population. They should not be limited to the traditional practices and uses for official depositories that had lasted since the 18th century. As Lamb argued:[53]

> The last 25 years have seen a great expansion in the public that wishes to make use of public records … [for] modern times and current problems … [people] seek access to recent records … [beyond war and politics] to multiple disciplines.[54]

Relevant to the story I am trying to tell, Lamb's recommendations exemplify how the ideas that underlay his terms of reference (and are also foundational to the Hope Report, as well as Whitlam's Garran Address) were in sharp tension, if not potential conflict. For example, Lamb supported 'the view that public records are the property of the people, not of civil servants nor of whatever administration happens to be in power', and, as such, 'archives should be one step removed from civil service and political control and from restrictions that might result from it'.[55] 'On the other hand', he was careful to delineate, 'the relationship of Archives with the Government is necessarily very close, and to perform its proper functions [preserving and curating the records of administration] it must work closely with every department and agency of the Government'.[56] In other words, Lamb articulated that it was the government's duty to carefully balance its competing obligations to effective execution of executive authority and to its citizenry. To do so, a proposed NAA should be an institution that remains within the structure of government, not a public institution with a distinct charter, like the National Library. Lamb was clear that if legislation to establish the NAA gave 'adequate authority to perform its functions, I see no reason why this status should not be satisfactory both to the Archives and to members of the public who wish to make use of its collections'.[57]

---

52   The Report stated that 'no records should be destroyed without the approval of the Archives': ibid 9–10.
53   Blouin Jr and Rosenberg, above n 3, 13–31.
54   Lamb Report, above n 17, 21. On the question of public access, Lamb noted that the current Office of Archives was 'highly unpopular, especially in academic circles. This is due in great part to the difficulties experienced by researchers in securing access to public records in the keeping of archives': 22.
55   Ibid 4.
56   Ibid.
57   Ibid 5.

Although the Lamb Report was careful about setting out these tensions and responsibilities for executive documents, what was not clear was how those same precautions might apply to the records of all national institutions.[58] Courts, for example, were not mentioned at all. Reading the Lamb Report in the context of 1974, as opposed to 2018, this omission is odd. This is because the expression of the state's underlying commitments to public accountability in the 1970s via open government (in all its senses) and its vision of a national estate, was not extant to how a new court—a federal court—had already begun to be imagined. Clearly, as noted, there is a more expansive history of the Federal Court as a national institution yet to be written.[59] But the Kerr Report of 1971 is an important source through which those commitments, and a jurisprudence of public relationship and public accountability in the 1970s, can be made visible.[60] However, the Kerr Report itself has been written about at great length, especially by public lawyers. It is rightly, I think, understood by them to be the cornerstone of the modernisation of public law in Australia: a 'vision splendid', as described by Lindsay Curtis, a former President of the Australian Capital Territory (ACT) Administrative Appeals Tribunal.[61]

---

58 Archives Bill 1979 (Cth), pt V. Debates about the Archives Bill in Parliament took a long time because of interlinked concern over freedom of information. These are interlinked narratives. In the Lamb Report, for example, it is expressly noted that there are limits to open government, and that the NAA should appropriately withhold certain classes of documents (such as those that were security classified or in confidence correspondence, and, of course, Cabinet minutes). But it also recommended that the 30-year rule on non-disclosure 'must not be interpreted as meaning that more recent records are automatically inaccessible': ibid 25.

59 There was always a constitutional possibility for a federal court since 1901, but the necessity did not really arise until the late 1950s. One of the earliest references to the need for a 'Federal Supreme Court' was raised in the second reading debate on the Judiciary Bill 1959 (Cth) and Australian Capital Territory Supreme Court Bill 1959 (Cth). The objective of the two Bills was to address a lacuna in the existing law that prevented the Commonwealth from being sued in the Supreme Courts of the Territories, those matters having to go directly to the High Court. Speaking on the Bills, Whitlam made a number of suggestions concerning the appellate structure for Territory Supreme Courts and noted that 'I would go further and express the hope that an appeal from a judge of a Supreme Court of a Territory might be heard *by the Full Bench of a Federal Supreme Court* instead of going to directly to the High Court' (emphasis added); Commonwealth, *Parliamentary Debates*, House of Representatives, 13 May 1959, 2108 (EG Whitlam); see also Kerr Report, above n 18, 71–5. As one example of parliamentary debates, see Commonwealth, *Parliamentary Debates*, Senate, 4 June 1975, 2542–54.

60 However, as John McMillan has described, these changes can be seen as the outcome of the 'maturing recognition' by Parliament of what the committees, led by lawyers and public officers of experience, proposed. As he notes, this is despite the fact that the Report 'attracted meagre publicity at the time. Not [sic] did it mirror any groundswell of public discontent, or catalyse a vocal public reform movement'; John McMillan, 'Foreword' in Robin Creyke and John McMillan (eds), *The Kerr Vision of Australian Administrative Law at the Twenty-Five Year Mark* (Centre for International and Public Law, 1998) iii–iv.

61 Lindsay Curtis 'The Vision Splendid: A Time for Re-Appraisal' in Creyke and McMillan (eds), above n 60, 36.

4. A MATTER OF RECORDS

The committee was chaired by Sir John Kerr who, in 1968 when it was commissioned, was a Judge of the Commonwealth Industrial Court and a Deputy President of the Trade Practices Tribunal—offices easily misremembered after the events of 1975. Kerr and the other committee members[62] had vast accumulated experience in public law and public administration, and knew how costly, alienating and near impossible it was for an ordinary citizen to challenge unlawful government action.[63] The terms of reference for the committee were quite narrow: to investigate the need for a new federal court to hear disputes arising from increased federal jurisdiction, and to alleviate the demands of the High Court.[64] But its 1971 recommendations—subsequently developed in the Ellicott and Bland Reports—were expanded by its members to do a great deal more.[65] In considering the jurisdiction of such a federal court, the committee also developed what we now understand as 'the New Administrative Law': merits review of government action at specialised tribunals; access to judicial review and reasons for decisions via the *Administrative Decisions (Judicial Review) Act 1977* (Cth) ('*Administrative Decisions (Judicial Review) Act*') that removed the ancient requirements of the prerogative writs; proposed freedom of information legislation; and a package of other institutional measures such as the establishment of an office of Commonwealth Ombudsman.[66]

What I want to draw out, for the purposes of this story, is how the Kerr Report and its recommendations were founded on the two principles that also shaped the rhetoric and policy of the Hope and Lamb Reports and Whitlam's 1973 Garran address. The first was a desire to formalise and give legal form to open government in a postwar world. For example, the Kerr Report makes plain that 'in formulating our proposals we have concluded

---

62 The committee's other members were Anthony Mason (an experienced advocate who, as Solicitor-General, had prepared foundational thinking within the executive on a new superior court, and subsequently joined the NSW Court of Appeal); Robert Ellicott (in 1968 Solicitor-General, and later Attorney-General in the Fraser Government); and, perhaps most importantly, Professor Harry Whitmore, Dean of Law of The Australian National University (a pioneer in the development of an Australian jurisprudence on review of government action, and a member of the Social Science Council); Kerr Report above n 18, i. The Report also notes in this frontspiece: 'NOTE: Mr Justice Mason was appointed a Judge of Appeal of the Supreme Court of New South Wales on 1 May 1969. Mr R.J. Ellicott was appointed Solicitor-General on 15 May 1969 and thereafter became a member of the committee'.
63 Curtis, above n 61, 45–6.
64 Kerr Report, above n 18, 1–4.
65 Robin Creyke and John McMillan (eds), 'Administrative Law Assumptions Then and Now', above n 60, 3–9.
66 Kerr Report, above n 18, 112–18.

that there is an established need for review of administrative decisions. We have not thought this to be a matter of real debate'.[67] Their point was not that governments in the late 1960s and early 1970s[68] were any worse than their predecessors *per se* in making lawful decisions. Rather, their argument was that older methods of opening those decisions to scrutiny had become antiquated. The committee stated that they wanted 'merely to point to the changing circumstances affecting the operation [of those older methods] in these days of vast expansions in the range of regulated activity and the range of services provided' and concluded that 'the traditional democratic methods in bringing possible injustices to notice seem to us to be inadequate'.[69]

The second foundational principal foundation was that the practice of Australian law needed to be understood, by 1971, as federal, or national, in ways it had not been before, and that this was perhaps an expression of an Australian jurisprudence that had not been institutionalised or legislatively recognised before either.[70] This included a careful consideration of the specificity of Australian constitutional arrangements, which did not permit a replication of either British or American models.[71] The Kerr Report noted that:

> Our consideration of the matters covered by our terms of reference has led us to the view that it is highly desirable to encourage in Australia a comprehensive system of administrative law, but one which is essentially Australian and which is specially tailored to meet our own needs, experiences, and constitutional problems.[72]

---

67 Ibid 10.
68 The Kerr Report also addresses French, UK and US responses to the rise of the administrative state postwar: ibid 31–75.
69 Ibid 8.
70 See Black, above n 14, where he makes these points in detail, and expressly.
71 In order to consider the nature of the 'jurisdiction to be given to proposed Commonwealth Superior Court', the terms of reference for the Kerr Report interlinked viewing comparative jurisdictions to see what new legislation had been introduced in administrative law (and why), and if and how that would be applicable and useful to the Australian experience shaped by its constitutional context. The terms noted that 'it is the uniform experience of the common law countries, including the UK, that the traditional supervision by the courts of the administrative process must be supplemented by provision for review on questions of law or on the merits of administrative decisions affecting the property and rights of citizens'; Kerr Report, above n 18, 2.
72 Ibid 71.

This included forming a view not only on matters of jurisdiction, but on the role that a federal court 'should play more generally',[73] of how it might undertake its institutional responsibilities in assisting Australian people to understand and challenge the decisions taken about them, and what correlative duties the state had to be just, fair and open with its citizens.[74]

The Federal Court began its institutional life in 1977 on the basis of these recommendations and visions. Former Chief Justice Michael Black, in his memoir of its first 30 years, shows how the Federal Court was responsive to new jurisdictions (most significantly, the *Administrative Decisions (Judicial Review) Act*, the *Trade Practices Act 1974* (Cth) and later, of course, the *Native Title Act 1993* (Cth)) and also new practices, procedures, ceremonies and protocols.[75] From the desire to innovate technologically to promote efficient court services, to the desire to represent itself differently from inherited British tradition by revolutionising rules regarding robing, wigs and architecture, the Federal Court has developed as a distinctively Australian and determinedly modern institution, reinventing the role of a court to meet the circumstances of time, place and the needs of a changing public.[76]

Many of these are innovations that we have had the opportunity to uncover in greater material depth in the course of our project. This is because our method involves an examination of the Federal Court's own archive of operational practices since its establishment, rather than an exploration of the rich litigation materials the court holds. These kinds

---

73 Ibid. The idea of a Commonwealth superior court had been the subject of discussion and planning in the Attorney-General's Department since the early 1960s; see, for example, NAA: A5819, VOLUME 12/AGENDUM 461.

74 During the second reading speech of the Federal Court of Australia Bill 1976 (Cth), government members referred to the need for the existing federal court system, which included separate industrial and bankruptcy courts as well as making the High Court the first instance jurisdiction for the review of Commonwealth administrative decisions, to be 'put on a more rational basis' (Commonwealth, *Parliamentary Debates*, House of Representatives, 21 October 1976, 2110 (Robert Ellicott)) and the significance of the role of the court in introducing 'streamlined methods' to address its jurisdiction (Commonwealth, *Parliamentary Debates*, House of Representatives, 10 November 1976, 2536 (Maurice Neil)).

75 Black, above n 14.

76 The need for change to the federal court structure to meet the demands of increasing population and an increasingly diverse jurisdiction was a central argument advanced by then Attorney-General Barwick in his initial recommendation to Cabinet for a Commonwealth Superior Court; see NAA: A5819, VOLUME 12/AGENDUM 461. As the proposal developed, the increasing diversity of state *and* Commonwealth jurisdiction was also drawn on by public servants working on the proposal to recommend that the new court also have an exclusive jurisdiction over some matters to ensure uniformity and consistency in the development of the law; see, for example, Memorandum from Mr L Naar to the Secretary of the Attorney-General's Department, 14 July 1967, NAA: A432, 1961/2132 pt 6.

of records are what the German legal theorist Cornelia Vismann would designate as files—bureaucratic documents—as opposed to the records of law that are required for courts to perform their juridical and, in common law countries, appellate function.[77]

I would, perhaps, describe these files in a slightly different way: as the records of how an institution conducts itself. These records have revealed to us how the Federal Court has made decisions about its role and public function over time, including how it considered the value and purpose of its own archive, and how and where they should be subject to democratic methods in bringing institutional court activity to notice. However, our problem is that these records are scattered, fragmented, not fully accounted for and potentially missing. Many sit alongside the official record of the Federal Court and its litigation files and within the custody of the Federal Court itself. But there are real and material difficulties caused to our project by the fact that although the NAA and the Federal Court shared responsibility for records of different kinds, they were never directly brought into relation in terms of their public roles. As we have seen in the Lamb Report, the NAA was designed to be a national enterprise responsive to collecting the public experience of Australian government for posterity and for use by future Australians. It is clear from the Kerr Report that the Federal Court was designed to be a national court responsive to the Australian public and its legal experiences. Yet the court records of the Federal Court, from the moment the NAA was established in 1983, were neither open for future use nor understood as part of Australian cultural property to be protected (in the language of the Hope Report) for intergenerational equity. They were excluded from the *Archives Act 1983* (Cth) ('*Archives Act*'). In the context of a prevailing culture of the time, it is important to note that this exclusion of court records was subject to challenge before it became law.[78] When the Archives Bill and the Freedom of Information Bill were scrutinised together by the Senate Standing Committee on Legal and Constitutional Affairs in 1978,[79] the committee (presciently) reported:

---

77 Files, in Vismann's terms, are 'not the instrument or medium for the arbitration of conflicts but a repository of forms of authoritarian and administrative acts that assume concrete shape in files' And she adds provocatively 'in this way law and files mutually determine each other': Vismann, above n 3, xiii.
78 Australian Law Reform Commission (ALRC) *Australia's Federal Record: A Review of Archives Act 1983* Report No. 85 (1998).
79 Senate Standing Committee on Constitutional and Legal Affairs, Commonwealth, *Report on the Freedom of Information Bill 1978 and aspects of the Archives Bill 1978* (1979), [33.29] ('Senate Standing Committee Report').

The purpose of the Archives Bill is to guarantee that our national history can be both preserved and reconstructed. This guarantee must exist with respect to the operation of the Head of State, of the Legislature and of the Judiciary, much as it exists in relation to the operation of other departments … [t]here must come a time when public interest in obtaining access to information necessary for the understanding of Australian government and history overrides the niceties of constitutional arrangements, and in our opinion that time has certainly arrived when an event is thirty years of age.[80]

But in 1983, such 'niceties' remained dominant. The view of Parliament then was that special treatment should be afforded to 'records of those arms of the Government which traditionally enjoy a certain degree of independence and autonomy'.[81] The rationale for the exclusion of Federal Court's records was then founded in both the common law (the traditional provenance and authority of courts to be masters of their own rolls and the custodian of their own records for the purposes of appellate matters) and the *Constitution* (protection of separation of powers to avoid 'interfer[ence] with the independence of the judiciary and the proper administration of justice').[82] This left records of a major innovation in Australian jurisprudence officially outside of a national archive that was designed to preserve the national estate.

A Matter of Records (A Commentary)

My purpose in revisiting the Hope, Lamb and Kerr Reports has been to offer a narration about the animating vision of Australian institutions as they 'liberated themselves' from Britain[83] and to contribute to an expanded understanding of the administrative mode of setting up such institutions

---

80 Ibid [33.23] and [33.26]. This, of course, became the subject of review of records in 1998 by the ALRC; see ALRC, above n 78. The ALRC pushed for reform to bring court records within the NAA. It also outlined the informal disposal and archiving practices under way in federal courts.
81 *Archives Act*, pt V excludes courts from operation of the open access provisions; see also Explanatory Memorandum, Archives Bill 1979 (Cth) and Senate Standing Committee Report, above n 79.
82 Senate Standing Committee Report, above n 79, [33.21]: 'The Explanatory Memorandum to the Bill explains the exclusion of vice-regal records and the records of parliament and the courts on the basis that it would be inappropriate for the regulatory powers of the Archives to be made application to the records of those arms of the Government which traditionally enjoy a certain degree of independence and autonomy. In part this independence can be viewed on constitutional grounds, particularly the separation of the powers of the Executive, the Legislature and the Judiciary. It is also felt that, as a practical matter, it should be for bodies like the Parliament and courts to determine what is to happen to their own records. For instance, attention is drawn to the difficult questions involved in determining what should happen to judges' notebooks'.
83 Clark, above n 11, 351.

in the 1970s and 1980s. But it has also been to make plain that the time 'when public interest in obtaining access to information necessary for the understanding of Australian government and history'[84] has clearly arrived.

I want to now discuss the implications of my narrative. In doing so, I want to hold against turning 'the archive' (and the archival) into normative principle by offering a different form of address—a commentary—that invites thought on the technicalities of public administration of records in terms of how they are experienced. More precisely, I want to describe my own activities in undertaking the Court as Archive Project as a set of comments about how my official relationship with the administrative machinery of archives is also a reflexive part of my training and scholarly traditions. I will do this by focusing on the tangle of where the records of the Federal Court during the period 1977–90 might be kept (and by whom), and the instruments that arrange those institutional relationships. By paying attention to these administrative technicalities, I can emphasise why court records of the very recent past reveal things about public law and life, in the omission and dispersal, that are themselves necessary to write into Australian histories of jurisprudence. I can also exemplify how maintaining a relationship to records is varied, not always romantic, but part of the practice and duties of the conduct of office of the historian and the jurisographer.

Provenance

Our archival adventures in the Court as Archive Project began at the Principal Registry of the Federal Court in Queens Square in Sydney. With the assistance of Lyn Nasir, the court archivist, we were able to take advantage of the work the Federal Court has done to digitise the records and papers that it possesses on site. We viewed, for example, records of committee meetings, as well as management files from 1977, and some of the papers of Chief Justices Bowen and Black. These internal papers included letters and memos concerning the relationship between the Federal Court and the Commonwealth Attorney-General's Department (AGD). Primarily, this is, of course, because the Federal Court began its institutional life administered by AGD. Predating the Federal Court, the earliest available records about the idea of establishing a new Chapter III court are the provenance and within the jurisdiction of AGD.

---

84   Senate Standing Committee Report above n 79, [33.23] and [33.26].

These earlier AGD records date from the early 1960s and include opinions about the status of a proposed court authored by Sir Anthony Mason as the then Solicitor-General and Sir Garfield Barwick as the then Chief Justice of the High Court. They also include terse exchanges between existing state supreme courts and the federal government over the vexed matter of jurisdiction.[85] These records remained within the AGD's physical and legal control until the NAA was itself established in 1983, at which point the NAA assumed control over the AGD records. From 1983 onwards, AGD records were therefore consigned to the NAA, under the authority of the general Records Disposal Authority (RDA) for government agencies and departments.[86] Records relating to the Federal Court that were the provenance of the AGD for both these early periods of the Federal Court's history (before 1977 and from 1977 to 1983) are noted in the NAA's database. They are easily identified, although until we began our project, most had not yet been declassified and others had not yet opened for public use—a point to which I will return.

What was more unexpected was how records of the Federal Court *after* 1983 also came to be within the custodianship of the NAA. A central legislative and administrative fact that underpins the narrative I have already told is that Federal Court records were excluded from the operation of the *Archives Act*.[87] Yet our archival investigations indicated that the governance relationship between the Federal Court and AGD that was instantiated as a matter of practice, if not law, continued after 1983. There is no specific RDA to authorise this relationship as a matter of records. The assumption from what was available for us to view through public channels is that the records about the Federal Court and AGD relationship were still subject to general NAA Departmental Disposal of Records Schedules, although the agency RDAs for this period are themselves classified AGD documents.[88]

---

85 See, for example, Memorandum from Anthony Mason to First Assistant Secretary (Executive), 26 July 1966, NAA: A432, 1961/2132 pt 2.
86 A Records Disposal Authority (RDA) is the administrative instrument necessary to organise the legal association and conditions of consignment, disposal and transfer of records between agencies.
87 This is in the following footnote and the exclusion is discussed earlier.
88 For a general overview of the development of the Federal Court's RDA, see Lyn Nasir, 'Presentation on the Records Authority (Speech delivered to the 9th Australasian Institute of Judicial Administration Librarians Conference, Sydney, 21 August 2015). For the historical development of the management of AGD and Federal Court records, see NAA: A432/27, 1979/3205; NAA: A432, 1987/016464-01; National Archives of Australia, *Records Disposal Authority 1234 for the Industrial Relations Court of Australia Principal and District Registries* (1996); National Archives of Australia, *Records Disposal Authority for the Federal Court of Australia, Principal and District Registries, Court Records other than Bankruptcy* No. 1124, 1994; National Archives of Australia, *Records Disposal Authority for Bankruptcy records, Principal and District Registries*, No. 1124, 1994. A Disposal Authority was agreed between

What was even more intriguing to us was that some records of the Federal Court continued to be sent to the NAA after 1990—the date when the Federal Court became self-administering and legally free from AGD management or association.[89] This state of affairs continued until 2011, when a specific RDA was established between the NAA and the Federal Court, instigating a more sustained conversation between the agencies about what records of courts might be worth preserving (to return to the language of the 1970) for the national estate.[90]

Describing the detail of the negotiations and practical compromises of that formalisation of public relationship between the NAA and the Federal Court are perhaps the duties that inform different kinds of writing in court administration and archival science.[91] However, the point I want to emphasise here is what a specific Federal Court RDA represents for Australian historians of jurisprudence of the 20th century. It is an instrument of administration that takes responsibility for records and imposes formal and legal consideration of the specific status of court records for the first time since both the Federal Court and NAA were established. I think that this has allowed a different, and perhaps more conscious, conversation about what it is courts do that other institutions do not that complicates yet gives shape to the nature of decisions about access and protocols that have happened, as well as those yet to come.[92]

---

the NAA and National Native Title Tribunal in 2009; see National Archives of Australia, *Records Authority National Native Title Tribunal*, No. 2009/00121658, November 2009. This activity of the NAA stands alongside the internal Federal Court initiatives that were occurring concurrently during this period, preserving all their own records of litigation through the introduction and innovations of e-filing.

89   Warwick Soden, 'Self Administration in the Federal Court of Australia'(Speech given at the JCA Colloquium, Noosa, 10 October 2014); Black, above n 14.

90   National Archives of Australia, *Records Authority: Federal Court of Australia*, No. 2010/00315821, 19 October 2011. The 2011 Authority designates all files not determined to be 'significant' or not native title matters into Part A, which is to be retained permanently by the NAA, and Part B, which is to be retained by the NAA for up to 25 years. Part A incorporates court documents that identify the issues before the court and the parties; final orders; reasons for decision; High Court orders remitting the matter to the Federal Court; and any signed orders disposing of the matter if there was no judgment. Part B incorporates the balance of the materials on the file.

91   Livia Iacovino, 'Rethinking Archival, Ethical and Legal Frameworks for Records of Indigenous Australian Communities: A Participant Relationship Model of Rights and Responsibilities' (2010) 10 *Archival Science* 353; Judith Bellis, 'Public Access to Court Records in Australia: An International Comparative Perspective and Some Proposals for Reform' (2010) 19 *Journal of Judicial Administration* 197.

92   Ian Irving, 'Information Held on Federal Court Native Title Files' (Speech given at the National Native Title Conference, Darwin, 2006). That the Parliament could legislate for the Federal Court to be exempt from the NAA—that it had to be *sui generis* and set apart—seems defensible in the 1970s in ways it is not today. In particular, the arrival of the native title jurisdiction in the Federal Court in

One aspect of that conversation is a concern of public law jurisprudence. On its face, the tangle of administrative control and legal authority over records is not simply an exercise of governance, but a practice that reveals how the legal exemption of the Federal Court from the NAA in 1983 is an executive recognition that, at common law and under the *Constitution*, Commonwealth superior courts have jurisdiction over 'the court record', which of course has not altered.[93] The historical association between courts and the executive that is a necessary part of their establishment, I think, reinforces the need to write about administrative and constitutional law, and about national institutions that emerged in the 1970s and 1980s, in a way that joins them together.[94]

Practice

The other aspect of that conversation is of course about the activity of writing those histories. This returns me to my own archival experience in this project. For example, Federal Court Archivist Lyn Nasir had told us that there were many consignments of records that travelled between Federal Court and NAA (without a formal RDA) via the agency of the AGD between 1977 and 1990. The Federal Court has the record

---

1995 made pressing and real what it means, and meant, to be a national court with responsibilities to holding an entire class of materials that tell stories of encounters between laws, as well as people, in this country. That we can see, perhaps, in 2018, other ways through this knot of who takes responsibility for decisions about court records, not only by negotiating an RDA with NAA, but also by establishing advisory committees with stakeholders to discuss significant matters (as Lamb suggested in 1974) or building relationships in different ways with as yet unimagined institutions that might house only native title records, says things we might in fact suggest at the end of the project. It also says a great deal about how the relationships between people and institutions have changed since the 1970s.

93   The court record (what the Federal Court, in their RDA, identify as Part A of a file) is, of course, what needs to be preserved by courts to review decisions of lower courts; above n 8. This has not legally altered since 1983. The point is that the 'court record' does not hold (and never has held) the same status as 'records of the court' (what in the Federal Court's and NAA's terms is now identified under the RDA as Part B). These are the abundance of materials that disclose the organisation of courts as institutions (ie, what we are looking at in the project); materials of litigation and decision-making not legally mandated as part of 'court record' (such as transcript and evidence); and judicial papers, bench books and ephemera.

94   The decision to exempt the court in 1983 from NAA, I think, was clearly aimed to quarantine Commonwealth courts' 'record' in its legal sense. The fact that this did not occur cleanly as a matter of administrative practice, and that the lines have been tangled because of the historical association between courts and the executive that is a necessary part of establishment, reinforces the need to write about administrative and constitutional law, and national institutions that emerged in the 1970s and 1980s in a way that joins them together. This is necessary to reveal the very complex ways that courts and executive (at the level of agency activity) practise their constitutional roles and, in turn, consider the changing shape of their public duties in time and place. The current RDA (now that there is one) offers a way to organise and make the context of those relations (and their implications) visible.

of the consignment batches and file numbers, but there is no record of the content in each consignment. The consignments are signified by a number or code only, which do not appear on the NAA catalogue. We knew nothing about those materials in any practical sense: what was in them; what they tell us; where they might be; and whether they had been sentenced let alone whether we could view them.

In 2015, we met with officers of the both NAA and the AGD in Canberra to try and find out what had happened to the Federal Court consignments. We also wanted to ask if certain AGD documents relating to the Federal Court that did appear on the NAA catalogue, but were at present unclassified or unopened, could have their status reviewed by the normal channels to assist with the process. On this latter point, the decision-making as to declassification was straightforward, as we expected it to be. The files we were asking to examine would, in most cases, have been opened by now under the 30-year rule. What is instructive is that these files had never been opened simply because no one, until the project, had made the request. If this project were being conducted in the US, the fact that a recently established federal court and its history had not been addressed would be highly unusual. It says something, too, about Australian legal historians' attentive focus on the 18th and 19th centuries and the early years of federation.

On the fate of the consigned Federal Court records, on the other hand, the story was instructive in a different sense. The lists did not appear on the NAA catalogue. The AGD had no knowledge of their lists. Yet we had access to a paper file, full of consignment numbers. This is worth imagining: the vast repositories in suburban Canberra, filled with containers of documents, from various departments, numbered by dispatch, as opposed to the delicate and precise numbering of individual items. This is the very material space between raw files, data and recoverable records that can be accessed in a form capable of carrying stories.

In the end, we asked for permission to view the AGD's RDAs to the NAA for the period we were interested in to see how they reflected the visions of Lamb, how they reflected the court disposal authorities after 1990, and to see what had been 'sentenced'. It is, of course, those instruments and the opened files that have shaped this very short dissertation on the institutional archival practices in Australia in the 1970s and that will help us produce more detailed accounts for the future.

Conclusion: Records and Australian Institutional Responsibilities

By way of conclusion, I want to make three points about my narration and commentary on the matter of records.

The first is about access. We would note that as academics with particular kinds of experience and institutional affiliation, we were supported and welcomed by the Federal Court to look at their records of internal administration. Our team were also given excellent assistance by the NAA and AGD. We are grateful for these opportunities, and the trust shown in us, but would acknowledge our archival adventures based in the Federal Court are not yet available to everyone. This is another demonstration of urgency in determining which records of courts can be viewed, by whom and under what conditions and protocols.

The second point is about court records as objects for history writing. That files produced by the Federal Court (and also files produced about them) are missing, lost, destroyed, in a lacuna or simply waiting in a repository speaks sharply to how lawyers, legal historians and scholars of the present and the future might address our past and present national stories, as a matter of record or a matter of litigation.

The precariousness of this slice of Federal Court paper records also reminds us not only that we need to pay close attention to a digital future, but also that we need more than the reports and the other documentary records I have drawn on in this paper, especially of the immediate past, to adequately tell stories of living with law and legal institutions. Indigenous people's experiences of Anglo-Australian encounters in law, particularly in native title, show this need clearly. In addition, if we are writing stories about the 1970s and 1980s, we have obligations for gathering oral histories and memoirs, for we need all kinds ways of thinking about what it means to record experience of building institutions, as much as living with them, and marking what they mediate or enable.

My third point returns to my opening remarks about the duties involved in writing histories of jurisprudence—what Shaun McVeigh and I have called the practice of jurisography. The sum of my experience in undertaking this particular project as jurisographer, rather than theorist, archival scientist or legal policy advisor, has meant paying attention to how the matter of court records is not only epistemological—it is not only about how we organise practices of legal knowledge and consider law's relationship to other practices. Court records also shape what we say about the national experience in time and place as matters of law. This is not just a matter of technology and technique. It also requires a historical understanding of how to step back, to think about institutions and their sense of duty, as representations of how a nation understands itself.

My own experience in the project of looking at the Federal Court as an archival question (as much as seeking to suggest how it might understand and arrange itself as an archive) is, then, allegorical. Joining the court to the public in and through archives is neither about past nor future, but, rather, about contemporary political ordering of the relationships between people, their law and their institutions, as a matter of national formation. Attention to archives as allegories of this political ordering requires our vigilance, our care and our sense of responsibilities as historians of public, and Australian, legal experience. By attending to our own duties and training, we can hopefully properly understand the implications of how and why law has been withdrawn or set apart from the national formation projects of the late modern period, as well as address what an archive about a court as an institution of law holds and represents as a consequence. In these ways, offering protocols about archival responsibilities of courts, as well as telling their own institutional histories as central to public concerns, contributes to the recording of a more complex national story in our own times, and as a story in which Australian jurisprudence is central.

5

Framing the Archives as Evidence: A Study of Correspondence Documenting the Place of Australia's Original High Court in a New Commonwealth Polity

Susan Priest

History in itself is fascinating, being the story of the human condition and the emergence of our species to what we hope is, and will be, a higher plane of peace and security, economic equity and respect for fundamental rights. History has an important component. That is why a life in law can never be far from history.[1]

When the Court sat at Noon on Saturday 29th April, it was announced from the Bench that circumstances had arisen which left us no alternative but to postpone the sittings of the Court appointed to be held in Melbourne on the following Tuesday (2nd May) … We did not resort to this means until the position had become intolerable.[2]

---

1   Michael Kirby, 'Is Legal History Now Ancient History?' (Speech delivered at Geoffrey Bolton Lecture, Government House Perth, 20 October 2008) 42.
2   Statement by S Griffith, 23 May 1905, regarding the court's decision to adjourn proceedings on 2 May 1905, National Library of Australia (NLA): Symon Papers MS 1736/11/865–6.

Introduction

In early May 1905, after an increasingly acrimonious and lengthy disagreement fought out through frequent exchanges of correspondence[3] between the then Leader of the Senate and fourth Federal Attorney-General of the Reid–McLean Ministry, Josiah Symon, and the Justices of the original Australian High Court—Chief Justice Samuel Griffith and Justices Edmund Barton and Richard O'Connor—the High Court reached a monumental decision. The court decided that proceedings scheduled for hearing in Melbourne on 2 May were to be adjourned and went 'on strike'.[4]

This momentous act has since been regarded as the newly created court's final protest against Attorney-General Symon and his ultimately unsuccessful attempts, throughout the course of the previous nine months,[5] to interfere with the court's itinerant sitting patterns,[6] including the curtailing of its travelling expenses, associated accommodation costs and the provision of staff to run the court.[7] In its immediate aftermath, the decision of the bench made newspaper headlines Australia-wide.[8]

Approximately two months later, in early July 1905, George Houston Reid resigned as Australia's fourth Prime Minister, and Isaac Isaacs succeeded Josiah Symon as Australia's new Attorney-General under Alfred

---

3   Additional references to specific written communications relevant to this discourse are identified in the footnotes that follow.
4   Letter from J Symon to G Reid, 22 May 1905, NLA: Symon Papers MS 1736/11/591. In this letter, it is Symon who refers to the court's actions as a 'strike'.
5   Symon sent a telegram to his wife in South Australia informing her of his appointment to the Reid–McLean Ministry. See Telegram from J Symon to E Symon, 18 August 1904, NLA: Symon Papers MS 1736/11/23. Hence, the timeline of August 1904 until July 1905, as suggested in the title of this chapter.
6   Section 12 of the *Judiciary Act 1903* (Cth) states, 'Sittings of the High Court shall be held from time to time as may be required as the principal seat of the Court and at each place at which there is a District Registry'.
7   For a more detailed account of the circumstances of this event, see Susan Priest, 'Australia's early High Court, the fourth Commonwealth Attorney-General and the "Strike of 1905"' in Paul Brand and Joshua Getzler (eds), *Judges and Judging in the History for the Common Law and Civil Law from Antiquity to Modern Times* (Cambridge University Press, 2012) 292–305; Susan Priest, 'Archives, The Australian High Court, and the "Strike of 1905"' (2013) 32(2) *The University of Queensland Law Journal* 253.
8   'Melbourne, Another High Court Difficulty', *The Brisbane Courier* (Brisbane), 2 May 1905, 7; 'Federal High Court Crisis Over Expenses', *The Age* (Melbourne), 4 May 1905, 4; 'The High Court Fixing The Judges Expenses', *The Argus* (Melbourne), 3 May 1905, 5; 'Is The High Court On Strike?' *The Advertiser* (Adelaide), 4 May 1905, 5.

Deakin's leadership.⁹ Isaacs promptly turned his attention to 'close the correspondence on the various subjects which [had] been under discussion between the Justices of the High Court and the Attorney-General [Symon] during the last few months'.¹⁰

Throughout July and August 1905, Attorney-General Isaacs offered what the court considered to be 'a satisfactory and … permanent solution [to] the matters in question'.¹¹ As suddenly as the dispute regarding the running expenses of the court had begun, the provisions put in place by the recently formed Deakin Government brought the disagreement to an end.¹² The government ensured that the High Court would continue its practice of visiting state capitals and that all associated travelling expenses would be paid. Lastly, it was also deemed that there would be no changes to the personnel required to run the court to ensure that the 'interests of the community would [continue to] be served'.¹³

On the world stage, it may no longer be unusual for the judiciary to take industrial action, particularly over wages and conditions.¹⁴ However, to this day, the decision made by Chief Justice Samuel Griffith to adjourn court proceedings in May 1905 remains unique in the history of the Australian High Court.

It was a spirited act by Chief Justice Samuel Griffith on behalf of the original High Court in an emerging Commonwealth polity that made a lasting contribution towards permanently shaping the place and role of judicial autonomy at the apex of Australia's judiciary. It also assisted in establishing what would become the contemporary day-to-day operations of the court itself. These, in an adapted form, remain to this day. As former Justice Michael Kirby reminded us in his 2001 reflections on law at the century's end:

---

9   JA La Nauze, *Alfred Deakin: A Biography* (Melbourne University Press, 1965) 398. This was Alfred Deakin's second time as Australia's Prime Minister. See also R Norris, *Deakin, Alfred (1856–1919)* (1981) National Centre of Biography <http://adb.anu.edu.au/biography/deakin-alfred-5927/text10099>.
10 Letter from I Isaacs to S Griffith, 22 August 1905, NLA: Symon Papers MS 1736/11/868.
11 Ibid.
12 Ibid.
13 Ibid.
14 George Winterton, *Judicial Remuneration in Australia* (Australian Institute of Judicial Administration Incorporated, 1995), 1–2; Uma Sudhir, 'Telangana Judges On Strike Over Appointments Return To Work', *NDTV* (online), 6 July 2016 <http://www.ndtv.com/telangana-news/telangana-judges-on-strike-over-appointments-return-to-work-1428671>.

Some features of the sittings of the High Court of Australia have remained the same. In June, as in Chief Justice Griffith's days, we return to his beloved Brisbane. In August, the Court travels to Adelaide for a week. In October, it is Perth. Chief Justice Barwick, a keen yachtsman, always attempted to visit Hobart for the Regatta Week in March. Now, the Court only travels to Hobart if business permits; and this is comparatively rare. On the establishment of the seat of Court in Canberra, Chief Justice Barwick attempted to terminate circuits to the outlying cities. This was resisted by the then Justices. Although views differ, most consider (as I do) that it is important for the Court to maintain the circuits. They provide an essential link between the serving Justices and the legal profession and litigants in the outlying States.[15]

Finally, the key individuals involved in these fractious written exchanges had a keen sense of rivalry to protect.[16] Each had been involved untiringly, but by no means in accord, in the National Convention Debates of the 1890s, shaping line by line the Bill that would become Australia's *Constitution*,[17] including the judiciary clauses of Chapter III.[18]

Therefore, it ought not be too surprising that in his position as the Attorney-General, Symon's intrusion into the running of the High Court was done under the belief that 'control over its non-judicial action … and expenditure … [came] … within … the sphere of [his role as] the Executive'[19]—a stance also met with marked resistance by the Chief Justice. Samuel Griffith, with equal resolve, believed it was not for the 'executive … to instruct the Judiciary, or to intimate either approval or disapproval of their action'[20] and, by insisting that the independence of the judiciary be protected, ensured that no easy or immediate solution to the conflict would be forthcoming. Nonetheless, as the preceding paragraphs have already revealed, the triumph of what remains a lasting legacy ultimately belonged to the Chief Justice.

---

15 Michael Kirby, 'Law at Century's End—A Millennial View from the High Court of Australia' (2001) 1(1) *Macquarie Law Journal* 1, 8.
16 WG McMinn, 'The High Court Imbroglio and the Fall of the Reid–McLean Government' (1978) 64(1) *Journal of the Royal Australian Historical Society* 14, 84–5.
17 Josiah Symon was greatly offended by Samuel Griffith's criticism of the judiciary clauses drafted when he chaired the Judiciary Committee in 1897; see John Williams, *The Australian Constitution: A Documentary History* (Melbourne University Press, 2005) 614–5.
18 Ibid.
19 Letter from J Symon to S Griffith, 31 January 1905, NLA: Symon Papers MS 1736/11/852.
20 Letter from S Griffith to J Symon, 21 January 1905, NLA: Symon Papers MS 1736/11/852.

5. FRAMING THE ARCHIVES AS EVIDENCE

However, for the remainder of this chapter, the focus is less on the details of this intriguing narrative, and instead, provides a twofold response to a question regarding methodology. Namely, how or in what way has the extraordinary story of this jurisprudential narrative been shaped by the evidence that remains in existing archival materials?

First, my analysis will provide a brief discussion of the impact made by a series of key preserved court and departmental letters known as the 'official correspondence'[21] in shaping this curious tale. Then, second, a series of observations will be presented to understand something about the nature of the sway of an alternative history—as revealed through the personal correspondence exchanged between then Parliamentarian Alfred Deakin[22] and the High Court Justices throughout the dispute.

From the perspective of the author, as a researcher immersed over long periods of time in extensive hybrid collections of manuscripts[23] held by the National Library of Australia,[24] the National Archives of Australia[25] and the State Library of South Australia,[26] it is suggested that perhaps the question of methodology can be postured more colloquially. In summary, throughout the course of this intensive research process, where, in this

---

21   Prime Minister George Reid was perhaps the first to describe the correspondence this way. See Telegram from G Reid to J Symon, 24 May 1905, NLA: Symon Papers MS 1736/11/595. This correspondence later became known as the *Correspondence Between Attorneys-General and the Justices of the High Court RE Sitting Places and Expenses of the Court*, NLA: Symon Papers MS 176/11/849–68. This Senate publication consists of 89 letters in total, with the first correspondence commencing 29 July 1904 and the last dated 23 August 1905.
22   Alfred Deakin was the recipient of the personal correspondence from the original High Court at a time when he had refused to join the Reid–McLean Government and, in his words, believed 'he could assist the Government more by sitting behind it than becoming a member of it'; see Commonwealth, *Parliamentary Debates*, House of Representatives, 29 June 1905, 81 (A McLean, Minister for Trade and Customs).
23   The use of the term 'hybrid' indicates that the collections are a combination of institutional and personal papers. See the earlier work of Paul Dalgleish, 'The Appraisal of Personal Records of Members of Parliament in Theory and Practice' (1996) 24(1) *Archives and Manuscripts* 86, 87.
24   The initial use of these archives was for my PhD; Susan Priest, *A Commonwealth Attorney-General and the early High Court, August 1904 – July 1905* (PhD Thesis, Macquarie University, 2011). These include the AJ Buchanan Papers, 'The Prime Ministers of Australia', 1940, MS 3034, vol 1; the H Campbell-Jones Papers, 'The Cabinet of Captains: The Romance of Australia's First Federal Parliament', 1935, MS 8905, Folders 1–3; the LF Crisp Papers, 1917–1984, MS 5243; the A Deakin Papers, 1804–1973, MS 1540, Series 14, 16; the JA la Nauze Papers, 1888–1984, MS 5248, Folders 115, 323, 328 and 375. Permission granted by L Cleland to view Folder 323 and the JH Symon papers, 1820–1959, MS 1736, Series 3, 6, 7, 8, 9, 11, 14, 29.
25   National Archives of Australia: A6006 1905/8/7.
26   The State Library of South Australia, Private record Group, 249, 'The Symon Family 1897–1976'.

instance, most of the federal archival documents appear largely intact and readily accessible to the researcher, what can be gleaned from the historical evidence as it emerged from 'reading other people's mail'[27] written more than 100 years ago?

The Archives as Evidence I: Official Correspondence

> The letters extending over a period of twelve months, were many, in some cases very long, and at times pointed.[28]

The use of letters by scholars for research purposes is by no means a 'new pedagogical phenomenon',[29] and their enduring or lasting sociohistorical value to the work of historians, legal historians biographers and writers alike remains well-documented.[30]

Further, even though it is readily conceded in the 21st century that the use of mobile phones, emails and other types of social media exchanges are quicker and may typically be regarded as a 'new form of letter writing',[31] written communications, including letters of state, remain of significant research value as a 'remarkable protean form of writing'.[32]

---

27   Maryanne Dever, 'Reading Other People's Mail' (1996) 24(1) *Archives and Manuscripts* 116, 116–29; see also her earlier lecture Maryanne Dever, 'Reading Other Peoples Mail' (Speech delivered at the National Library of Australia, 25 October 1995) <https://www.nla.gov.au/maryanne-dever/reading-other-peoples-mail>.
28   'The High Court. Circuits and Travelling Expenses. Interesting Correspondence', *The Argus* (Melbourne), 25 August 1905, NLA: Symon Papers MS 1736/3/120.
29   R Holmes, 'The Past Has a Great Future' (2008) (November) *Australian Book Review* 26, 27.
30   J Kent, 'Creating Lives: The Role of the State Library of NSW in the Creative Process of Biography', (2002) (August) *LASIE* 83, 83–90; Maryanne Dever, 'A Friendship that is Grown on Paper: Reflections on Editing Majorie Bernard's Letters to Nettie Palmer' (2005) 19(1) *Antipodes* 13, 13–19; John Thompson, 'Some Australian Letters of Love and Friendship' (1998) 8(10) *National Library of Australia News* 11, 11–15; Dever (1996), above n 27; Adrian Cunningham, 'The Mysterious Outside Reader' (1996) 24(1) *Archives and Manuscripts* 130, 130–44; Miriam Estensen, *The Letters of George and Elizabeth Bass* (Allen & Unwin, 2009); H Anna Suh (ed), *Van Gogh's Letters* (Black Dog & Leventhal, 2010).
31   Jennifer Moran, 'Potency of the Pen' (2008) 18(12) *National Library of Australia News* 7, 7.
32   Thompson, above n 30, 11–15. As a recent example, see Michela McGuire and Marieke Hardy, *Signed, Sealed, Delivered: A Collection from Women of Letters* (Viking Press, 2016).

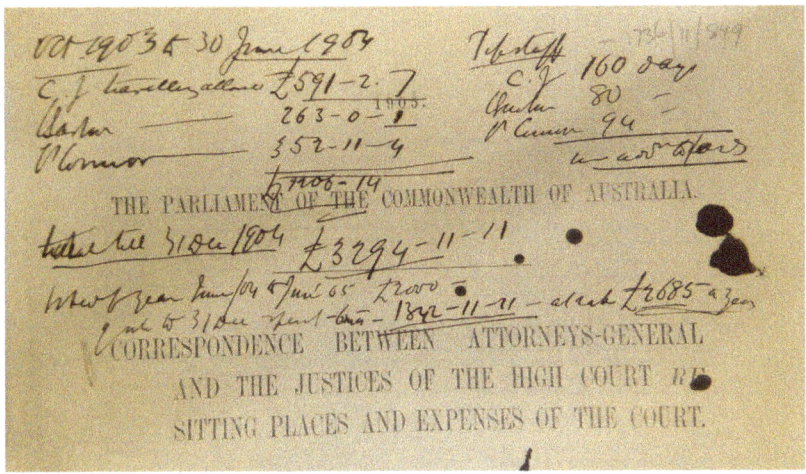

Figure 1: Correspondence between Attorneys-General and the Justices of the High Court re sitting places and expenses of the court.
Source: NLA Symon Papers MS 176/11/849.

Even if letter writing might be regarded as a diminishing art, correspondence is a permanent manifestation of writing that permits the reader to understand something about the ways in which the quality and character of individuals of the past, who were unwilling to converse with each other face-to-face, used the privacy of the letter to express themselves.[33] John Wishart documented these ideas in 1921 when he stated:

> Letters ... reveal the inner history of great national events of the time in which they were written ... names to most readers, become real persons to those who have read their letters ... The little incidents of every-day life ... give an insight into the thoughts and actions of our forefathers such as no amount of description can provide. To read such letters is to enter into the life of days gone by, to accompany the writers in their business ... to look at the world as they knew it through their eyes.[34]

While such observations readily confirm the merits, for research purposes, of examining correspondence for what its close association with both their writers and history will reveal to a reader, the same commentaries go further in their contribution to the focus of this chapter.

---

33 Thompson above n 30.
34 John Wishart (ed), *Selected English Letters* (JM Dent & Sons Ltd, 1921) 11.

These sources verify that the 'high-water mark'[35] of letter writing encompassed specifically the time of the dispute between Attorney-General Symon and the original Australian High Court.[36] They also reveal that the common notion of correctness, or practised conventions, dominated letter writing at this time to an extent unknown before or since.[37]

In a telegram sent from then Prime Minister George Reid to Attorney-General Symon dated 24 May 1905,[38] the Prime Minister suggested that Cabinet may have discussed the likelihood of publishing these letters with the intent of showing 'that there were faults on both sides'[39] of the disagreement. His prediction, in the end, ultimately proved to be correct.

The collection of 89 letters of state that became known as the 'official correspondence',[40] exchanged between the Attorney-General's Department and the Justices of the High Court between the months of July 1904 and early August 1905, presented in foolscap typeset,[41] appear to conform to the practised conventions as business letters of the day required.[42]

They were frequently answered similarly to the one received and promptly answered.[43] Each member of the High Court, when writing to Attorney-General Symon or vice versa, addressed each other as business letters of the day required.[44] They often used 'My dear Sir'[45] or 'Sir'[46] and ended with 'Yours faithfully',[47] 'I have the honour to be … Your obedient Servant',[48] or more commonly, 'We have, &c.',[49] or 'I have &c.'.[50]

---

35 Ibid. This high-water mark is purported to have ended around 1918.
36 Ibid.
37 Ibid.
38 Telegram from G Reid to J Symon, 24 May 1905, NLA: Symon Papers MS 1736/11/595.
39 WG McMinn, *George Reid* (Melbourne University Press, 1989) 218.
40 Telegram from G Reid to J Symon, 24 May 1905, NLA: Symon Papers MS 1736/11/595.
41 *Correspondence Between Attorneys-General and the Justices of the High Court RE Sitting Places and Expenses of the Court*, NLA: Symon Papers MS 176/11/849–68.
42 Mrs Erskine (full name unknown), *Etiquette in Australia* (William Brooks & Co., 1911) 71 indicates that business letters needed to be answered promptly and in the same form as the one received.
43 Above n 41. The dates on this correspondence indicate replies to letters received ranged from the same day to only several days apart.
44 Ibid.
45 Ibid.
46 Ibid.
47 Ibid.
48 Ibid.
49 Ibid.
50 Ibid.

To contemporary eyes, such expressions of politeness appear to be at odds with the contents of the letters that generally seem to remain aloof, uncompromising, acerbic and, at times, lengthy and rather repetitive.

Described by other scholars who examined these letters of state several decades ago, the correspondence on Attorney-General Symon's part, according to one, was written with 'fiendish ingenuity and sinister powers'.[51] According to others, the letters were 'marked on both sides by suppressed fury, and deadly icy courtesy',[52] being eloquent, but not overly elaborate in style and frequently long;[53] descriptions perhaps that ought not to be too startling.

Contemporaries of Attorney-General Symon, for instance, have suggested that he was well-recognised for his 'lucid and pungent'[54] writing style, which, at the time of his death in 1934, was paralleled with his eminence,[55] not only for his work as a lawyer but also with his contributions as a legislator, a lecturer and an author.[56]

Similarly, AD Graham, a barrister who claimed to have known Chief Justice Samuel Griffith for 'some years',[57] reflected on Griffith as a writer.[58] He stated that the Chief Justice not only 'wrote an excellent letter',[59] but 'had … a complete knowledge of the etiquette of official correspondence, and knew exactly the intricacies of the appropriate addresses and signatures of letters passing to and fro in Government departments'.[60]

However, in seeking alternative ways to interpret the contents of the formal correspondence, insights are readily documented that see beyond a narrative merely concerning an unseemly and prolonged clash of words.

---

51 La Nauze, above n 9, 383.
52 Gavin Souter, *Lion and Kangaroo; The Initiation of Australia* (Text Publishing, 2000) 110.
53 McMinn, above n 16, 14, 29.
54 JJ Pascoe (ed), *History of Adelaide and Vicinity: With a General Sketch of the Province of South Australia and Biographies of Representative Men* (Hussey and Gillingham, 1901) 374.
55 'Death of Sir Josiah Symon', *The Advertiser* (Adelaide), 30 March 1934, 7.
56 Ibid.
57 Douglas Graham, *The Life of the Right Honourable Sir Samuel Walker Griffith, GCMG PC* (Powells and Pughs, 1939) 2.
58 Ibid 88–93.
59 Ibid 92.
60 Ibid 93.

On 25 August 1905, the Melbourne *Age*[61] suggested that its reading public consider, as identified in the introductory paragraphs of this chapter, that this unique event in Australian legal history not only be regarded as a petty argument between the executive and the judiciary but also as an argument involving questions of principle:

> The epistolary altercation ... of a long and bitter controversy, revolving sometimes round petty matters ... sometimes round large questions of principle. Sir Josiah Symon seems to have irritated the judges and the judges ... appear to have snubbed the then Attorney-General on the slightest provocation. The spectacle presented by the letters is an unyielding one ... It closes with a letter written by the present Attorney-General, placing the whole of the matters in dispute on a basis which has given satisfaction to the judges, and at the same time scale of economies.[62]

Moving into the 21st century, in *One Hundred Years of the High Court of Australia*,[63] JM Williams clarified the notion of principle further. He suggested that any narrative concerning the High Court brings with it 'an important reminder'[64] that it is not an 'anonymous institution',[65] but is staffed by personnel 'who bring character, and in some cases drama, to the work of the Court'.[66] None more so perhaps than the original High Court tasked with establishing the 'Court in the Australian hierarchy ... [and] winning ... the respect of the local profession and judiciary'.[67]

Chief Justice Murray Gleeson, writing extrajudicially in 2007, also underscored the significance of the relationship between personalities and principles. He indicated that no matter how strong the personal opinions may have been between those involved in Australia's federal movement, it remains necessary to look beyond their robust exchanges and examine carefully the context in which these exchanges occurred.[68] In part, the former Chief Justice observed:

---

61 'High Court Judges', *The Age* (Melbourne) 25 August 1905, NLA: Symon Papers MS 1736/3/120; see also 'The High Court. Circuits and Travelling Expenses. Interesting Correspondence', *The Argus* (Melbourne) 25 August 1905, NLA: Symon Papers MS 1736/3/120 and the 'High Court Official Correspondence. Some Plain Speaking. The Justices' Views Adopted', *The Advertiser* (Adelaide), 24 August 1905, 5, who cautioned its readers that the correspondence would take two-and-a-half hours to read.
62 Ibid.
63 John Williams, *One Hundred Years of the High Court of Australia* (Menzies Centre for Australian Studies, 2003).
64 Ibid 30.
65 Ibid.
66 Ibid.
67 Ibid 31.
68 Murray Gleeson, 'The Constitutional Decisions of the Founding Fathers' (2007) 9 *University of Notre Dame Australia Law Review* 1.

In interpreting a legal instrument, including a Constitution, what finally matters is the meaning of what the instrument says. The task is to construe the text. The authors of the text employed particular language, and it is the effect of that language, [and] not their beliefs about that effect, that is legally binding.[69]

Most recently, acknowledging that the story of the strike has been 'been told a number of times … [and] … in a variety of ways',[70] Justice Stephen Gageler described the unfolding tensions as 'a quarrel which wound its way "through a labyrinth of spite and petty vituperation on both sides", but "originated in a noble vision" and which bore on "an important principle"'.[71]:

> Griffith's triumph and Symon's ignominy cannot gainsay the mixture of pettiness and principle which fuelled the actions and reactions of each. To the extent the principle can be separated from the pettiness, their battle was about the boundaries of judicial independence and about the balance between judicial independence and judicial accountability. And to that extent, recalling their battle has some enduring significance.[72]

Lastly, if we return to the archives of original letters, Attorney-General Josiah Symon writing to Alfred Deakin in June 1905 echoed similar views. He was 'grateful'[73] for Deakin's remarks 'as to our differences upon my purposes in regards to the High Court'[74] and, despite all that had occurred, hoped that it would have little impact on their collegiality. In anticipation of any future communications between them, he also hoped that 'our jurat intercourse … shall not be affected'.[75]

Finally, if any types of administrative oversights or errors occurred during the compilation of the letters that became known as the official correspondence, existing archival evidence on these issues remains silent. Attorney-General Symon did leave a legacy in this regard and specifically noted on his copy of the published volume of the official correspondence that one letter to the court, dated 16 February 1905,[76] was missing but subsequently located elsewhere.[77]

---

69 Ibid 17.
70 Stephen Gageler, 'When the High Court Went on Strike' (2017) 40(3) *Melbourne University Law Review* 1098, 1099.
71 Ibid 1101, citing DI Wright, 'Sir Josiah Symon, Federation and the High Court' (1978) 64 *Journal of the Royal Australian Historical Society* 73.
72 Ibid 1130.
73 Letter from J Symon to A Deakin, 25 June 1905, NLA: Deakin Papers 1540/16/414.
74 Ibid.
75 Ibid.
76 NLA Symon Papers MS 1736/11/849–68.
77 Letter from J Symon to S Griffith, 16 February 1905, NLA: Symon Papers MS 1736/11/728.

Even so, as a researcher having full access to official court archives, this discovery left an impression that additional archives remain beyond reach or are yet to be found. As Maud Bailey lamented in AS Byatt's *Possession*, 'you know if you read the collected letters of any writer ... there is always "something ... biographers don't have access to, the real thing, the crucial thing ... There are always letters that were destroyed. *The* letters, usually"'.[78]

The Archives as Evidence II: Personal Correspondence, Letters to Alfred Deakin

> It is impossible to create a federation without having divisions and distributions of powers, without having different organs of government possibly in conflict. Therefore from the necessities of federation, and as one of the inevitable consequences from which we cannot escape, we find ourselves in a new situation of comparative peril and serious responsibility. Hence we must necessarily have an Australian court for the determination of principles which shall be common to the whole Continent, based upon a survey of the requirements of the whole people. If the legislative and executive powers of the States, the Commonwealth, and the Imperial Governments are to be judicially restrained each to its own sphere we have before us a difficult task.[79]

> Alfred Deakin was not a gregarious person ... His friendships were few, and almost none came from his political life, Barton and O'Connor being the exceptions in that they were his personal friends as well as political allies.[80]

---

78 Catherine Burgass, *AS Byatt's Possession: A Readers Guide* (The Continuum International Publishing Group Ltd, 2002) 45.
79 NLA Deakin Papers MS 1540/14/1038 9.
80 Al Gabay, 'Alfred Deakin and his Friends' in David Headon and John Williams (eds), *Makers of Miracles The Cast of the Federation Story* (Melbourne University Press, 2000) 82.

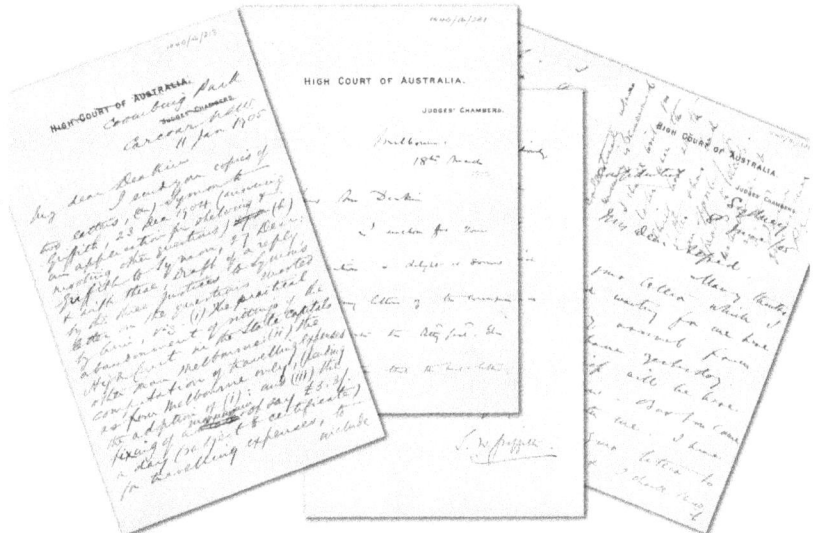

Figure 2: Correspondence from each of the High Court members to Alfred Deakin.
Source: NLA Deakin Papers 1840/16/213; 1840/16/281; 1840/16/328.

The significance of the use of court and departmental letters as archival evidence to the researcher cannot be underestimated it would seem. However, this historical importance for research purposes is further magnified when discussing the place of personal letter writing in research; the historical value of those communications 'passed on … in a confidential relationship'.[81]

In a series of incomplete letters that remain as part of the Deakin papers,[82] a brief but manifestly personal understanding is revealed into how each of the judges felt about the nature of their formal frequent written exchanges with Attorney-General Symon. They provide a reader with an immediate and compelling alternate history that can lend both originality and depth of historical analysis to the story of the judicial strike of 1905.

The original three Justices of the High Court turned to Alfred Deakin as their 'trusted friend, the legislative father of the court and the only man who might be able to protect them by private representations, since Prime

---

81 Telegram from G Reid to J Symon, 24 May 1905, NLA: Symon Papers MS 1736/11/595.
82 NLA Deakin Papers MS 1540/16/187, 213–23, 237–52, 272, 281, 303–5, 328–35, 345–7, 356, 378–9, 385–91, 404–5, 411–14.

Minister Reid seemed unwilling or unable to intervene between them and the formidably venomous Symon'.[83] This collection of letters, most frequently penned to Alfred Deakin by Justice Richard O'Connor, are incomplete because none of Deakin's original written replies are part of the Deakin collection. Nonetheless, the letters that do remain reveal the High Court bench from a different perspective; an original Federal Judiciary appalled by the personal attack of the Attorney-General and frustrated by his fierce resistance to achieve a lasting and mutually agreeable outcome to the drawn-out circumstances of the controversy.

In contrast to the official typeset correspondence, these letters are, for the main, all handwritten, extremely difficult to read and, at times, are illegible. They were exchanged during January, February, March and, more regularly, June 1905. Unlike the formal correspondence, the tone in each of the letters appears gracious and forthcoming, and they were written between individuals with complete trust and confidence in each other.[84]

In stark contrast to the formalities required with official correspondence, Alfred Deakin is addressed as 'Dear A. D.',[85] 'Dear Deakin'[86] or 'My Dear Alfred',[87] and the letters frequently conclude with 'yours as ever'[88] or 'yours always'.[89]

Through these exchanges, the congenial relationship that existed exclusively between each of the Justices is also confirmed. In one instance, the Chief Justice and Justice Barton had written separate notes to Deakin on the same page,[90] and, in another, Justice Barton puts pen to paper in the full knowledge that copies of Attorney-General Symon's letters had already been sent from Justice O'Connor a few days earlier.[91] Alfred Deakin was privy to the original High Court's deeply personal attitudes towards the nature of the dispute from its outset.

---

83   JA La Nauze, above n 9, 383.
84   Al Gabay, above n 80, describes Barton and O'Connor as being Deakin's 'personal friends' and 'political allies'.
85   Letter from E Barton to A Deakin, 16 February 1905, NLA Deakin Papers MS 1540/16/187.
86   Letter from E Barton to A Deakin, 26 February 1905, NLA: Deakin Papers MS 1540/16/245.
87   Letter from R O'Connor to A Deakin, 12 June 1905, NLA: Deakin Papers MS 1540/16/335.
88   Letter from R O'Connor to A Deakin, 21 June 1905, NLA: Deakin Papers MS 1540/16/389.
89   Letter from E Barton to A Deakin, 21 June 1905, NLA: Deakin Papers MS 1540/16/385.
90   Letter from S Griffith to A Deakin and letter from E Barton to A Deakin, 16 February 1905, NLA: Deakin Papers MS 1540/16/187.
91   Letter from E Barton to A Deakin, 21 June 1905, NLA: Deakin Papers MS 1540/16/385.

On 11 January 1905,[92] Justice Edmund Barton sent Alfred Deakin copies of two letters the court had received from the Attorney-General dated 23 December 1904, and the Chief Justice's response of 27 December 1904, respectively.[93] He also enclosed a copy of the court's draft response to Symon[94] and identified the early proposals the Attorney-General had put forward to the court to address ways of curtailing its expenditure. These, in Justice Barton's words, were threefold: 'the practical abandonment of sittings of the High Court in the State capitals other than Melbourne';[95] that travelling expenses would be computed from Melbourne only; and that the judges would be paid a fixed daily rate of three guineas.[96] However, the main reason for writing at this stage was to ensure that Deakin was informed of 'everything so far'.[97]

A month later, Justice Barton wrote again. By 16 February 1905, he had already referred to the Attorney-General's letters in earlier correspondence as being peculiarly 'insulting in tone',[98] but by 26 February, Attorney-General Symon's letters contained 'screeds on the subject of the abolition of the system of holding court in the District Registries'.[99] In addition, before the court was able to write a 'joint letter'[100] in response to the latest communication from the Attorney-General, Symon was writing to them again in a manner that was 'more extraordinary and more insulting than anything that had gone before'.[101] Barton once again enclosed copies of the letters to give Deakin a 'complete grasp of the matter',[102] but on this occasion, his correspondence concluded with an individual request for assistance. 'If you find what seems to you as a solution please let me have it always … yours sincerely Edmund Barton'.[103]

---

92 Letter from E Barton to A Deakin, 11 January 1905, NLA: Deakin Papers MS 1540/16/ 213.
93 NLA Symon Papers MS 1736/11/850–1 are the original references for Symon's letters.
94 Above n 92.
95 Ibid.
96 Ibid.
97 Ibid.
98 Letter from E Barton to A Deakin, 16 February 1905, NLA: Deakin Papers MS 1540/16/187.
99 Letter from E Barton to A Deakin, 26 February 1905, NLA: Deakin Papers MS 1540/16/245.
100 Ibid.
101 Ibid.
102 Ibid.
103 Ibid.

Deakin's response to the circumstances, according to JA La Nauze, was one of disbelief. The Attorney-General's letters had 'shocked'[104] him and left him 'humiliated'.[105] He thought that Symon had an 'immense advantage'[106] over the High Court because he treated the judges as they were 'constitutionally supposed to be'[107] treated 'while all the time [Symon] is throwing mud like a larrikin at you and exercising the petty tyranny that his position allows'.[108] He encouraged the Justices to destroy the correspondence for both 'the sake of the Commonwealth and the High Court'.[109]

Other revelations from the judges throughout the next four months followed. Chief Justice Griffith sent copies of Symon's latest letters to the bench to Deakin in a brief note on 18 March 1905, enclosing them for Deakin's 'delight or sorrow'.[110]

A large gap in the archival materials exists until Justice O'Connor again wrote to Deakin in early June.[111] By that time, the court's decision to adjourn proceedings and go on strike had already taken place, and their reasons for doing so had already been made public. Nevertheless, Justice Richard O'Connor thought that a solution to the dispute was still possible.[112]

Aware that Prime Minister 'Reid ha[d] now left the matter to Symon'[113] to resolve, Justice O'Connor expressed his regret that the correspondence could not be withdrawn as it was 'too late'.[114] He went on and rightly predicted that 'Parliament will probably demand to see' it.[115]

Days later, O'Connor made a rather startling revelation. Despite the misconception Attorney-General Symon might have had in thinking he would 'eventually induce us [the court] to give up opposing him',[116]

---

104 La Nauze, above n 9, 384.
105 Ibid.
106 Ibid.
107 Ibid.
108 Ibid.
109 Ibid.
110 Letter from S Griffith to A Deakin, 18 March 1905, NLA: Deakin Papers MS 1540/16/281.
111 Letter from R O'Connor to A Deakin, 8 June 1905, NLA: Deakin Papers MS 1540/16/328.
112 Ibid.
113 Ibid.
114 Ibid.
115 Ibid.
116 Letter from R O'Connor to A Deakin, 12 June 1905, NLA: Deakin Papers MS 1540/16/335.

O'Connor wrote about the urgency and necessity of discussing and settling the matter with the Attorney-General, especially if 'Symon himself became a member of the Court'.[117] However, such an appointment occurring sometime in the future, given the manner in which the Attorney-General had behaved towards the judges, was deemed 'unlikely'[118] to occur.

On 19 June, renewed written attacks from Attorney-General Symon were interpreted by Justice O'Connor as the 'absolute freehand'[119] the Attorney-General had been given by Prime Minister Reid 'to wreck as far as he can the High Court establishment as you [Deakin] and we designed it should be when we first took office'.[120] Then, on the following page, O'Connor confirmed, as Symon had threatened that he would do in his 26 April 1905 letter, that 'the official telephones were disconnected [in their Sydney chambers except one] today'.[121]

Still the optimist, Justice O'Connor's letter concluded on a positive note, looking towards an opportunity for a change to the current and untenable circumstances:

> We are all curious to hear what you have to say at Ballarat—when I say 'we' I do not mean the High Court, but all Federalists and indeed all them who wish to see Parliament lift out of the slough … into which Reid has dropped it.
>
> I am sure you will do what you think best in the interest of the Commonwealth apart from any other considerations.[122]

On 21 June 1905, Edmund Barton wrote his last letter about the crisis to Alfred Deakin.[123] He revealed, perhaps in the most intimate terms, the impact the dispute was having upon him. In his view, it had now become 'impossible to do one's work efficiently'[124] because of the disturbing nature of the contents of Symon's latest letters to the court both dated 9 June 1905.[125]

---

117 Ibid.
118 La Nauze, above n 9, 416.
119 Letter from R O'Connor to A Deakin, 19 June 1905, NLA: Deakin Papers MS 1540/16/378.
120 Ibid.
121 Ibid; J Symon to S Griffith, 26 April 1905, NLA: Symon Papers MS 1736/11/858 is where the Attorney-General initially indicated he would change the existing arrangements with regard to the payment for telephone usage.
122 Letter from R O'Connor to A Deakin, 19 June 1905, NLA: Deakin Papers MS 1540/16/378.
123 Letter from E Barton to A Deakin, 21 June 1905, NLA: Deakin Papers MS 1540/16/385.
124 Ibid.
125 See NLA: Symon Papers MS 1736/11/860 and 861 for copies of these letters to the court.

According to Barton, the Attorney-General in these two communications had now surmised:

> his determination to pack our tipstaffs off at a few days notice and turn them adrift upon the world. Shocked as I had been at the ... venom of the war, it was natural to fear that he would resort to such a cruelty to these innocent officers for the mere purpose of satisfying his hatred of us.[126]

Then, he finished his letter by adding:

> One feels all this bitterly. We are in every way degraded and humiliated by this unspeakable scoundrel: and if Australia offers the Judges of her one and only national Court to be treated thus she will deserve as she has not yet done the scoffs and jibes of the English speaking world. My wife wishes me to resign rather than submit to any further indignity but at least I shall wait to see whether Parliament adopts or condones, the outrage we have suffered, of which every day brings a new one in the shape of an insulting letter.[127]

Fortunately, for the Griffith Court, the original High Court bench would remain a united one. In addition, Justice Richard O'Connor had been right in his June 1905 prediction to Deakin.[128]

The controversy between the High Court and Attorney-General Symon would only be resolved by an 'appeal to Symon's successor',[129] and it was. The decisions reached by the new government, as documented at the beginning of this chapter, brought the dispute to an end.

The Archives as Evidence III: Concluding Notes on Methodology

> Then there are emanations from the documents themselves, which the historian sometimes exposes to the light for the first time since they were preserved.[130]

> [T]he greatest strength of a position depends on its facts, its greatest weakness arises from its epithets.[131]

---

126 Letter from E Barton to A Deakin, 21 June 1905, NLA: Deakin Papers MS 1540/16/385.
127 Ibid.
128 Letter from R O'Connor to A Deakin, 12 June 1905, NLA: Deakin Papers MS 1540/16/335.
129 Ibid.
130 Tom Griffith, *The Art of Time Travel* (Black Inc., 2016) 11.
131 Telegram from G Reid to J Symon, 24 May 1905, NLA: Symon Papers MS 1736/11/595, 597.

The notion of missing primary sources from manuscripts and records, such as the letters documenting Alfred Deakin's personal replies to the Justices of the High Court, has been described generally in secondary sources as a concept referred to as the 'fissured archive'.[132] As the expression denotes, it refers to materials that survive as evidence in archival materials but ultimately remain as a part of what may have originally been their total.[133]

This is a useful choice of words because not only does it highlight the limitations on tasks a researcher can achieve when key documents are missing, but, as a consequence, the information when ultimately presented, as highly relevant and compelling as it may be for research purposes, has the potential to be often fragmented and rather disjointed. Again, to use a similar colloquial expression cited above, the experience of this as a researcher and writer is one of never playing with a 'full hand'.[134]

Instead, having to accept that in the private correspondence between Alfred Deakin and the High Court, they could only reveal discrete snippets or instances from the parties about the information they wished to convey, it made subsequent interpretations and reinterpretations for writing purposes an extremely difficult undertaking for the researcher. Particularly when trying to fill in the gaps with words that could only be representations and unable to guarantee a full comprehension or even an 'impartial review'[135] of all the details enclosed in the correspondence.

This dilemma is perhaps especially relevant in 2018, where, in the age of disclosure, our sense regarding the privacy of individuals and the extent to which they will be exposed 'has been systematically eroded over the years by the public's right to know'.[136] Further, it was Prime Minister George Reid who predicted that under such circumstances personal motives had the potential to be 'unfairly decried',[137] which remains a relevant observation even today.

---

132 Dever (1996), above n 27, 119.
133 Ibid.
134 Ibid.
135 HG Turner, *The First Decade of the Australian Commonwealth: A Chronicle of Contemporary Politics 1901–1910* (Mason, Firth and McCutcheon, 1911) vii.
136 Dever (1996), above n 27, 117.
137 Turner, above n 135, vii.

Therefore, as acknowledged by writers before me who have studied other kinds of early letters written by Australian public figures,[138] there is little reason to doubt that both types of correspondence referred to throughout this chapter have presented a valuable 'tangent to reflect a key moment in Australian legal history' for research and writing purposes.[139] However, these observations, it is suggested, offer much more.

The contents of the archival materials, including private correspondence, have been powerful reminders of personal histories as well—supplements to a specific time in Australia's legal history by providing information, opinions and attitudes that can have a dramatic and intensely personal impact on how a very public set of circumstances in existing formal letters of state are interpreted.

In short, as this chapter sets out to demonstrate, histories have ultimately been shaped by numerous tensions, as much by what is known as what is not known. The 'absences and the subtle silences',[140] which structured my reading from the archives remain and serve in the end to act as but a representative of the whole to depict a narrative as comprehensively and as systematically as those resources will allow.

As Marianne Dever wrote in 1996, in the end, reading the archival materials—in this instance, both the formal and personal correspondence pertaining to the strike of 1905—was, from time to time, a little like:

> being the proverbial eavesdropper on a telephone call, inferring from the overheard fragments of information those portions of conversation to which one is not privy. I read between the lines. But this partial and disconnected dialogue leaves me unable to clarify so many details … I can picture but not pin down.[141]

Finally, it was demonstrated, particularly from the list of the early references included in the preceding pages, that a broad interest in letter writing by researchers 'with its own unique qualities of style and personal expression'[142] continues against all the odds to make a regular appearance on the publication list of books.

---

138 Thompson, above n 30, 11.
139 Ibid.
140 Ibid 12.
141 Dever (1996), above n 27, 126.
142 Thompson, above n 30, 11.

In writing his much-acclaimed biography of Alfred Deakin, JA La Nauze revealed what has already been stated in the previous section of this chapter. Alfred Deakin wished under no circumstances for the correspondence between the High Court and then Attorney-General to ever be made public.[143] However, in the same publication, La Nauze expressed his view that, if a study of the dispute were ever to be undertaken, it would provide the substance for a 'fascinating study in character'.[144] Indeed, it has. Even so, the unease about the controversy and shame Alfred Deakin expressed about the realisation that the written exchanges might be made public can be put to rest.

The original Justices took a resolute position of principle. Under the leadership of Chief Justice Samuel Griffith, they established the foundations of the High Court as they thought it should and would continue: to attain 'high standards of integrity, learning, ability and industry'.[145]

For the former Attorney-General, Josiah Symon, the High Court affair, as it had for all individuals involved, seemed to have taken an enormous toll. In a public and rather emotive demonstration of this, Symon made an important distinction between the contributions he had made to the dual parliamentary roles he had held in the Reid–McLean Ministry. When he resigned his position as Leader of the Senate on Wednesday, 5 July 1905, he made it known to the Chamber that:

> In relinquishing this position which I have been proud to hold, and whose duties I have been proud to discharge—I do not mean the official position of Attorney-General, but the position of leader of this great and august assembly—I part company from all my honourable friends here, certainly on my part, with what will always be a constraint of feeling of personal regard, and I am sure that it will be reciprocated by the goodwill of all my friends. I move—That the Senate at its rising adjourn.[146]

---

143 La Nauze, above n 9, 384.
144 Ibid 382.
145 Harry Gibbs, 'Griffith, Samuel Walker' in Tony Blackshield, Michael Coper and George Williams (eds), *The Oxford Companion to the High Court of Australia* (Oxford University Press, 2001) 311.
146 Commonwealth, *Parliamentary Debates*, Senate, 5 July 1905, 134 (JH Symon).

In short, when combined and used as evidence, both official and personal letters both disclose and confirm that behind the historical narrative of strong or robust opinions of the Federation Fathers,[147] a constitutional battle testing the parameters of the separation of powers doctrine to maintain the well-ordered dignity of the High Court was far greater.

The resolute personality of Australia's founding Chief Justice of the High Court, Samuel Griffith, displayed a determination to establish the independence of the court from its beginning, including its sitting patterns and the staff required to ensure its operation at the apex of the judiciary in an emerging Commonwealth polity.

However, the final words regarding methodology belong to Charles Darwin. In a completely different context in his writing in the *Descent of Man*, he stated that 'we are not here concerned with hopes and fears, only with truth as far as our reason allows us to discover it'.[148]

---

147 Gleeson, above n 68, 17.
148 Charles Darwin, cited in Inga Clendinnen, 'The History Question. Who Owns the Past?' (2006) 23 *Quarterly Essay* 1, 68.

6

Accessing the Archives of the Australian War Crimes Trials after World War II

Narrelle Morris

Introduction

In 1945–51, Australian Military Courts convened 300 trials of Japanese accused of committing various war crimes during World War II, which sat at Morotai, Wewak, Labuan, Darwin, Rabaul, Singapore, Hong Kong and Manus Island. The military courts were creatures of statute under the *War Crimes Act 1945* (Cth) and akin to field general courts-martial.[1] As such, they were exercising executive, not judicial, power. Significantly, the military courts had no duty to produce written reasons for decisions.[2] It is the lack of written decisions that elevates the trial proceedings—tens of thousands of pages of forms, transcripts and exhibits that were created during the trials—to a position of unusual importance as legal records. Moreover, there was some recognition at the time that the proceedings had worth beyond legal records; they formed a body of historical records relating to the war in their own right and merit and with national, if

---

1   See Michael Paes, 'The Australian Military Courts under the *War Crimes Act 1945*—Structure and Approach' in Georgina Fitzpatrick, Timothy McCormack and Narrelle Morris (eds), *Australia's War Crimes Trials 1945–51* (Brill Nijhoff, 2016) 103–33, doi.org/10.1163/9789004292055_005.
2   Even in judicial proceedings, the requirement to give reasons is regarded as a 'normal but not universal incident' of the process: *Public Service Board (NSW) v Osmond* (1986) 159 CLR 656, 667.

not international, significance. The proceedings contain thousands of accounts of war crimes perpetrators, victims and witnesses, as well as firsthand accounts of military service, movements, battles, capture by the enemy and, inevitably, atrocities. In seeking to gain copies of the proceedings, the Australian War Memorial asserted in 1946, for example, that they would be of 'great value to the official historians, and later to other historians and students of the Second World War'.[3] However, the Department of the Army, which had been responsible for the trials, simply treated the proceedings as it did those of courts-martial. The proceedings were regarded as classified and confidential Commonwealth legal-administrative records that were shuffled between government departments and eventually archived but were closed to public access for the next quarter of a century.

Australia's tight control of its trial proceedings in the postwar period was not unusual for government records in this period. This was due to both the absence of an independent archive and the tendency to regard archiving as an economically effective means for the storage and disposal of records, rather than as the creation of a valuable national repository to preserve and make information accessible. However, given the obvious personal and international character of the trial proceedings and associated war crimes records, the closure raises questions about access to information for those prosecuted and their country. Australia provided only a 'bare minimum'[4] of information to Japan about the trials, mostly concerning the identities of the convicted and their sentences. Thus, the Japanese Government made several diplomatic requests to Australia in the 1950s and 1960s for access to or copies of the trial proceedings and other war crimes records. Other Allied nations were receiving similar Japanese requests for their war crimes records. The consequent Allied consultation was fairly rudimentary but demonstrated that a consensus approach to the requests was thought necessary.

These processes revealed that, in the decades after the war, Allied nations were generally opposed to making their war crimes records available, although some countries were slightly more permissive than others. In Australia, the issue of granting Japanese access to records was typically

---

3   AW Bazley, Acting Director, Australian War Memorial to the Secretary, Department of External Affairs (Ext Aff), 28 August 1946, National Archives of Australia (NAA): MP742/1, 336/1/1000.
4   As characterised by Yuma Totani, *Justice in Asia and the Pacific Region, 1945–1952: Allied War Crimes Prosecutions* (Cambridge University Press, 2015) 186, doi.org/10.1017/CBO9781316104118.

regarded as one of 'policy and practicability, rather than of law'.[5] There was no legal requirement to provide the trial proceedings even to those who had been prosecuted, let alone to Japan. Thus, citing policy and practicability, the Departments of External Affairs and the Army refused to release the records for decades. The policy reasons for access refusal usually turned on what was seen as Australia's right and obligation to control the dissemination of sensitive 'national' information that Japan might use to criticise the trials. Moreover, the estimated expenses in time and money to make copies of these records was used to argue that their provision was impracticable. Little consideration in this decision-making process was given to those who may have had a valid interest in access to the records or to the light that the records may have shed on a key part of wartime history. The closure of the records simply ensured that Australia maintained an exclusive grip on knowledge of that history.

Drawing on government correspondence, this chapter examines the postwar views and control of Australia's archives of war crimes records in response to the Japanese requests for access. This story will be told through short vignettes that describe the shifting relationships between Australia and Japan, as much as those between the institutions of the Australian Government and their conceptualisation and approach to the value and materiality of war records. This story demonstrates how records that documented the prosecution and punishment of people from another nation during legal processes that were open to the public to watch (*prima facie* court records) can, nonetheless, be classified afterwards as confidential national records (not court records) of such significant international political consequence that they had to be zealously protected for decades. Although Prime Minister John Gorton announced the accelerated release of general World War II records in 1971,[6] it took until 1975 for the trial proceedings to be opened to the public. In an interesting turn of fate, it was the Commonwealth's legal executive—the Attorney-General's Department—that finally recognised the importance to history of allowing public access to the records, an importance that overrode any supposed protective requirements, such as confidentiality. The 'past', stated

---

5   See handwritten note to Mr Horne, 28 May 1965, NAA: A1838, 3103/10/13/2 PART 15A.
6   *Access to Commonwealth Archives – Statement by the Prime Minister, Mr. John Gorton* (30 December 1970) Department of the Prime Minister and Cabinet <http://pmtranscripts.pmc.gov.au/sites/default/files/original/00002342.pdf>.

Attorney-General Keppel Enderby QC, 'should be everyone's property'.[7] Yet, the lengthy delay in making the records accessible meant that, in the interim, most individuals involved in the trials had died, taking with them what could have been invaluable personal accounts and permanently impacting on our understanding of the trials and the histories that can be told of them. In hampering research for so long, protectionism had, in this case, an indelible effect on knowledge.

The First Japanese Request for Access in 1955

Japan's first request to the Department of External Affairs for records relating to Japanese war criminals and their trials arrived in 1955, four years after the final trial on Manus Island. A Japanese Embassy official asked in person for information about the whereabouts of the records and what authority was in charge of them; whether there were extra copies of these records; and whether Australia would consent to Japan obtaining these copies. Given that the official also enquired about the estimated cost of reproducing the records, it was perhaps contemplated that Japan would pay an appropriate fee.[8]

As the Army had convened the trials, External Affairs forwarded the Japanese request to the Department of the Army for its view.[9] The Secretary of the Department of the Army was surprised that a 'request of such magnitude' had been made orally. He advised that it seemed 'almost certain that the information is wanted for propaganda purposes as no other possible reason can be visualised'. He observed that '[p]ublication of distorted versions of particular trials, extracts therefrom taken out of context, or half truths' might assist the various nationalist organisations that had since sprung up in Japan, which sought, for example, to 'restore the lost honour of the Imperial armed forces' and to 'correct the cruel injustices done to their dignity and memory'. He pointed out that there was nothing in the *War Crimes Act* or its regulations that provided for copies of the proceedings to be made available and nor were there extra

---

7   Attorney-General (Att Gen) press release, 'Access to Historical Records', 2 June 1975, NAA: A1838, 3103/10/13/12 PART 16A.
8   Secretary, Ext Aff to the Secretary, Department of the Army (hereafter Army), 8 July 1955, NAA: A1838, 3103/10/13/2 PART 13.
9   Ibid.

copies. He estimated that it would cost £13,000 and '20 typist years' to retype about 75,000 pages of records or £38,500 and '185 machine days' to do photostatic reproductions and his departmental staffing was insufficient to undertake such a 'tremendous' task. For all these reasons, he recommended that no records should be made available to the Japanese.[10]

External Affairs considered the Army's response and canvassed a number of high-level departmental officials. James Plimsoll, then Assistant Secretary, for instance, recommended that Japan should be told that it was not possible to provide any records and that no information should be provided at all, apart from the Army's estimated cost of reproduction.[11] In due course, the Japanese Embassy was told that that none of the information requested could be made available. The Embassy apparently made 'no comment' on the refusal.[12]

After Australia's refusal was communicated to Japan, External Affairs informed its diplomatic representatives in the United States, the United Kingdom, the Netherlands, France and the Philippines about the request and the refusal. The representatives were asked to ascertain whether Japan had made similar requests to those nations; if so, what that government's response had been; and if there were any 'views' as to what was 'behind' the request. The Australian Embassy in Tokyo was similarly asked to 'shed any light' on what had prompted the request.[13] The Embassy responded that '[n]othing specific' had suggested itself as the 'immediate cause' of the request, but that it seemed 'likely' that the records were sought to give 'further support for appeals for clemency'.[14] Most of the other Allied Powers had, in fact, received Japanese requests for access to, or copies of, their records of war crimes trials. The cautionary responses were fairly similar in each case, demonstrating scepticism of the Japanese motives. As a result, the requests were met usually with outright refusals or with limited access being offered with such stringent conditions and/or high costs to be met by Japan that such offers were not taken up. The United States, for example, had received a Japanese request for records, but the

---

10 AD McKnight, Secretary, Army to the Secretary, Ext Aff, attaching Appendix A and B, 21 July 1955, NAA: A1838, 3103/10/13/2 PART 13.
11 Handwritten note signed and dated 27 July 1955, NAA: A1838, 3103/10/13/2 PART 13.
12 Secretary, Ext Aff to the Secretary, Army, 12 September 1955, 1, NAA: A1838, 3103/10/13/2 PART 13.
13 TW Eckersley for the Secretary, Ext Aff, to Washington, London, The Hague, Paris, Manila and Tokyo, 1 August 1955, NAA: A1838, 3103/10/13/2 PART 13.
14 RWL Austin, Second Secretary, Australian Embassy, Tokyo to the Secretary, Ext Aff, 2 September 1955, NAA: A1838, 3103/10/13/2 PART 13.

State Department could 'only guess' what the reason for it might be, as none had been provided.[15] State Department officials suggested to the Australian Embassy that the Japanese 'might wish to use parts of the ... records to support requests for the release of prisoners' or, alternatively, that the Japanese 'simply' wanted 'all records concerning important matters in which its nationals have been or may be concerned'.[16] One of these officials, legal expert George Hagan, referred to:

> the common Japanese feeling that the war criminal trials constituted a kind of national disgrace and the Japanese desire to 'expunge them', as it were, from the record: possession of the official documents might help them in some way for this purpose.[17]

The State Department told the Australian Embassy in early 1956 that the Japanese Embassy was going to be informed that the records were 'not available', since they were still being used by the US Clemency and Parole Board relating to war criminals. Moreover, '[s]ome form of words will be found' to 'discourage the Japanese from renewing their application', even after the war criminals had been all released.[18] As External Affairs later characterised the overall outcome of the Japanese requests to the Allied Powers, '[i]n effect, the Japanese got no change from anybody'.[19]

The Second Japanese Request for Access in 1959

The second, quite similar, Japanese request for copies of Australian records arrived in August 1959. The Japanese Embassy advised that the Ministry of Justice was 'engaged in collecting' all postwar trial records.[20] Indeed, the Ministry had established a Judiciary and Legislation Investigation Bureau (*shihō hōsei chōsabu*) in May 1958, tasked with the project to collect as many

---

15   JR Rowland, First Secretary, Australian Embassy, Washington DC to the Secretary, Ext Aff, 29 August 1955, NAA: A1838, 3103/10/13/2 PART 13.
16   Ibid.
17   Ibid.
18   JR Rowland, First Secretary, Australian Embassy, Washington DC to the Secretary, Ext Aff, 25 January 1956, NAA: A1838, 3103/10/13/2 PART 14A.
19   Ext Aff File Note, 'Japanese War Criminals, Records', 7 September 1959, NAA: A1838, 3103/10/13/2 PART 15A.
20   Embassy of Japan, Note Verbale, no. 109, 25 August 1959, NAA: A1838, 3103/10/13/2 PART 15A.

Allied trial records as possible.[21] One External Affairs analyst was initially minded to reject the request outright, as Japan had provided 'even fewer reasons for the request now than they did in 1955, when we rejected it' and that the reasons for the rejection remained valid.[22] The analyst posited that the request was based on the fact that 'there is, in Japan, pressure to "correct" the verdicts of Allied Military Tribunals'.[23] The analyst also suggested that if none of the above was sufficient to explain a rejection, Japan could be told that it was based on 'the need to protect individuals who had supplied information about war crimes'.[24] The Legal and Treaty Division of External Affairs also advised that there was 'no obligation in law' to comply with the request and, in fact, no specific legislative provision under which the records could be provided.[25] However, this did not prevent the handing over of copies to Japan, if this was the policy decision that was made.[26] The Department of the Army agreed that the objections raised in 1955 remained 'sufficient' to refuse the request and, if any further reason was required, it was the ongoing Allied opposition to providing access. The Army suggested that the Japanese Embassy simply 'be informed that it is not the practice of Australia to pass documents of this nature to a foreign Government or to provide copies of them'.[27]

This time, External Affairs began international consultation while consideration was ongoing.[28] The United States advised that another Japanese request had arrived in mid-1959, for the stated reason that Japan wanted the records 'for the purpose of historical record'. However, a State Department official suggested to an Australian official that if Japan gained the records, it 'might in the future attempt to cast doubt on the trials' and that 'this was the real motivation' in seeking them. The State Department intended to 'stall the Japanese request indefinitely by long drawn-out consultation' with other government agencies. The only 'difficulty' was

---

21 Totani, above n 4, 188.
22 Ext Aff File Note, 'Japanese War Criminals' Records', 7 September 1959, NAA: A1838, 3103/10/13/2 PART 15A.
23 Ibid.
24 Ibid.
25 AH Body, Ext Aff File Note, 'Japanese War Criminals' Records', 15 September 1959, NAA: A1838, 3103/10/13/2 PART 15A.
26 Ibid.
27 B White for the Secretary, Army to the Secretary, Ext Aff, 3 March 1960, NAA: A1838, 3103/10/13/2 PART 15A.
28 HA Dunn for the Secretary, Ext Aff to the Australian Embassy—Washington, the Hague, Paris, Tokyo and the Australian High Commission, London, 5 July 1960, NAA: A1838, 3103/10/13/2 PART 15A.

that 'some' proceedings had already been reproduced for university libraries. Therefore, the State Department expected that it might have to permit Japan to have copies of those trials, although it was likely that access would be refused to investigation files.[29] Of the other Allied countries, the United Kingdom, the Netherlands and France had also received Japanese requests but were generally not cooperative. Nevertheless, France had provided to Japan a list of the numbers and dates of the judgments of 34 Japanese war criminals and advised that it would provide copies only of judgments if Japan paid the expense of doing so.[30]

After receiving the international responses, External Affairs continued to debate the matter. One official suggested that it would 'close the matter out to refuse the Japanese request', which he favoured.[31] Another official felt 'strongly that we should not yield an inch on the subject of war criminals', given that 'Japan's record in this field was disgusting' and that it would be 'abhorrent to the Australian people if it became known that we even discussed this subject with the Japanese'. Moreover, this official suggested that Japan be told that 'we would not welcome any further approaches on this subject'.[32] Another official agreed with this latter view, pointing out in particular that 'we have already done a lot of yielding' on war criminal issues.[33]

The Australian Embassy in Tokyo was warned in advance that the Japanese request would be refused and was advised that the grounds for the refusal included Australia's 'feeling that we have gone far enough in meeting other Japanese requests on such matters as remission of sentences of war criminals'.[34] On 19 December 1960, Assistant Secretary DW McNicol advised Mr Yoshida, the Counsellor at the Japanese Embassy, that:

---

29   Australian Embassy, Washington, to the Minister and Ext Aff, 1 August and 3 August 1960, both in NAA: A1838, 3103/10/13/2 PART 15A.
30   GJ Price, Second Secretary, Australian Embassy, Paris to the Secretary, Ext Aff, 23 September 1960, NAA: A1838, 3103/10/13/2 PART 15A.
31   Handwritten note for Mr McNicol, 24 November 1960, NAA: A1838, 3103/10/13/2 PART 15A.
32   Ext Aff File Note for Mr Heydon, 25 November 1960, NAA: A1838, 3103/10/13/2 PART 15A.
33   Ibid.
34   DW McNicol, Assistant Secretary, Ext Aff to the Australian Embassy, Tokyo, 2 December 1960, NAA: A1838, 3103/10/13/2 PART 15A.

The Department wishes to inform the Embassy that it is not the practice of the Australian Government to make available information relating to documents of this nature and it is therefore unable to meet the Embassy's request.[35]

McNicol told Yoshida that it was in Japan's interests that memories of war crimes—which had 'deeply shocked and angered the Australian people'— be 'erased' and that the 'chances that time would diminish the memories would be improved if one was not reminded of these crimes'.[36] McNicol added, on a personal level, that it would be 'preferable' if the Japanese Ministry concerned was 'persuaded not to raise the subject of war crimes again'.[37] Yoshida said that he was 'grateful' for the reply and 'understood'.[38]

After Australia's refusal, the United States surprised Australia in May 1961 with the information that it proposed to tell Japan that copies of its trial records—not its investigation records, which remained classified— could be made available at Japan's expense. The reasoning behind this abrupt change in position was that, as the Japanese had participated in the trials, they could be 'assumed to have their own rudimentary records' of them. In addition, records had already been partially made available in the United States. The State Department had also concluded that request arose from 'Japanese Bibliophile-type psychology and their passion for completeness'. While the State Department continued to 'bear in mind' the possibility that Japan might want the records to 'enable' the casting of doubt on the trials and to 'attempt to rewrite history', Japan was already in a position to do this. Therefore, Australia, the United Kingdom and the Netherlands were invited to give their views to determine whether an 'agreed policy could be worked out', so as to 'avoid' Japan using the United States' position to 'bring pressure to bear on the others'.[39]

External Affairs forwarded the United States' proposal to the Army, which repeated its opinion that Japan should be refused access.[40] The Australian Embassy in Washington was advised in December 1960 that Australia was

---

35 Ext Aff Record of Conversation with Mr Yoshida by Mr DW McNicol, 'Japanese Request for Records Relating to War Crimes Trials', 19 December 1960, NAA: A1838, 3103/10/13/2 PART 15A.
36 Ibid.
37 Ibid.
38 Ibid.
39 Australian Embassy, Washington to Ext Aff, 3 May 1961, NAA: A1838, 3103/10/13/2 PART 15A.
40 B White, Secretary, Army to the Secretary, Ext Aff, 26 May 1961, NAA: A1838, 3103/10/13/2 PART 15A.

adhering to its refusal and hoped that the United States would 'not act unilaterally', given that there were 'advantages' to 'maintaining a united front on this issue'.[41] External Affairs in London passed along the comment that the United States' proposal had led a senior Foreign Office official to refer 'unkindly to the "double-crossing" attitude of the Americans'.[42] External Affairs later assumed that it was continued Australian and United Kingdom opposition that led the United States to reconsider its plan to provide its trial records to Japan.[43] Instead, the United States released a policy directive on war crimes records in March 1963, which stated the details of the trial records that could be made available to American citizens upon application; however, the trial records were not available to Japan or Japanese citizens. Moreover, apart from official purposes, war crimes investigation records were 'closed to all persons'.[44]

The Third Japanese Request for Access in 1965

That the Japanese had not been discouraged by lengthy delays in responding to the requests for war crimes records and the repeated firm refusals to provide the records, as well as the advice to desist from requesting them, was made clear in April 1965, when another request arrived via the Japanese Embassy. The request came with strong reassurances about the purposes for which Japan wanted the copies and the conditions it was willing to abide by to receive them. The Ministry of Justice explained that it was collecting 'all available material concerning war trials' to facilitate research on the factors such as the social system that 'contributed to war crimes', the 'legal aspects of the prosecutions' and the 'procedural rules', which it was convinced would 'contribute to the development of international law and to the prevention of war'. The Ministry reassured Australia that it had 'no intention of repudiating the war trials themselves'

---

41   Ext Aff to the Australian Embassy, Washington, repeated to London and The Hague, 29 May 1961, NAA: A1838, 3103/10/13/2 PART 15A.
42   H Marshall for Senior External Affairs Representative, London to the Secretary, Ext Aff, 9 June 1961, NAA: A1838, 3103/10/13/2 PART 15A.
43   Ext Aff File Note by AJ Melhuish for Mr Horne, 'Japanese War Crimes', 13 May 1965, NAA: A1838, 3103/10/13/2 PART 15A.
44   Detailed in RN Birch, Counsellor, Australian Embassy, Washington to the Secretary, Ext Aff, 17 September 1965, NAA: A1838, 3103/10/13/2 PART 15A.

and advised that any copies would be held at the Ministry and 'made available only to those scholars who can make good use of them for a purely academic purpose'.[45]

An initial External Affairs analysis of the Japanese request concluded that the 'reasons advanced by the Japanese' were 'not very compelling'.[46] Therefore, it was suggested that the request be refused with the same terse statement that had been given five years earlier.[47] However, the usual consultation with the Department of the Army revealed that while the Army maintained its opinion that the records should not be provided, it conceded that it was 'now twenty years since the war' and that it would be 'increasingly difficult to sustain this attitude as time goes on'.[48] Change also appeared to be in the air at External Affairs: Malcolm Booker, a senior official and former ambassador, suggested in October 1965 that the department should take 'a fresh look at our negative attitude' and 'ease up a bit'. In his view, Australia's approach had become 'anachronistic' and, he alleged, out of step with that of the United States, which was 'prepared to make open to the study of all persons [sic] trial records, transcripts, documents and other evidence presented in court'.[49] Unfortunately, this was a clear misreading of the United States' policy. While the United States had by then allowed Japan access to its records of the International Military Tribunal for the Far East (IMTFE), its own trial records remained closed as per the 1963 directive. Despite the inaccurate premise, Booker's suggestion to reconsider Australia's approach was adopted.

A draft briefing memorandum was prepared for the Minister for External Affairs Paul Hasluck, which provided the background of the 1955, 1959 and 1965 requests and advised that as 'twenty years have now passed since the end of the war it is considered that a completely negative attitude to the Japanese request is anachronistic and that we might modify our attitude'.[50] The draft memorandum conceded, accurately, that the United States had only made publicly available the records of the IMTFE,

---

45   Embassy of Japan, Note Verbale, no 51, 25 April 1965, NAA: A1838, 3103/10/13/2 PART 15A.
46   Ext Aff File Note by AJ Melhuish for Mr Horne, 'Japanese War Crimes', 13 May 1965, NAA: A1838, 3103/10/13/2 PART 15A.
47   Ext Aff File Note for Mr Booker, 'Japanese War Crimes', 7 October 1965 attaching draft note verbale addressed to the Embassy of Japan, NAA: A1838, 3103/10/13/2 PART 15A.
48   B White, Secretary, Army for the Secretary, Ext Aff, 18 August 1965, NAA: A1838, 3103/10/13/2 PART 15A.
49   Ext Aff File Note by LE Phillips for Mr Piper, 'Japanese War Crimes', 14 October 1965, NAA: A1838, 3103/10/13/2 PART 15A.
50   Draft for the Minister, 'Japanese War Crimes', nd, 3, NAA: A1838, 3103/10/13/2 PART 15A.

but argued that that there was 'no real argument against enlarging the permission' to include national records. It recommended to the Minister that Japan be granted access to Australia's records.[51]

Before Hasluck was given the briefing memorandum, External Affairs sought further information from the United States. This time, the State Department was slightly more revealing about the reasons for its historical reluctance to release the records. The State Department told the Australian Embassy that all the records had been 'bundled together in Army warehouses' and that the 'initial U.S. reluctance to release' the records arose from the 'physical problem of sorting the material'.[52] Then, around 1956, the 'records were handed over to the archivists' and it was 'feared' that 'some of the material inadvertently found its way into the hands of research scholars'.[53] This fear had prompted a discussion about access restrictions and had led to the decision that the records should not be released to Japan unless the other Allied nations were similarly prepared to acquiesce, which they were not. This was the policy still being observed in 1965. However, the State Department was now tending to 'discount any possibility that the Japanese are attempting to "whitewash" criminals at this point of history'. Rather, the State Department assumed that 'some obscure [Japanese] historical section has discovered gaps in its files and succeeded in having its request processed by the Foreign Ministry'.[54]

Australia's decision on Japan's request was still being considered in early 1966 when it was proposed that, subject to widespread agreement, copies of the trial decisions should be offered to Japan.[55] Acting Legal Advisor Patrick Brazil recommended that as George Dickinson—who had been the defence advisory officer at the Manus Island trials in 1950–51—had praised in print the 'ability and fairness' of President Kenneth Townley, who presided over the Manus Island trials,[56] it might be worth considering that:

---

51 Ibid.
52 RN Birch, Counsellor, Australian Embassy, Washington to the Secretary, Ext Aff, 10 December 1965, 1, NAA: A1838, 3103/10/13/2 PART 15A.
53 Ibid.
54 Ibid.
55 Ext Aff File Note by HW Bullock for Mr Booker, 'Japanese War Crimes', 8 February 1966, NAA: A1838, 3103/10/13/2 PART 15B.
56 George Dickinson, 'Manus Island Trials' (1952) 38 *Journal of the Royal Australian Historical Society* 67; George Dickinson, 'Japanese War Trials' (1952) 24 *The Australian Quarterly* 69.

> if judgments are to be made available, they should be limited, at this stage at least, to the judgments given in the Manus Island trials. This course would have the advantage of limiting the work involved in sorting out the records and would also mean that we could reasonably be confident as to the quality of the jurisprudence that we were putting before the eyes of our Japanese friends.[57]

Thus, External Affairs suggested to the Army that departmental officers examine the Manus Island decisions to determine whether their 'contents would cause difficulties if made available to the Japanese authorities'.[58] However, what this process revealed was that External Affairs was completely unaware of the fact that the trials had no written decisions that could be provided. Even the Army, which had run the trials, now appeared unaware of this crucial fact, as it did not correct External Affair's impression but simply said that the decision was 'properly' one for External Affairs.[59] Thus, External Affairs remained under the impression throughout the remainder of 1966 that the Army was busily engaged in reviewing the (non-existent) decisions from the Manus Island trials. Booker was told in August 1966, for example, that despite several reminders to the Army, External Affairs was 'waiting for Army to examine the judgments [sic]'.[60]

External Affairs must have finally realised its misapprehension about the existence of written decisions, as a review of the trial proceedings commenced. Lyndel Prott of the Legal and Treaties Branch observed in her April 1967 report that the trials were 'generally satisfactory' and did not cause 'any substantial miscarriage of justice'. However, she pointed out that:

> since war crimes trials are a controversial issue in general, they provide material for a troublemaker to use against the country which conducted them … Almost all of the trials of 'B' and 'C' class criminals have elements appearing on the face of the records which would provide a hostile reader with anti-Australian ammunition.[61]

---

57   Ext Aff File Note by P Brazil, Acting Legal Officer, 'Japanese War Crimes Trials', 11 March 1966, 2, NAA: A1838, 3103/10/13/2 PART 15B.
58   AH Borthwick, Acting Assistant Secretary, Ext Aff to the Secretary, Army, 17 March 1966, NAA: A1838, 3103/10/13/2 PART 15B.
59   B White, Secretary, Army to the Secretary, Department of Defence, copied to the Ext Aff, 22 March 1966, NAA: A1838, 3103/10/13/2 PART 15B.
60   Ext Aff File Note by AH Borthwick for Mr Booker, 'Japanese War Crimes', 23 August 1966, NAA: A1838, 3103/10/13/2 PART 15B.
61   Lyndel V Prott, 'Release of Records of Japanese War Crimes Trials', 5 April 1967, 1, 2, 5, NAA: A1838, 3103/10/13/2 PART 15B.

Prott concluded that Australia should 'be wary of providing adverse propaganda against ourselves', but pointed out that a refusal to grant access to the trials 'might imply that we have something to hide'.[62] Afterwards, Prott studied reports on the American, British, Dutch, French and Chinese war crimes trials and observed that 'at least some' of our trials could 'raise no more criticism than that which has already been thoroughly discussed' and that any impact could be 'diminished' by the fact that criticism could be levelled widely. In any event, she thought that it was possible to select certain trials for provision to Japan that were defensible against criticism.[63]

By this stage, a clearer division had appeared within External Affairs as to whether the Japanese request should be granted. The department's East Asia Branch, for instance, felt that Australia's agreement would further relations with Japan, but the Legal and Treaties Branch was opposed. Two draft briefing memoranda that presented lists of 'considerations' for and against the release of Australia's trial records, noticeably so in that specific order, were prepared. The considerations against release in the first draft were:

(i) hostile consideration of these records by the Japanese could lead to criticism of the trials and create unpleasant propaganda if made public;

(ii) a future government may attempt to repudiate these trials (although the present government says it has no intention of doing so);

(iii) their study would draw attention to provisions of the War Crimes Act which would be better left in their present happy state of neglect;

(iv) once the records were transferred we would have no further control over their use or future disposal by the Japanese;

(v) the release of certain cases or of certain parts of proceedings only may incite the Japanese to further demands;

(vi) in the absence of judgments the trial records of little value for research [sic].[64]

The considerations promoting release generally revolved around being 'obliging' to the Japanese Government, with whom relations were 'likely to become of increasing importance', or avoiding the suggestion that

---

62 Ibid 1, 11.
63 Ext Aff File Note by Lyndel V Prott, 'Release of Records of Japanese War Crimes Trials', 14 June 1967, NAA: A1838, 3103/10/13/2 PART 15B.
64 Draft for the Acting Minister, 'Japan—War Trial Records', nd, 1–2, NAA: A1838, 3103/10/13/2 PART 15B.

Australia had something to hide or distrusted Japan or its motives.[65] The second draft memorandum was more vehemently against releasing the records. It pointed out that as redeeming Japan's reputation was presumably part of the overall goal, 'critical attention' would necessarily be focused on 'debatable aspects' of the trials.[66]

External Affairs consulted again with the Australian Embassy in Tokyo. Counsellor RJ Percival responded that he thought that the undertakings provided by Ministry of Justice about how the records would be used should not be taken seriously. He pointed out:

> If at some future date the Japanese authorities wish to repudiate any or all of the war crimes trials, question any particular sentences, criticise the conduct of the trials, or take any similar action, we can be fairly sure that they will not let any previous undertakings of this sort stand in their way.[67]

He conceded that, at this point, he saw 'little gain' for the Japanese Government in doing so. On the other side, Percival pointed out that it would not help Australia's relations with Japan to be 'the only government to hold out on this matter' or for Japan to become aware that, 'but for our opposition', other Allied nations would have provided their records. He also thought that refusing the request would suggest that Australia had something to hide and that this would be 'evidence that a strong element of distrust and antipathy remains in Australia's attitude towards Japan'. In his opinion, Japan would 'keep at us for the release of these records until such time as we agree to their transfer'. Therefore, he suggested that Australia release its records, provided the other Allied nations also agreed to do so.[68]

After further consultation with the other Allied Powers, another draft briefing memorandum was prepared for the Minister for External Affairs in July 1968. The Minister was asked to approve the records' release upon the release by the United States of its records.[69] When consulted, the Army now indicated that there was 'no reason' why the Australian records could

---

65 Ibid 2.
66 GA Jockel for the Acting Minister, 'Japan—War Trial Records', nd, 1, NAA: A1838, 3103/10/13/2 PART 15B.
67 RJ Percival, Counsellor, Australian Embassy, Washington to the Secretary, Ext Aff, 26 June 1967, 1, NAA: A1838, 3103/10/13/2 PART 15B.
68 Ibid 2.
69 MR Booker, 'Japan—Release of Australian War Trial Records', 12 July 1968, NAA: A1838, 3103/10/13/2 PART 15B.

not be 'perused' by Japan, apart from those of two particular trials, which it identified. In those two trials, the Judge-Advocate General (JAG) had advised not to confirm the findings but his advice had been disregarded.[70] However, the Army pointed out that the JAG's reports were 'never included' when transcripts of courts-martial were made available, as they were regarded as 'confidential and privileged'.[71] The Attorney-General's Department then agreed in principle to release the trial proceedings to Japan, subject to the JAG's reports being withheld.[72]

Thus, External Affairs recommended to the Minister that, subject to the concurrence of the Minister of Defence, the trial proceedings (apart from the JAG's reports) be approved for release in parallel with the release of the United States records.[73] In response, Hasluck raised a crucial issue of parity: should Australia release the records to Japan 'for the use of scholars', as Japan had proposed, without 'facing up' to the issue of releasing them to Australian scholars?[74] Booker advised Hasluck that the records had been withheld from Australian scholars on the 'grounds that information they might derive from them could come into the hands of the Japanese to whom the records have been barred'. Booker's reasoning might have been constructed on the spot, as External Affairs had told the State Department only the previous year that there was 'no record of any interest ever being expressed by scholars' in the Australian trial records.[75] This lack is not really surprising, as scholars would have been unlikely to have directed requests for access to External Affairs, given that the records had been created by the Army and, once archived in the Commonwealth Archives Office, were controlled by the Attorney-General's Department. Certainly, political scientist and historian David Sissons, who had served as an interpreter at the Rabaul trials, had been seeking access to various war crimes records since the early 1950s but his queries were directed, for

---

70   For these two trials, see NAA: A471, 80757 and 81068.
71   B White, Secretary, Army to the Secretary, Ext Aff, 25 July 1968, NAA: A1838, 3103/10/13/2 PART 15B.
72   Secretary, Att Gen to the Secretary, Ext Aff, 15 August 1968, NAA: A1838, 3103/10/13/2 PART 15B.
73   MR Booker, 'Japan—Release of Australian War Trial Records', 12 July 1968, 4 September 1968, NAA: A1838, 3103/10/13/2 PART 15B.
74   MR Booker, 'Japan—Release of Australian War Trial Records', 5 September 1968 with marginalia on 4, NAA: A1838, 3103/10/13/2 PART 15B.
75   Ext Aff to the Australian Embassy, Washington, 11 April 1967, NAA: A1838, 3103/10/13/2 PART 15B.

example, to the Australian War Memorial.[76] Regardless of past reasoning, Booker then suggested to Hasluck that if the records were released to Japanese scholars, they should 'also be made available to bona fide Australian scholars'.[77] In support, he pointed out that if Japanese scholars 'distorted or otherwise misused the records, their interpretations would be open to comparison with the judgments of Australian scholars'.[78] Hasluck eventually approved the recommendation to release the records, subject to the proviso that the release go no further, as 'we have to keep in step with the Allies as much as we can and not get ahead of them'.[79]

Although Australia had finally, after three years, made a decision on the Japanese request, the process of consultation continued without any communication of that decision to Japan. Various concurrences to releasing the records were still required, including those of the United States and the United Kingdom. In the interim, there were other practicalities to address, including whether a ministerial or other committee had to approve the release, given that it was a 'sort of archives policy matter'.[80] Whether all the records were in existence and accessible, how to offer Japan access and the costs of doing so also had to be ascertained. It was also suggested that the Returned Services League and the Australian War Memorial be 'sound[ed] out' on the release in case of 'any political backlash from old soldiers'.[81]

All of this background process was presumably underway when the issue of access to the trial records was finally publicised in mid-1969. Jack Sue, a former member of Z Special Force on Borneo, asked the Army for access to the trials that dealt with the Sandakan-Ranau 'death' marches to complete his book.[82] Making the Australian Government appear as if it was being churlish to a veteran, a *Canberra Times* story alleged that Sue had been given 'unqualified refusals' to access the files for 17 years, which

---

76 Letter from David Sissons to the Director, War Memorial, 27 December 1954, AWM: AWM315, 449/009/142.
77 Underlining in the original: Ext Aff File Note by MR Booker for the Minister, 'Japan—Release of Australian War Crimes Records', 25 November 1968, 1, NAA: A1838, 3103/10/13/2 PART 15B.
78 Ibid, 2.
79 Additional copy of draft submission for the Minister by MR Booker, 'Japan—Release of Australian War Trial Records', 5 September 1968, with marginalia dated 26 November 1968 on 4, NAA: A1838, 3103/10/13/2 PART 15B.
80 Ext Aff File Note for Mr Borthwick, 2 January 1969, NAA: A1838, 3103/10/13/2 PART 15B.
81 Ibid.
82 Jack W Sue to the Minister of the Army, 3 June 1969, NAA: A1838, 3103/10/13/2 PART 15B.

had delayed publication of his book since 1952.[83] At this point, External Affairs had not yet determined how to decide whether any applicant for access was a *bona fide* scholar, but it advised that it had no objection to Sue perusing the records, provided that 'no reference' was made in the book to 'the records as such or to the fact that he has been given access to them'. This condition was imposed because no international concurrence to the release of records had yet been received.[84]

Amply displaying the problem with consultative and consensus decision-making involving multiple stakeholders, and the apparent imperative for Australian policy to neither get ahead nor behind other nations, any momentum on releasing the records then appeared to grind to a halt. Australia never received any official indication from the United Kingdom of whether it would agree to release the records. As a memorandum in 1975 pointed out, External Affairs had last heard from the United Kingdom on the issue in September 1969.[85] As a result, no decision had been apparently communicated to Japan on its 1965 request and nor had any further requests from Japan been presented when, in 1975, the issue finally became moot.

Opening the Trials

The decision to finally release the Australian trial proceedings to public access in 1975 appears to have been prompted not by Japan—which, sensibly, might have given up asking by then—but by Australian scholars such as Sissons pressing the Attorney-General's Department for access. Fortunately, at least as far as the Attorney-General's Department was concerned, some transition had taken place in how the records were viewed. In announcing his decision to lift the access restrictions, Attorney-General Keppel Enderby QC pointed out, in fact, that he did not regard the trial proceedings as 'government records', as the 'conduct of these trials did not form a part of the normal administration' of government.[86]

---

83   'Borneo Story Still a Secret', *Canberra Times* (Canberra), 19 June 1969, 3. In fact, the book was not published for decades after this: Jack Wong Sue, *Blood over Borneo* (WA Skindivers Publications, c2001).
84   AH Borthwick for the Secretary, Ext Aff to the Secretary, Army, 15 July 1969, NAA: A1838, 3103/10/13/2 PART 15B.
85   WM Bush for the Secretary, Department of Foreign Affairs to the Secretary, Att Gen, 22 May 1975, NAA: A1838, 3103/10/13/2 PART 15B.
86   Att Gen press release, above n 7.

6. ACCESSING THE ARCHIVES OF AUSTRALIAN WAR CRIMES TRIALS AFTER WORLD WAR II

This meant that the standard 30-year closed period then in force for archives—which would run until the early 1980s—did not apply. More crucially, Enderby remarked:

> The Australian Government recognises the need of this and future generations of Australians to question and understand this country's past … For too long Australian scholars have been hampered in their attempts to interpret Australia's history. Restrictions like this one no longer serve a useful purpose. They should be replaced by a policy based on open access wherever practicable. The past should be everyone's property.[87]

Given the general trend in the early 1970s to appreciate the value of government records to national history, and that other World War II–era records had been opened in 1971, the decision to make the trial proceedings accessible was probably not surprising. However, this decision may never have been made if the Attorney-General's Department had not acted without consultation with the Department of Foreign Affairs, as it now was. Presented with a *fait accompli*, Foreign Affairs complained about this 'unwelcome surprise', especially as it came on the eve of a ministerial visit to Japan.[88] Foreign Affairs alleged that there were 'political considerations which, even after the passage of many years, remain[ed] strong' and argued that the United Kingdom should have been consulted as a matter of 'courtesy'.[89] This reads as oddly deferential to the United Kingdom, given that there was no mention of consultation with the United States, which had earlier been of equal importance on this issue. Fortunately for scholars and the public, international consultation did not further delay the release of the records. Yet, clearly miffed at the Attorney-General's trespass on what it considered its patch of responsibility, Foreign Affairs sought an undertaking that, in the future, its concurrence should be sought before the Attorney-General's Department released 'historical records affecting other countries'.[90]

It took close to a quarter of a century after the end of the Australian trials in 1951 for the Australian Government to finally make the trial proceedings publicly accessible. In the interim, most Australian trial participants had died, taking with them their invaluable personal accounts.

---

87   Ibid.
88   Department of Foreign Affairs to Tokyo, 6 June 1975, NAA: A1838, 3103/10/13/12 PART 16A.
89   JR Rowland to the Secretary, Att Gen, 6 June 1975; and Ext Aff File Note by W M Bush, 'Japanese War Criminals—Release of Records', 2 June 1975, both in NAA: A1838, 3103/10/13/12 PART 16A.
90   JR Rowland to the Secretary, Att Gen, 6 June 1975, NAA: A1838, 3103/10/13/12 PART 16A.

Yet, even if Australia had granted any one of the Japanese requests for access to the trial proceedings in the 1950s and 1960s, any records that Australia provided to Japan would have been restricted from public access in Japan for another quarter century. It was not until 1999 that the Allied war crimes trials records gathered by the Ministry of Justice's Judiciary and Legislation Investigation Bureau were transferred to the National Archives of Japan, Tokyo, and made (mostly) accessible to the public.[91] Fortunately for researchers, Japanese participants in the trials have left considerably more personal accounts in writing of their experiences at the Australian trials.

Today, the Australian trial proceedings are digitised in full at the National Archives of Australia,[92] as are many other war crimes files. Fortunately, somewhere along the way Australia discarded the imperative not to get ahead of other Allied nations: Australia is, in fact, the only Allied nation thus far to disclose all its World War II war crimes trial proceedings online. Any researcher in the world can now access the trial proceedings, and efforts to make public comprehensive finding aids to the investigation and trial records are ongoing. While Australia has by its promotion of digitisation perhaps partially remedied the restrictions it placed for decades on historical research into the trials, the impact of the delay and particularly the loss of valuable firsthand accounts of the trials can never be overcome.

91 Totani, above n 4, 188.
92 Apart from a handful of large maps tendered as exhibits during the trials, the size of which currently precludes digitisation.

Part 3—Institutional Experience and Responsibility for Records

7
A Conversation with Warwick Soden (Principal Registrar and Chief Executive Officer, Federal Court of Australia)

Interviewed by Kim Rubenstein and Ann Genovese[1]

On 28 January 2016, Kim Rubenstein and Ann Genovese interviewed Warwick Soden for the Court as Archive Project, at the Principal Registry in Sydney. Mr Soden is the Chief Executive Officer of the Federal Court of Australia, a position he has held since 1994. In the full interview, we discuss the status and management of court records over time, as well as Warwick's experiences in undertaking his duties in Court Administration, over the period of his career.

The Federal Court archivist, Lyn Nasir, was also present.

---

1   Please cite as Warwick Soden and Lyn Nasir, interview Kim Rubenstein and Ann Genovese in Ann Genovese, Trish Luker and Kim Rubenstein (eds), *The Court as Archive* (ANU Press, 2019).

Included below is a selection from the interview concentrating on aspects relevant to this collection. Further publications from the interview are planned, given that the interview with Warwick Soden is a rare example of an oral history undertaken with a key administrative office holder of the Federal Court.[2]

The interview was conducted on the eve of the court's 40th anniversary as a national institution and should be read as capturing the respective participants' thinking at that time. Indeed, some of the issues discussed have since progressed, but its essence and content maintain its value on a number of levels relevant to this research.

> **Kim Rubenstein (KR)**: Warwick, we would like to start by asking you when you joined the Federal Court, and what you had been doing before, to understand the relationship between your expertise and coming to the court.
>
> **Warwick Soden (WS)**: Well, for about eight years prior to coming to this court, I was the Chief Executive and Principal Registrar of the Supreme Court of New South Wales. Now, that is a long time ago.
>
> **KR**: Yes, when was that?
>
> **WS**: I went to the Supreme Court of New South Wales in 1987—early 30s at that time. I thought I was old at that time!
>
> [Laughter]
>
> In 1972, I think I was about 18 and a half, 19, I started working in the courts in New South Wales—primarily what were then called the Courts of Petty Sessions—and did my law degree part-time.
>
> **Ann Genovese (AG)**: At the University of New South Wales?
>
> **WS**: No. I ended up doing it remotely, through Macquarie Law School because I was in the country and I needed to do all my study externally. It took me about four or five years to do it.

---

2   The Federal Court has undertaken oral histories with former Federal Court judges and Federal Court judges have also been interviewed as part of the ARC Linkage Project, The Trailblazing Women and the Law Project (ARC Linkage LP120200367). See Australian National University and University of Melbourne, 'The Trailblazing Women and the Law Project' (30 November 2016) The Trailblazing Women and the Law Project <http://www.tbwl.esrc.unimelb.edu.au>.

AG: Would it be fair to say that, for you, the commitments and demands of the job were supplemented by your degree, rather than the other way around? Because for many people, they're doing the degree to get the job, and you've already …

WS: I was working in the courts, and in that whole scheme, they had what were called in those days, exam barriers. So as you progressed through university, you were able to be promoted because of your partial legal qualifications, as long as you had some managerial acumen. Which, luckily, I did. So I was fortunate in being quite young, finishing my law, and there weren't other people who had done their law in the system who were competing for a job. So I ended up being in some quite senior positions in the New South Wales court system prior to going into the Supreme Court. I was what was called, I think, the Registrar or the Clerk of the court, or whatever it was called in those days for Wollongong. So that included being … the Coroner for the City of Wollongong. So I did all the coronial enquiries from things like deaths in the steel works and mine collapses and all that sort of stuff.

AG: And this is when you were still very young.

WS: I was early 30s. At that time, there were a lot of industrial accidents occurring and the Supreme Court had an industrial accident jurisdiction with juries. That's all gone now. So I spent some time in the Supreme Court, learning Supreme Court practice and procedure with people there, and set up the Supreme Court registry in Wollongong. So I got involved in some of the policies and procedures in delay reduction and case management, and ended up being asked to be in the Supreme Court [in Sydney]. For a while, acting, and then was appointed.

AG: What year was that?

WS: That was '88: '87 to '88 from memory. So one of the things that was important, as an issue for me in the Supreme Court, was not only the delay and reduction initiatives, and all the case management work that we did, but there was also a whole lot of records work that was being done, for example, a whole lot of microfilming of old probate records. One of the things I found amazing at that time was the indexes to the probates—big index books—were in a complete state of disrepair and just rotting away.

AG: Where were they all housed?

WS: In the dungeon of this building [No. 1 Queen's Square, Sydney]. I went and got one, which was just a sample, and it was almost unusable. It went back to the days of things like the will of James Ruse, you know, which is from the time of the early settlers, and these things were just going to be destroyed. So I had copies done that were preservable and all that sort of thing. So I don't think that was the start of my interest in records or archives but it was an issue at that stage. It was a no-brainer to me at the time that some things must be preserved that weren't being preserved. That led to a lot of issues about court records, what comprises the court records, *et cetera*. Although I was in the Supreme Court for, I think, eight years, most of the time with Murray Gleeson subsequently as Chief Justice, the focus of my work then was case management and delay reduction. We did turn it around substantially to be much better than it had been. So I didn't focus as much as I could have on records issues. But we did touch upon, even in those early days, the issue of what comprised the court record.

I can remember it was Gleeson who made it indelibly clear in my mind that the court record doesn't comprise anything more than—this is the official court record of a superior court—who sued what for whom and what was the result?

AG: So where were all the records kept?

WS: Most of it was here. There were some offsite archives. But I'm not sure what was offsite and what was here. I know probate was here. I think most of the probate work was here, or probate records were here.

AG: So the relationship between courts and departments or administering agencies is really fascinating to us. As we were saying before this interview started, our archival searches at NAA [National Archives of Australia] show that in the early years of the Federal Court, the court was trying to manoeuvre or navigate its relationship with Attorney-General's Department, when that's in Canberra and you're setting up state-based registries, it was quite a distinct theme or narrative.

WS: Well, can I say, by 1994 at the time when self-administration was under consideration, there was quite a large movement in [the] Australasian Institute of Judicial Administration by a number of judges and others on the subject of the governance of courts. *The Australian* got involved. There were seminars and conferences on the subject of the governance of courts because a lot of courts were having problems with resource allocation and being able to control what they did, because they were part of the Department of Justice or a Department of Attorney-General. Many of them still are.

In the federal area, I could see that that debate had progressed from the courts being administered by the Federal Attorney-General's Department to the sensible conclusion that the court should be given the responsibility for managing themselves and making the decisions about how to manage their operations, rather than be remotely administered by a department who had no real control over what needed to be done. So that happened with the Federal Court, the Family Court, and the Administrative Appeals Tribunal, on the model of the High Court. I think, subsequently, that was thought to be quite a successful change.

I have recently written a paper[3] about this, and the people who talk about that in that paper, the people who proposed it, said after a number of years, they thought the whole system was much more efficient. The courts were operating more effectively. Federally, that took away a lot of the previous tension that had existed between the judges and the people working in courts, and the Attorney-General's Department in relation to how the courts were administered.

KR: So can you tell us a little bit about that vision when you first arrived at the Federal Court?

WS: Very importantly, independence came with responsibility and accountability. So organisational responsibility was holistic. So everything we did as an organisation, put aside the fact that we were a court, needed to be done in organisational terms in the best possible way. Innovative leading. World leading. We had a saying within the court that we wanted to be and to be seen as a world-leading superior court. Which drove some of the strategies. That's one of the reasons why things like managing court records and managing the record and related issues was an important issue. It was part of the holistic approach to management of the organisation. So one of the things I focused on was managing organisational issues of the court. Not as a court, but as an organisation.

AG: I mean that's a massive shift for many, not just judges, but in the legal profession, to come to terms with. To think about courts organisationally, rather than only institutionally. You have been talking about the Federal Court being a national court, but also about how the court is perceived by the public and how the public can use it. Did you want, for the record, to describe some of those other innovations?

---

3   Warwick Soden, 'Self-Administration in the Federal Court of Australia' (Speech delivered at the JCA Colloquium, Noosa Heads, 10 October 2014)

WS: Yes, and this is all really important background as to why we are now in the position we are, in a records sense. It's almost a consequential offshoot of what we've done in the past. Wishing to be perceived as, and to be, a world-leading superior court meant that there were many strategies that needed to be undertaken. That included all of the practice and procedure reforms; it included the buildings; but included important things like focusing on courteousness and politeness; cost reduction; time reduction; and also really important things like an appearance of modernity, rather than an appearance of being a colonial relic.

AG: There are major innovations that you've overseen too in terms of the individual docket system and e-filing and other things, which, again, most people in the general public wouldn't be aware of, but [which] are hugely innovative in terms of how people can access courts quickly.

WS: Yes, well, the reason that we now have a Records Disposal Authority and an electronic court file goes back to a whole lot of the related issues about being a modern, accountable, responsible institution, which happens to be a court. So if we're going to move to the modern environment and we're going to work in an environment that the business community expects us to work in, the clients of the practitioners, we had to take decisions that I persuaded the judges to take, about making assumptions about what it meant to move from the paper to the electronic environment. Because, importantly, the business-to-business interactions would be electronic and the legal profession would be expected by business to work in that environment. They would then expect us to work in that environment. So we would be perceived as being antiquated and out-of-date if we did not plan to do the same thing. So we developed what was called an e-services strategy. We needed to say we can do electronic filing, we can do electronic hearings, we can do things in the courtroom without paper. We were very careful, and I emphasised this, we needed to be careful that what we did electronically was what should be done, not what was done in the paper context. We did a fair bit of work on that, all of those types of initiatives as a court and as an organisation improving its performance ultimately led to in the e-services strategy, which was the creation of electronic work file, and all of the things that went with that. It was the creation of the electronic court file that drove the requirement to make a decision about what comprised the court record and what wasn't part of the court record. For the purpose of Lyn Nasir, getting a records authority for the digital record to be accepted by National Archives. You couldn't get the judges to focus on the record unless it was in the context of …

KR: The modern court.

WS: Exactly.

KR: That's very important. As a way back into how the court conceived of itself as managing an archive, there is actually an earlier question which comes back to your views around when you came in to be a manager of an organisation. That is, of course, a court is different to any other organisation in that it is constitutionally placed and has constitutional frameworks within which it operates.

WS: Yes, but one of the things that is misunderstood often is the constitutional position of the court in terms of judicial independence. Judicial independence is about judges. Not about the institution of the court. The best way of highlighting that fact is there was no issue of judicial independence when the courts were administered by the executive. Do you know what I mean?

KR: Yes.

WS: The transfer of responsibility to the court wasn't for judicial independence. It was for organisational performance reasons. So there's no such thing in the law as institutional independence of the court. There's only judicial independence of the person making decisions under Chapter III.

KR: So the follow-up question then to you, Warwick, is why do you think the court was excluded from the *Archives Act*?[4] Because if you follow that train of thought, the court should not have been excluded from the *Archives Act*, should it?

WS: I think the only reason that comes to my mind is the court of record issue that we touched on before: a superior court being a court of record. Now that's got nothing to do with judicial independence or ... the independence of institution. Superior courts of record.

AG: It is a common law question.

WS: And if it's a superior court of record. All Supreme Courts, Federal Courts, are courts of record. There's common law requirements on what the record of that court should be. Nothing to do with judicial independence.

---

4   *Archives Act 1983* (Cth).

KR: No, but it is interesting, I think. It's really interesting because, theoretically, it could have been clearer. The National Archives could have been clearer about the things that were not subject to the *Archives Act*, as opposed to the entire court not being subject.

WS: Yes, look, I don't know what was considered at that time. But you know, there are issues in relation to the perception of judicial independence that sometimes blur decisions about what it is and what it isn't; it's certainly not about prerequisites of office.

KR: No, but by virtue of the fact that the court was exempt, we're interested to know how the court saw itself in terms of its management of its archive.

WS: The court, being exempt, didn't change its common law requirement to be a court of record.

AG: No, not at all. But that's the fascinating conundrum, I suppose.

WS: It is muddied, yes, and I think maybe that's behind the reason why the court was excluded from the *Archives Act*. But I'd like to say that we take our historical archival responsibility seriously. Even though there's no statutory requirement to do so.

KR: That's what we're interested in: how that evolved. So part of it is the modern story that you're telling us. That, by wanting to be the sort of court that it is, that's the obvious consequence; that you want to be in the spirit of the *Archives Act*. But what else, I guess organisationally, lead to that?

WS: Well, I think it comes from two sources. One is that the sense of having an archival responsibility comes from the tradition of being a court of record, if I could describe it that way, which goes back to colonial times. There is archival relevance in the court of record information. That's one issue. On the other side of the coin is the, I think, accepted responsibility from Michael Black, other Chief Justices. And those of us in present charge of maintaining the historical record of the institution, which is an important institution for the country, dealing with some of the most important cases affecting civil society and the commerce of the institution—commerce of the country, which would be important for the future and for the history of the country. One of the things I'd never looked at closely here, and we didn't do it in the Supreme Court, was do a survey of who was asking for what and for what purpose. But I know that in the Supreme Court, before you had any electronic information, you maintained manual indexes of plaintiff–defendant or applicant. I think many organisations, law firms, financial institutions did due-diligence work in relation to whether there was anything in the indexes in respect of someone being sued for what. Now, all that can be done electronically these days.

KR: So that probably takes us nicely back to, if you can, charting for us the relationship between the court and National Archives. Given that it wasn't a strictly …

WS: Harmonious.

KR: … formal one.

[Laughter]

KR: How that evolved, really, to the extent you know from the start and then how it changed.

WS: Well, I had nothing to do with them really.

Lyn Nasir (LN): Well I suppose when I came in, the …

KR: When did you start then?

LN: I started in late 2007.

WS: There was a person before you.

LN: There were several before me, but getting a records authority had been going on for many years. I think we stopped with our other records authorities the year 2000. The National Archive said, 'we're not taking anything from you anymore; you've got to revise that and come up with something new'. It was called DIRKS [Designing and Implementing Recordkeeping Systems]. There was apparently lots of interviews with the Deputy Registrar at the time and …

AG: Can I just pause there? So DIRKS, just so we can clarify, is not just for the court. Looking at the materials we've been looking at, the National Archives itself was having a recalibration of its relationship with …

LN: All agencies.

AG: … and how they define what an agency is and, therefore, also what they keep and select, and to rethink those sentencing of records questions. So I suppose what's really interesting to us is that we know that in 1994, there was a record disposal authority with NAA?

LN: Yes, there were several. We sent everything then. All our court files went to National Archives.

WS: Everything went there and they kept the lot.

KR: So there was no decision-making at all? It was just everything went?

LN: Yes, all paper went. We still sent everything. They considered everything from the court as significant at that point.

AG: So that period between 1976 and 1994, it's very hard to ascertain what happened.

WS: They were getting miles and miles of storage cost.

LN: They couldn't take a thing anymore so that was it. Economics probably drove a lot of that.

WS: I know I gave it a fleeting thought in the early days and was just very relaxed that everything was going off to National Archives and being kept. I didn't have to worry.

LN: Everything was retrieved from there too. We'd get files back. They'd go back and forth, back and forth. It was all working pretty well. You know what? We would have been under the Attorney-General's disposal authorities.

WS: At that stage.

LN: That's why our Records Disposal Authorities are dated a bit late. They're in the early '90s I'm pretty sure. Yes.

WS: I would have thought the Attorney-General's Department at the time would have said, 'off to archives'.

LN: They wouldn't have been able to send it without some authority. So there would have been something somewhere like a class number or whatever. You can't send them anything unless they know all that. A lot of them are handwritten. I've scanned them. They're handwritten files that we've sent off. Sometimes, they don't even match up with this versus that. How useful is this, I mean research-wise?

AG: Hugely. Because that's the story. That becomes the question, I think.

KR: They're part of the things that I think will be part of a protocol as to what would be important for future researchers. In a way, this is amplifying this function between a court of record and a …

WS: And an archive.

KR: … that houses documents that are of national significance. In a way, it's the beautiful distinction you're making between the judges, as independent and as judges, and the court as an institution in a modern democratic Australia. I mean the way you've articulated that is so helpful for showing how this plays out in terms of the nature of history in a modern postcolonial society.

AG: And I think we're now at a point, because of the innovations and the commitment of you and others in this court, and how this court has imagined itself into being, that the record and file have become electronic, so it's a whole other question about how you store metadata and access the metadata.

WS: There was a confluence of records authority requirements, and an electronic record. It came together. That was what I would describe as a break point in defining the court record, and focusing on the requirement to identify important files for archive purposes, separately from the courtroom—what can be classified as 'significant files'. I must say, I didn't focus on that path when I came here. I was only focusing …

AG: You're building a court, right? It's a different thing.

WS: [Laughs].

KR: I'm going to put that in at terms of your vision. Your vision was forward looking.

WS: It was. It was. It was. It was.

KR: Which, therefore, in and of itself means that archives are not within your frame, and I don't mean that in a judgmental sense.

WS: No, I can say I did not think of the future archive requirements at that time because everything was being kept.

LN: Yes, that's true and it was being taken care of then.

WS: It was not an issue that needed to be managed and it was not a cost issue for them.

AG: So to return to this question of significance, which is really an internal issue for the court, a response to DIRKS it's …

WS: Developing.

LN: Yes, and that's in the records authority. We have to define what we think is significant. We still haven't defined it completely.

177

WS: It's not finished.

LN: Yes. The conversation that went around that was National Archives coming back to us and saying, 'We can't take everything'. And we're coming back to them and saying, 'But you should take something. We feel that there are some cases that we have here that really should be sent'. They're coming back to us and saying, 'Yes, we agree with that. We've got to put a percentage on it. We can't give you …'. That's where the 10 per cent of files came in. They were negotiations really with Imelda Payne, Director of Information Services at the time, and myself, just trying to flesh that out. Also, with Warwick's backing, and the Deputy Registrar at the time saying 'well, we do need to send—we know we have to send—something. We feel it should be on a public record in a national research area, which is the National Archives, that these significant files are kept. Even though you don't want everything, you should have some'.

WS: Significant could be a number of different things. I've expressed some views. There are some variations. Significant files, to me, ought to be a representation of what the workload was, not just the important cases. So when we were thinking about the 10 per cent, should that be a random collection of 10 per cent of the files of a year? Should it be a request for an identification of the significant cases from the judges and then a top-up to make the 10 per cent by a random collection of everything else? So that's out there for consideration at the moment.

I think what is significant to me is much more than just the big and important cases. Because cases that have commenced, been worked up, case managed and settled don't have the big judgment, don't have the big hearing.

AG: No, they don't.

KR: Then what about the court's own internal administration? How do you conceive of that in your archival decision-making?

WS: We don't. [Laughs].

KR: I mean it's again, back to you, that distinction. You are an organisation.

LN: Well, no, we keep the judge's minutes. They will all be going there; significant. But as you say, that's probably out of the administration because that's the judicial side of things. Our rules and practices, yes, they're kept.

WS: Practice committee papers and real committee papers, yes.

LN: They're kept but they're kept with us. We have the obligation to keep that. Nothing goes off to National Archives. The only thing going to National Archives are our significant cases and our native title files. That's all they've been taking out.

KR: I mean but this is really pre-empting a later output of the project, which I haven't made, but I think the focus of our research is highlighting the significance of the court as an institution. As an organisation. It's almost your job in a way and the way you conceived it is that that's a significant part of this institution that arguably is significant for the archive for further down the track.

WS: It should be actually. It should be.

AG: Well, it's extraordinary to us that we were the first people who have ever asked and got access in National Archives to looking at those documents that discuss the setting up of this court.

LN: We're not that old yet really. [Laughs].

AG: It's kind of part of broader projects for us about what it means to take your own Australian innovations in jurisprudence seriously.

WS: Most of the other courts—most, I think it's fair to say, you've probably already experienced this—but most of the other courts of Australia that are still connected in institutional terms with the executive aspire to be like us.

KR: That's right. I guess their records would be done through the Justice ...

WS: Department of Justice.

KR: Yes, and the requirements of those departments.

AG: That's right.

KR: They would, you would hope, have approached looking at their own management as part of the archive. Because I think for our project, the outcome is to think of the court beyond the cases that it hears. Sure, it's set up for the cases that it hears and those become significant, but it's the organisation as well.

LN: It's a lot of other things as well.

WS: It's the institution, in all aspects.

KR: Exactly, that is significant and significant to the development of Australian identity.

LN: These days, we are really trying to maintain the electronic side of administration up to speed too. What we're trying to do is keep everything electronic. It's hard because a lot of it is emails now.

AG: I mean it's a question facing people [who are] thinking not just in terms of courts and histories and legal history projects but all sorts of historical things, like just writing biographies in the future where you can't read anyone's letters. Because it's now electronic.

We were talking about what is significant. Back to the significance problem. So I was just saying to Lyn: I had a look at the current Records Disposal Authority just in preparation, again, for coming today. When you're reading that, you're thinking, 'well that's perfectly sensible'.

KR: Yes, for this record, let's read out what constitutes part A and part B of the court file according to the Records Disposal Authority.

WS: Well, part A is the words that define what is essentially the court record. The document that commences the proceeding that identifies the parties and the cause of actions, together with the orders made at the end of the proceedings, comprises the court record. But to be clear about that, you've got to add things like amended pleadings, *et cetera, et cetera*. Because there might be a change to the parties. But importantly, what the court record doesn't include—the official court record—is the reasons for the decision …

AG: Unless they're published.

WS: Yeah, but a lot of reasons aren't published. Or the transcript, the description of the parties; who sued what for whom, and the orders made and variations in appeals and first in matters, *et cetera, et cetera*. In order to get that, sometimes you might have to have a look at interlocutory decisions in relation to either adding or deleting parties. So the case that's commenced may not be the case that has all the parties at the end.

AG: So I'm gathering no judge would have had any dispute with part A at all?

WS: No. No.

KR: Because that's the law.

AG: So part B: what was the nature of the debates about what was going to be in part B?

WS: No, there were discussions at the meetings about whether or not reasons for judgments or transcripts should be included. Because I can remember one of the judges saying, 'But the High Court has a transcript in all its cases, why shouldn't we?'. Well, the answer to that is because we don't need to in many of the cases.

AG: But that's also interesting because the High Court can't be appealed from. So the notion of what is on their record has completely different significance.

WS: The judges could see the sense of having an electronic court file system that automatically categorised part A and part B.

AG: About part B, was there any debate? The conceptual thinking about what to preserve, what might be of future value? This is the Apple and Samsung issue.

WS: I can tell you: no, there wasn't. The reason was this: once they were satisfied that part A was defined and it was going to be kept, everything else was part B.

KR: So you keep everything.

AG: Or nothing.

LN: Well we only have to keep part A forever.

WS: Part A was the record. Part B was everything else, and in the context of significant files being kept, that was going to be A and B.

AG: Right. So back to the circular question about significant files and how to decide …

KR: … what was significant.

WS: They really left … They've left that to us.

KR: The process is still an evolving one, you think?

WS: We're still having discussions about what it ought to be.

LN: We're starting prepared cases to go now. There's two massive ones in the ACT [Australian Capital Territory] that we know are going to be and so we're preparing them to go. But what we've got to do is have an access policy, which we're still working on as well.

KR: So this is where I hope our work can be practically significant too, because there are quite interesting process questions about how those decisions are made. In the sense of, I mean even our discussion today, at the moment, you're only thinking about the cases that are significant as opposed to the other documentation that exists in the Federal Court that should be, perhaps, in our view, be reflected upon to be identified as significant.

WS: That's fair comment.

KR: I was saying a bit earlier to Lyn, when I first got involved and interested in archives from being a legal academic, it was in the context of not courts but the Department of Immigration and which documents it kept from my work on citizenship. Being amazed at things that were about to be sent and destroyed that were of real national significance. I have a memory, and I need to follow this up, that committees were established where there were historians. Or people not from the actual organisation who were involved in that process of making decisions about significance.

One thing I'm just literally throwing up, that's coming to my mind in this discussion, is whether the Federal Court, in its thinking about making those decisions about significance, should be thinking about external people who could be on the committee to assist in that process.

WS: I think we should think about it.

AG: Well, I think that's how … I mean just about the part A and part B. Because all lawyers will understand that but the historiographical problems of thinking about how we interpret what we save, keep and curate and then how you access it and what you might think is of value and what kinds of stories or histories are able to be told. Most lawyers find that very difficult to understand. Now, Chief Justice Allsop, I've had one conversation with him about this project, when we asked for permission to come and work, and he gets it implicitly. He gave me an example from his own experience about how he had thought about that. So, as an institution, the fact that …

KR: You're doing all this stuff.

WS: It's important. It's important. It's important, yeah.

AG: The access question is a really difficult one that sort of exercised us a fair bit because, and again this goes to the native title question, because clearly how to modernise and become a national court occurred at the same time as the introduction of the native title jurisdiction.

LN: Ian Irving [Former Native Title Registrar of the Federal Court of Australia] was working on that and we've got a MoU [Memorandum of Understanding] ready drafted. It's a draft. It's going to the judges. The native title judges. It is ready for final sign off. Because we are wanting to send away native title files and National Archives, in their wisdom, and it's from a practical thing, and they're saying, 'Well, why should we accept all of them if they're not going to be accessible? We're not a storage area anymore'.

AG: See, this is fascinating.

LN: We are here for significant files to be placed with us so people can access. So if you're not going to give an access policy, thank you very much, we don't want your files. We know we've got to take them but they're putting the onus back on us.

WS: That's fair enough. I think that's fair enough.

LN: We're nearly there because Ian has got something pretty good. The only thing that's not worked out is the expert reports, but anyway.

AG: It was really interesting before to me and I think this is a really exemplary thing about this court, is when you were thinking about what native title meant when it arrived jurisdictionally. To be able to think okay, this is a majorly ground-shifting political and historical moment in the history of this country. Like post-Mabo, everything is different.

WS: It is. It is.

AG: Everything is different. In how we think about what institutions do, who accesses, all of that has to be fundamentally different. The fact that this court both could have the foresight and imagination to say 'we need to think of practice guidelines that include things that don't ordinarily look like law but are law' and, at the same time, going 'we've got to treat these matters exactly the same as we treat all other matters, with efficiency'. That, I suppose, is a really important thing to consider. If we think about how native title matters are to be archived and access[ed], that gives an indication, I think, of how everything else should be.

LN: We've actually spelled a lot of that out. All [those] diaries and sound recordings, we've actually …

WS: It's true. I mean you've got to apply both sensible practices to that issue.

AG: Yeah, because the nature of what it is to be a court fundamentally incorporates all of that.

WS: Yes.

AG: That's, I think, a really important thing to consider—how to think about access for native titles matters and native title materials, which are diverse and this complexity of not everything can be electronically managed.

LN: Well that's it. You want to do that in the electronic world, it's going to be difficult, isn't it?

WS: Yes, I know, and there has to be some sort of sensible consideration given because these things that are presently thought to be quite sensitive are not going to be sensitive in 50 years', 100 years', 200 years' time. They're going to be critically important.

AG: Yeah, so and I suppose the debates for Indigenous communities about ownership and repatriation and having some of those conversations with colleagues, researchers, who work in that area, but you've got to understand the responsibility to hold material because it's a superior court of record and what it means to preserve things and who and how that is accessed.

KR: It's not dissimilar to concepts that go with things like cabinet documents that are closed for particular periods of time because of the sensitivities …

WS: Yes, true. True.

KR: … where there is a need for closure because of other interests and how you work out what that period will be in light of the interests that are involved.

WS: Yes, I think there's some common sense being applied to that. But the judges are going to have to be satisfied that there's something in place to protect some sensitivities of litigation in the present time.

KR: But also what would be interesting, coming back to that external advisor, how much the Indigenous communities are consulted on those sorts of questions.

LN: Well Ian is definitely talking to them about expert reports.

WS: Yes, they have. They have been.

LN: I think any confidential order that's been put now … Because we're sending a file with a page on the front that will summarise what can and can't be accessed in that file. They're going to be putting the details of any confidentiality orders so that National Archives still have the right to come back and ask about that. But it seems—I wanted to clarify that with them—but it seems like they're asking National Archives to do that. They're giving them contact details so that if they feel … they can contact the Indigenous body direct.

AG: But, I mean, it's the community, not the individual that sort of is the point. Those things are going to be ongoing relationships. So, I suppose it's an interesting difficulty … what are obligations of courts … to multiple publics [different groups, and communities]? I mean I have used collections [of different community organisations] at Mitchell [Library] and other places, some of which [are restricted and require permission from the group], some … that I can copy. [Court records, however,] are not of the nature of those kinds of records. I think the difficulty [for courts in making access rules] is going to be about who the parties are … a problem that has beleaguered the native title jurisdiction. It is going to be those same kinds of issues, in terms of consultation about who can then access materials.

LN: Isn't there a move too, Warwick, for the judges now to put a limit on orders? You know there's going to be a time when they can be lifted.

WS: Yes.

[Over speaking]

LN: Because at the moment, there's no end date. That's the difficulty with anything like this: no end date. So I think there was a move to see if she could put something in place. Okay, we'll put this on but there is an end date or a review date or something, so it doesn't go on forever.

KR: Yes, like a sunset clause.

LN: Yes, and that's our problem. Because these things have got to be around forever.

AG: Because also, just for non–native title matters as well, when does a file become closed? You know, to make the decision about when things are sent. I mean, you say you're preparing things now to send. So the idea that this … clearly you can't be sending significant matters until they've been …

KR: Concluded.

LN: Well, these are about 2003, these ones we're looking at now. So that's quite a …

AG: Yes, so the lag itself obviously is part of the protocol that you have to …

LN: Well, hopefully there won't be that real lag later. We will probably get all of those. Those big ones like that, we'll identify them. But then we're looking at significant files like 12, 24 months after the event really, aren't we? We're flagging them.

WS: Yeah, we're not going to do it until the prospect of the appeal period having been passed. Because on the list of documents, I mean, if you're just looking at our file, parties and orders, there might subsequently be a Full Court, a High Court appeal that reverses the decision.

AG: Exactly.

WS: That's noted on the original file. So you want the benefit of all that on the original file.

AG: Can I just come back to this thing about selection by number. You know, by … because obviously, this is something that a colleague of mine who works very closely as a 19th historian with Supreme Courts, in particular in Victoria, said they did a similar thing. But they didn't even think about what they were keeping. They just went, 'we're just going to keep …'. They just literally looked at what was there.

WS: No, I wasn't prepared to let that happen.

AG: I think you need to have that kind of sweep. Because we don't know. We want to know, you know, you're looking at social histories of who the parties are. What the legal issue is has become sort of …

KR: Who had access to the courts? What's in the nature of the submissions? Who were the lawyers? How do we think about those?

LN: We always had that in mind that we would be looking at a selection of the cases we look at every year. So there's a cross-section of … We deal with migration—they mightn't be significant migration—but we deal with migration so we want a sample of all the things that we do. So that was always a category that we were going to look at.

AG: That's back to the idea of the history of this organisation, also lets you see that.

LN: Yes. Exactly. That's important.

WS: I think the history of the organisation is going to be in a lot of the documents and records we have in the administration files. The committee meetings, I mean; you would have seen that.

LN: We've got a scanning project going on at the moment with just doing that. All the background papers to the judge's meetings, which are where all the work happens.

WS: The introduction of the electronic court file and the fact that we'll be able to keep, in the future, the record electronically and transfer significant files electronically is the solution to the future cost problems of keeping records.

As discussed in the introduction to this extract, the various issues raised in this interview are of continuing relevance to the court and involve ongoing projects. This interview was conducted on the eve of the court's 40th anniversary as a national institution and captures the respective participants' thinking at that time. At the time of publication, the court had not finalised its significant court file policy, although progress has been made in developing a policy on accessing native title files, which will have an influence on other accessibility policies, including the court's significant files.

8

A Conversation with Louise Anderson and Ian Irving (Former Native Title Registrars, Federal Court of Australia)

Interviewed by Ann Genovese and Kim Rubenstein[1]

On 27 February 2017, Kim Rubenstein and Ann Genovese interviewed Louise Anderson and Ian Irving for the Court as Archive Project. Louise and Ian are former Registrars of the Federal Court of Australia. Louise was the first Native Title Registrar appointed in 1998 and Ian was appointed a Registrar in 2003 and became the second Native Title Registrar in 2005. At the time of the interview, both worked at the Victorian Supreme Court, Louise as the Chief Executive Officer and Ian as a Judicial Registrar. In 2019, Louise Anderson returned to the Federal Court in the role of National Director, Court and Tribunal Services.

In the interview, we discuss, among other topics, what it meant for the Federal Court of Australia to accrue the native title jurisdiction in 1996 and what changes that occasioned for the Federal Court's practices, procedures and records management. We also discuss what the arrival of

---

1 Please cite as Louise Anderson and Ian Irving, interview Ann Genovese and Kim Rubenstein in Ann Genovese, Trish Luker and Kim Rubenstein (eds), *The Court as Archive* (ANU Press, 2019).

the jurisdiction meant for the relationships between the court, Indigenous litigants and other parties; there are also aspects of this discussion that highlight key issues around active citizenship as a form of participation.

We interviewed Louise and Ian together to capture their significant collaborations and their different institutional and professional experiences. The full interview is not included below, but further publications are planned around other aspects of their interview.

Alongside the interview with Warwick Soden, the following extract from this interview offers another rare example of an oral history undertaken with key administrative office holders of the Federal Court conducted around the time of its 40th anniversary as a national institution.

In the same spirit as the interview with Warwick Soden, this interview represents a point in time. Some of the issues discussed will have progressed, but they are a timely record of significant aspects of this project's research interest.

> **Kim Rubenstein (KR)**: There's an interesting backdrop to our conversation today. We're sitting in the Victorian Supreme Court, Louise as the CEO and Ian a Judicial Officer, but we're taking you back to your Federal Court life.
>
> **Louise Anderson (LA)**: So in terms of taking this back, the Federal Court just had its 40th anniversary and, well, in fact, it was created in 1976 by statute. Both Ian and I were invited to the official anniversary event, which was great. It was great that the Chief Justice had invited Professor Mick Dodson to address the court as part of the anniversary celebrations. That motivated me to attend. I'm so pleased I did. Why I mention it now is that submissions were made at the event and almost all mentioned a native title jurisdiction, mediation and case management and digital innovation. These initiatives/innovations were things that we were passionate about and drove very hard. So that was incredibly exciting when you think of the time, the life of the Federal Court and, really, well, 1994 was a significant part of the court's history.[2]
>
> **Ann Genovese (AG)**: In looking at internal documents, of its own administration, and what you have just commented on regarding the anniversary is confirmation, adding context and flesh to what we know from the documents: that your stewardship, alongside former Federal Court of Australia Chief Justice Michael Black, marks a central moment

---

2 The time of the commencement of the Federal Court's native title jurisdiction.

for the court. If you go back, looking at the files and arguments about the establishment of the court in the first place, a key issue was: what is a modern Australian jurisdiction going to look like?

LA: That's right.

AG: How that's realised? It doesn't really, in my view, come of age until after *Mabo*[3] and the arrival of the native title jurisdiction.

LA: It's really interesting, because I felt that so strongly when I was there on the 40th anniversary, and I felt that strongly, that I was sort of growing up, as it were, in the Federal Court. Chief Justice Allsop spoke passionately about the native title jurisdiction. For the Federal Court, notwithstanding being in the rarefied air of a commercial jurisdiction, you've got to hang on to something that makes you relevant to the community of which you're a critical part.

KR: The heart of it.

AG: So that's exactly what I would observe, that after *Mabo*, the whole game changes. Australian law—what does [Chief Justice] Brennan say?: 'The law of Australia is Australian law'. So institutions have got to start being responsive and responsible in different kinds of ways.

KR: It's interesting. From my perspective, the sort of migration jurisdiction is the other point of analysis too there, because of that key workload. It also asks of the court: who is the community? And that in law we define ourselves by who we are not: the 'aliens' head of power. That all plays out so amazingly here too.

LA: Yeah, very true. Very true.

KR: Louise, you made a lovely statement that you grew up in the Federal Court. Can you both tell us, well, one by one, how you came to the Federal Court?

LA: Sure. I did law as a graduate after my first degree and then I moved to Sydney and I was admitted to practice a year before the High Court delivered *Mabo*. So, for me, having come from a very political activist background and worked in ...

AG: In Tassie, for the record.

[Laughter]

---

3   *Mabo v Queensland (No 2)* 175 CLR 1.

KR: In terms of Tasmania Dams case.[4]

LA: Yeah. That was my first experience of consensus decision-making, learning about it with Bob Brown.

KR: Were you at UTas [University of Tasmania] for your law degree?

LA: No. I started ... I did one year at UTas for an Arts degree and then I got a small scholarship on the understanding that I would come back and continue in political science because that was my passion, but I didn't. I became a 'mainlander'. Yes. Then I worked in the union movement actually and then went to Sydney and worked in community legal centres. Ian and I, in fact, had a crossover. We both worked at the Inner City Legal Centre. Just by chance, really, which has been my career, a bit by chance. I then fell into a role as an Associate at the AAT [Administrative Appeals Tribunal] when Justice Deirdre O'Connor was the President in Sydney. Anyway, from there, I realised how much I liked working in tribunals and courts. Then the NNTT [National Native Title Tribunal] was established, so that was 1 January 1994. I worked on and off in the community legal centres for a number of years. Then a position came up at the NNTT as a senior case manager. So I went for that really with passion about what native title could be. That was when Justice French was the President and I was one of the first 50 employees. So that was a very exciting time. Michael Black had decided that post-*Brandy*,[5] and with the increase in the jurisdiction in the Federal Court, there needed to be a native title specialist role within the court. Now, again, what was interesting was that it was at a time when the NNTT really were still very, very, very challenged by the notion that their decisions could not be enforced and the belief was that the court would rubber stamp the agreements. However, the court was never going to be a rubber stamp, because courts don't operate in that way. I was in Sydney and it was a Melbourne position, but the twins were quite young. There was family in Melbourne, so I applied. It was a very intense time. I first started working in the old High Court, which is now part of the Supreme Court, which was the Federal Court in 1998. I remember my first meeting with Chief Justice Black was in a stairwell. He said, 'So how are you going to resolve all these cases in three years?'. I was quite surprised and said, 'I'm not. We need to have a conversation'. That's what happens when you're kind of young and ...

AG: You just say it.

LA: Yes. Rather than now, I'd probably be far more nuanced. So ...

---

4   *Commonwealth v Tasmania* (1983) 158 CLR 1.
5   *Brandy v Human Rights & Equal Opportunity Commission* (1995) 183 CLR 245.

AG: But I take it he didn't respond negatively to that?

LA: No. He said, 'Well give me a plan'.

Ian Irving (II): He was throwing out a challenge.

LA: At the same time, the court's expectation for prompt disposition remained paramount, and a three-year target for all cases had been set. This started a really interesting journey in itself and a lot hangs on that, because the court under [Principal Registrar] Warwick [Soden] and the Chief Justice's leadership was absolutely and understandably focused on efficiency and effectiveness. In doing that, disposition targets and dockets were central to it. So to have a jurisdiction [like native title] that didn't necessarily fit within the docket system [introduced to the Federal Court in 1997], that was clearly going to challenge the ordinary notion of case management and disposition targets. There was a real opportunity for shaping that, but the three-year disposition target for all cases remained something I think that was a reputational risk for us. Although, on reflection, Warwick Soden's focus on the target did focus attention on what target was reasonable; a question that played out for many, many years. So we had to hear strongly from others. So what we went to do was organise. For example, I went and spoke at conferences and was really the spokesperson for what in my view was a fairly untenable position; to set that target so early on [in] the court's journey with the [native title] jurisdiction.

KR: Can I just clarify, who had set the three-year disposition target in the first place?

LA: The court had set up a native title coordination committee, which—primarily at that point—comprised judges who had land rights experience from the [Land Rights] Commission, so Justices Olney, Gray, Merkel, Beaumont, O'Loughlin … with leadership from Justice Toohey—notwithstanding he was on the High Court … What we did very quickly was put in place specialist native title judges. And [Justice] French was also a member notwithstanding being the President of the NNTT. So to meet the disposition target [in native title], I think, was around saying to government: 'what resources do we need to drive [these native title cases]?'. So it was quite strategic on that part. What we organised very early on, so—well, it didn't culminate until 2001—was a series of user groups. It drove both a different level of community engagement that wasn't there in the Federal Court before. It drove a different level of public information that wasn't there in the Federal Court before. Also, specialist rules and procedures and a very different way of doing business, notwithstanding it was still a superior court of record. Each of these things required significant submissions from me, presentations to our judiciary, really cross-examination in a way that just made me grow up very quickly.

KR: Your advocacy skills must have really been honed in that period.

LA: They did. I really learned how to get a message across in the most, I hope, effective way. Even the user group narrative had to be well-argued and presented, because the Federal Court wasn't in the position of saying to the people who had come before it, other than through formal engagement with the Bar: 'what are we doing well and where could we do better?'. So that was my message. The two things we've got to be saying out aloud and actually open to hearing are enormous. I mean, Ian certainly worked and followed that through …

II: I was originally on the other side of that.

AG: So that seems like a convenient moment to …

KR: A nice segue …

AG: … and Ian enters the picture!

II: But I didn't enter the picture until 2005 at the Federal Court, but from 2001 through to 2005, I'd been at the Kimberley Land Council. I was at UNSW [University of New South Wales]. I did a science–law degree, genetics and immunology. I was going to be a research scientist. Started doing operations on rats and all of the rest. Realised pretty quickly I didn't want to be a research scientist. Finished my law degree. Thought, what am I going to do? Travelled around for a while. Tried my hand at a few things …

[Laughter]

II: Ended up somehow after that at community legal centres, so doing volunteer work at Marrickville Legal Centre, getting a job a Marrickville Legal Centre, eventually working at Inner City Legal Centre. I think [Louise] you had just left there …

LA: I was on the Board. I'd just left.

II: Then I worked at Legal Aid. I had a really good friend who had recently got a job in Alice Springs. Thought: 'I want to get out of Sydney. What am I going to do?'. A job came up in Broome at the KLC [Kimberley Land Council] and I thought, 'well, what the hell. I'll give it a go'. Had a mad interview by video from Glebe to Broome.

AG: So had you been to Broome before?

II: I had been luckily once before. Anyway, it was amazing. But, so that was 2001, and I think in 2001, in some senses, I was on the other side of [the user groups Louise was organising]. So the KLC for better or for worse had, at one stage, five matters that were all in litigation at the same time. They had hardly any lawyers. The lawyers that they had had no real litigation experience. I'd at least worked at Legal Aid, so I knew how …

AG: To run a file …

II: Yes, run a file and broadly how courts worked, but also that experience of working there and being kind of trapped in this litigation process meant that I was going to user group meetings with a sense of 'hang on a second, there's almost too much litigation pressure'. But we were also passionate about getting outcomes in a way that's not only through litigation.

LA: It was a very clear intention and explicit that native title was around an intersection of two laws and customs, so we wanted the Federal Court's presence to be, and the structure, to be there. But we also needed to find a way to properly listen and hear on a more equal footing. That was a real challenge.

AG: Can we come back to that? Because that's hugely significant …

LA: Well, I—to return to my arrival at the Federal Court in 1998—in my first three weeks, I was in the old High Court building in Little Bourke Street in Melbourne, on a chair that fell apart and a desk that was wonky! The first thing was to write some native title procedural rules.

AG: In the first three weeks!

LA: So I rang Graeme Neate [at the NNTT] and asked for his advice. I rang others—judges and legal practitioners, academics. But the conversation about 'what are rules?' can be difficult if you're not immersed in it. So then I started to think about, well, what were they, the court rules? Now, my—for my sins …

II: You can't subvert the rules without knowing what they are.

LA: Yeah. I love rules! So when we tried to work out how to rewrite the rules, Justice French was very helpful. People gave me the Northern Territory land rights regime, all of that. Then we started to think about—and [Chief Justice] Michael Black was great on this, because there was great concern from within the Federal Court about including music, language, art and dance as evidence. That was something that I felt really passionate about.

II: And statements of cultural and customary concerns.

LA: Yes that's exactly right. If you're working within a predominately oral culture and you don't have the written record, how are you going to get it across there?

AG: I want to come back to that, it is very important. But Ian, to return to your arrival at the Federal Court; so obviously if you're at the KLC, legally that's a very specific set of experiences.

II: So I arrived there from Sydney. I had always lived in Sydney. So then I was transplanted to Broome. As soon as I got there, we had the AGM [Annual General Meeting]. It was at a pastoral station outside of Kununurra, so it was just boiling hot. So we get back to the office in Broome, which is where all the lawyers were, and I asked, 'where are the files?'. Well, they kind of didn't really have a proper filing system. No sense of when you have a conversation, write it down, make a file note, put it on a file, make sure the file has a date when it has to come back to you. Like, to try and get people to understand why that was important was kind of …

AG: When you say people here, we're talking [about] the other lawyers?

II: Other lawyers. There were only really two other lawyers at that stage: Julie [Melbourne] and Kristy [Guest]. Julie had been at the KLC since the '80s, and the KLC had been really a community kind of political organisation.

AG: I think that is really important, because how practitioners, not just judges working on claims, but practitioners working with communities learn particular skillsets, which are unbelievably important, but they're not litigation focused.

II: Yes. Really skilled at actually working with groups—mediation skills. But litigation is very different. By the time I got there, Julie was in Kununurra, so she didn't have any time for me, because she was busy at the hearings …

LA: With *Rubibi*[6] and *Miriuwung Gajerrong*[7] looming.

II: *Miriuwung Gajerrong* had just been remitted by the High Court.

AG: Wow.

---

6 *Rubibi Community v State of Western Australia & Ors* (Unreported, National Native Title Tribunal, 7 November 2001).
7 *Attorney-General of the Northern Territory v Ward* (Unreported, National Native Title Tribunal, 9 December 2003).

II: We were saying to Justice Merkel, 'Please don't put *Rubibi* into litigation. Please don't put *Rubibi* into litigation'. But he did. Then *Bardi Jawi*[8] somehow ...

AG: So this extraordinary. These are major matters. And there are three of you?

II: There were three of us, but we quickly brought on more people. So, hence, going to the Federal Court user group and just saying ...

LA: I remember. You made a submission. It was in 2001. We had, I remember, the first and only, I think, national user group. I had the Full Court there. It was in Adelaide.

AG: So having you two in the interview together is perfect, because how you are coming to know each other happens at the same time as the jurisdiction you're imagining, from the ground up. You need all these different experiences. So Louise, how did you argue for the user group in the first place?

LA: I wrote a lot, because it's still submission-based. You had to write things and we'd put things up to the Native Title Practice Committee. We needed to find a managerial approach within the Federal Court. It is important to remember that we had the docket system from 1997; the principle of a single judge in control of a case as soon as it's filed. So the native title jurisdiction got caught up in that. I mean, I think the docket system is an extraordinary success and it works as a core principle of accountability and transparency in a court system. But you've also got this notion that ran counter to the complexity of native title. So there was so many things that were at odds with each other, but you're trying to make this work. Anyway, what we identified was the risk. We could have had 50 individual judges with native title matters and neither the 'system'—because it was by now being seen as a 'system' ...

II: The court couldn't afford that.

LA: No. Well, that was part of the driver: one, just financially; two, credibility; and three, managing the workload. So we needed to get education streams running: one, how's the *Native Title Act*[9] to work?; and two, what are the Indigenous perspectives running under, in and around the Act. There's sense, for the court, for the first time, that there was criticism of it. That it wasn't loved by this jurisdiction and the stakeholders.

---

8   *Sampi on behalf of the Bardi and Jawi People v State of Western Australia (No. 2)* (Unreported, National Native Title Tribunal, 30 November 2005).
9   *Native Title Act 1993* (Cth).

So we had a number of pressures, and we needed to engage at every stream of government through that point, with the Wik Task Force, with the rep bodies, with ATSIC [Aboriginal and Torres Strait Islander Commission] as it was then.

AG: Were all of these in your consultative framework?

LA: Yes, then also internally supporting our judiciary to understand that we needed a different managerial structure for native title. So we improvised with the docket system and we created these judges called provisional docket judges. Those judges were the managerial judges. They were not intended to hear matters. They were to be case management judges and then we aligned very quickly the idea of specialist Registrars to support all that. That took me a long time to get up. So just in terms of the user groups, we get through to 2001, and we've now got conversations at local level. A lot of internal professional development. In fact, Noel Pearson was really excellent in that, because he gave a lot of his time and came to a number of our internal training [sessions] as it were with the judiciary and spoke in a way that crossed the divide.

AG: Well, he is a lawyer.

LA: He's an advocate. Beautiful advocacy. Compelling. So, by 2001, in Adelaide, we had the first national user group, which was to deal with the three-year disposition target, amongst other things.

AG: So, how many people?

LA: One hundred.

II: At the court, was it?

AG: There was no Federal Court building in Adelaide then.

II: But you know what, it's interesting that you talk about they 'all came in' and they—such strong engagement and leadership—and I reckon there's something about that. It's obvious in a way. Aboriginal people and their interaction with institutions and law. So it's not about coming from a place of 'I've got rights; I'm going to assert them'. It's 'how am I going to negotiate in this?'.

AG: Exactly.

II: 'How am I going to engage with this in a way that I'm going to come out with an outcome I like, for my law, not depending upon my rights?' So that coming in together is really deliberate.

LA: Very deliberate.

II: I think that was important for my clients' approach to native title. I think, in the Kimberley, they had been using the *Heritage Act*[10] as their way of actually getting outcomes. Then suddenly native title comes along and it was really uncertain, but they thought, 'Well, what the hell? We'll sign on. We'll become a rep body. We'll do it, because that was another opportunity. Let's see what happens'.

AG: That's important to note: instead of saying 'Here's Australian law and Aboriginal people have been completely done over [by it]'—which removes Indigenous people from their own law story. You are reminding us that at every single point is an encounter of laws and what you, as the lawyer, bring to the meeting, how you take instruction and how the meeting is ceremonially staged at every single level is important

LA: That's right. The ceremonial staging was critical. I think. And I absolutely agree with your point, Ian, that there wasn't anything on either side accidental about this. Native title was supposed to be a mediated outcome through the tribunal, but there was such opposition from government to local Aboriginal land councils that had just created their own governance in that space. So there was heritage interaction already, and native title was this overlay. In principle, in theory, sensational, but then you go …

KR: How do you fit it all together?

LA: Yes, from a governance perspective. So Indigenous leadership was very, very cogent, particularly for saying to the court, 'You've got it wrong in applying a disposition target'. So we shifted from there. But in shifting, the court couldn't move too far. We still needed to look at outcomes and that's something, as Ian said, both he and I were very passionate about; that you couldn't have these matters languishing for so long; and the court must look at all sides and bring that sort of perspective. So the user groups were, sort of, looking from the outside in.

II: That's huge.

LA: They were extraordinary and they shifted the court's engagement. The court really then … Many of its jurisdictions adopted that approach.

AG: Had that happened before?

---

10   *Aboriginal and Torres Strait Islander Heritage Protection Act 1984* (Cth).

LA: No. It had only happened with the Bar Association and the Law Council of Australia. Well, these national user groups ... there were hundreds of people in that room. I mean, it was like a conference.

AG: So I'm just imagining how hard you worked.

LA: Yes. We had everyone with speaking notes and we had everyone structured and everyone knew what was going to be said and what was going to be the response. So these were very orchestrated events. The local user groups were a bit different and that's where Ian and I met. I mean, Ian and I had sort of known of each other from Inner City and just around the traps, but it was [at] the WA user group. I remember. For me, one of the things was, as an officer of the court, I was invisible a lot of the time. Whilst I was quite comfortable with that, now and then you'd sort of go, 'Oh, hang on a minute. Is this where I actually want to position myself?' because it was so much back-room wheeling and dealing to get things sorted, and I remember being in that meeting and, Ian, you went, 'Louise Anderson'. I looked around I thought, 'Who's that?'.

[Laughter]

Then you made a very compelling presentation to Justice French and you basically said, 'We have five trials on, we can't do it'.

AG: God, Ian. Five.

II: Yeah. We had *Miriuwung Gajerrong*. We had *Neowarra*.[11] We had *Karajarri*,[12] the remainder of *Karajarri*. We had *Rubibi*. And we had *Bardi Jawi*.

AG: That's huge. How many solicitors at the time?

II: At that stage, we probably had four.

AG: Ian.

KR: Wow.

II: We had brought in ... so we were just buying in barristers, really, to try cases and financially, what happened was that FaCSIA [Family and Community Services and Indigenous Affairs] turned around and said to KLC, 'Well, you can't manage your money. So we're putting in an administrator'. So we were just caught between what felt like a broader conversation between the court and the bureaucracy about native title

---

11 *Neowarra v Western Australia* [2004] FCA 1092.
12 *Nangkiriny on behalf of the Karajarri People v The State of Western Australia* (Unreported, National Native Title Tribunal, 12 February 2002).

funding models. We were just stuck in the middle, saying, 'We're trying to get out of this, but we can't get out of it and now we're closing all of these regional offices and laying off a quarter of the staff', which was awful. Yeah. As well as …

KR: Running the cases.

II: … just trying to keep on top of it. Yes. So you had an organisation, which had started as a community organisation, where suddenly it's like, 'Wait a minute. We're getting rid of the local officers, which are the main connection with the community and becoming a law firm'.

AG: So on that point—which, I think, is another important point about native title practice—if you're losing the local office, and, obviously, the on-the-ground work you're doing with your clients is so fraught to get consensus or agreement that fits into the form for native title litigation, that must have been hugely problematic.

II: It was, because you had all of these groups who needed to be together to form the Kimberley Land Council. But we had to say to claimants, 'We don't have any time or resources to actually do any of your future act work. We are for the next X number of years—well, really we do—yeah, stuck with this. We're going to effectively work for these five groups in the litigation and that's it'. So the others are just, like, 'Well, what am I doing here?'.

AG: So that's a huge amount of political negotiation going on.

LA: With your community.

II: Yes. And even considering who claimants might be. But that was fascinating. As someone who had kind of come from Legal Aid and working with individual clients, to go to groups and group dynamics and that was a whole level of complexity, which wasn't the same; exhausting, but so exciting.

AG: But this is the thing. To think as lawyers across the board, to have that sense that the client is not a corporation in a traditional sense, even though under the [Native Title] Act, you are a corporation in different kinds of ways, but a group who have not only different relationships to law, but different relationships to each other, to fit as a litigant for everyone would have been difficult.

KR: It's just such interesting democratic flow-on in terms of thinking originally as participatory democracy in terms of user groups to then the ways in which a Western liberal system conceives the individual as separate from and whereas this is so connected. It's very interesting.

LA: That's right.

AG: So I want to return to that national user group in 2001. So there you went, 'Louise Anderson', and then gave a compelling submission. What did you say?

II: From what I can remember, French J asked a question. I can't remember exactly what the question was. But the sense was, 'If we did this, would it make a difference?'.

LA: Which was a small thing, but we had taken forever to say we can't run native title matters all at the one time. So really it was just a prioritisation process.

II: Yes, but our priorities at KLC were just kind of keeping our heads above water and trying to hang on to some staff. So we were saying, 'Just back off for a minute and let us get through this thing'.

[Laughter]

LA: It was important in the Federal Court to always be thinking in that broader sense of 'What's the point of engagement?'. It's not just at an individual. It's not just at a claim. We needed to think more broadly about what's the role of the court. How can the court, as such a critical institution in the Western legal democratic principles, engage with legal practice and principles that actually run almost counter to the way that the court sees itself? So it's ... While the user groups were the sort of theatre, but what had gone behind it was so much engagement around decision-making, the management of knowledge within Indigenous communities. So the orders that started to come out around gender-restricted evidence, what was interesting in terms of the practice of the court, in my observations, were judges who in the main would have been making orders per case in isolation of others now needed to be quite collective in their thinking around that.

So—and I remember Justice Branson—there was quite a big engagement at one of our judicial conferences around the making of those orders around restricting gender evidence. Not only the mechanics of it, but also the conceptual thinking around it in the way that knowledge is. So they had to learn so much about the demarcation of knowledge, and that knowledge in our Western legal democratic institutions should be as open as possible. We've got to be as transparent as we can. Then we ran up against how that actually can offend the principles you're trying to recognise.

So that's in itself a very, a really critical, acknowledgement that native title was alive and law and custom was alive, if there was debate and …

8. A CONVERSATION WITH LOUISE ANDERSON AND IAN IRVING

II: So while you're doing all of that internally with the court, the KLC and, I suppose, the legal team that's involved is working at it from the other side by bringing Pat Dodson into court as an Indigenous person who has that *gravitas* within a broader kind of audience to actually try to educate the court from an Indigenous perspective.

LA: That was a brilliant move, because the Pat Dodson transcript was just used and used and used.

KR: When you say his transcript of …

II: His evidence, yeah.

LA: It was an extraordinary piece of advocacy, wasn't it? It wasn't in respect of *Karajarri*. It was in respect of the neighbouring claim, wasn't it, around …

II: Well, he's Yawuru, so he's Rubibi. So he did get brought in to …

LA: To speak, yes. Well, Ian you were part of orchestrating that as the lawyer. But what worked for us at the court was it spoke volumes of all of what we were trying to ask the judiciary to understand internally around a vibrant dynamic law and custom working on the ground in a native title community, if we can use those terms, and had so many rules of disclosure within Indigenous law. It was such an articulate piece to be able to say, 'This is how it works in practice'. We referred to it a lot. I mean, what I was doing during that time, after the rules, my second piece of work was putting together a bench book. We launched that at a judges' conference, I think, again in 2001; we did the front of it in, not Federal Court colours, but Indigenous and land rights colours. The bench book broke down the life of a case, which has always been my thing. Beginning to end. Each part of it: What was the nature of the orders? What secondary source material? What are the critical issues you need to think about at this juncture? What are going to be the pressures at play? We did it online and in hard copy.

AG: A manual, a training manual. So, Ian, you joined the court in 2005. What was your official role when you joined?

KR: Or can you tell us the transition of the move, what happened?

II: So I was in the Kimberley until about 2005. Decided I wanted to come back to a city.

LA: Well, just before then, Chief Justice Black's—one of his Associates, [Kristy Dunn] was at a juncture. I said, 'There's a great media role going at the Kimberley Land Council. You'd be excellent'.

II: Okay. So Kristy came to work at the KLC. She was fantastic and I said, 'Come and work in the legal unit'. So she came to work as one of the lawyers, which was fantastic. She worked on *Rubibi* a lot. In fact, I'm sure she would have looked at various papers and things that I wanted to talk to at user groups, so she was a really good insight into the other side in terms of what's happening at the court. Anyway, Justice North was up in the Kimberley. He must have been doing the *Karajarri* Part A determination maybe and, through Kristy Dunn, we ended up having dinner. Just felt like a real connection there. But he had been so—I don't know what he was like before *Karajarri*—but he had been so, kind of, open to the experience ...

LA: Yes, brilliant.

II: ... to the extent where the claimants used to call him Mudjanunja or something, like Boss North. Like, 'he's our judge'. They felt such a level of connection, such a respect for someone who was going to listen to them, who was going to hear what they had to say, they ... But they also recognised that he was a law boss as well, so ...

AG: So the procedure—so I'm just thinking back to the institutional—we are sort of slowly moving to the actual nub of the archive question in doing this, because obviously Ian took particular responsibility for that question around that time. But before we do so, I want to ask about how institutions become transformed, a theme of this conversation. Obviously, the Federal Court, on one level, thinks of itself as always being responsive and transforming itself. But from my observation, and keeping in mind protocols in and outside the court, it would seem your influence and role, both of you, in speaking with judges in chambers, or at user groups, helped to change jurisprudence, not just rules. I mean, it's under-sung. So it is important to acknowledge it here. But from the outside perspective looking in, the key things are not just transforming the culture of the court, how you think with outsiders, who comes to court and what happens, but writing the rules—the on-country hearing question.

LA: So the on-country hearings ... I mean, whilst we inherited some of that from the land rights regime and the Land Commissioner, the majority of our judges were very opposed to it. They were opposed to it because land rights was an administrative procedure ...

AG: Absolutely.

LA: ... with a judge exercising quite a different power and authority than the Federal Court. The Federal Court had never contemplated operating outside of its own premises within states and territories. We drove that. There were many conversations. It was advocacy coming in predominately from either our internal professional development opportunities or externally through land councils and others. So, for me, there were three things running. One was I knew instinctively, I suppose, that once you get judges on country, you're going to get a whole other quality of decision-making, because there has to be, at some point, a sense of the meeting of those ... an intersection of those laws and that needed to be palpable and experienced on that very sensory level, not just through reading, so there's that. The second thing that we sort of were able to argue strongly was oral tradition versus written submissions. You've already got a ... you're going to deliver a significant disadvantage to people if you're trying to determine whether their law and custom is sufficiently robust or intact, and at a certain point you were requiring all to be done, mediated, through advocates on a written submission basis. So that was good because judges could understand that there was a fairness principle running in it, and there was a quality of the evidence. You were going to get your best evidence by being on country. So we had those messages coming in from all places. The other piece of it was I had to negotiate, and we did very well with this, was to get the funding for it.

[Laughter]

II: Have you seen the manual? It's so comprehensive in terms of every possible risk including shark bite, mosquitos, flat tyres ... Each region had its own set of risks.

LA: I mean, when you look at risk assessment, we had to do everything. We had to have protocols. My brother was in CASA [Civil Aviation Safety Authority] at the time, so he was helpful on twin-engine planes and the nature of the plane and what time we would invest into pilots! I had this scarce precious resource: a judge. Then you also had the cultural manual. But it was to give judges comfort that we were not doing this without very significant consideration of what we were asking them to do. So you had the bench book running, you had the rules, you had the OH&S [occupational health and safety] manual and our checklists and then the kind of cultural protocols. So basically, we did research. Some of it we got from the tribunal but, in the main, we generated things ourselves, around cultural norms, outside of native title, and how it was going to be put in the case—how to interact, what to expect. So there'd be things like, 'What was the temperature like?', 'What are things?', 'What's the colonial history?', 'What are you ... ?' 'How do you want to address things?'; that ...

AG: But it worked.

LA: Yes. So they were read. Yes. Then we had to [get] a portable coat of arms, you know?

II: That's right.

LA: [Laughs]. We don't go anywhere without a coat of arms. I had no idea. I'm, like, 'What? I have to have a coat of arms?'.

AG: Because you're a court. And when you speak to Indigenous people on country …

LA: Yes.

AG: … you're coming here as law, you've got to be …

LA: Be, I know, law. You've got to come robed. It was all of that and it was …

II: … getting permission to go on pastoral stations …

LA: That was huge. God, that took me a long time to negotiate.

AG: If we could turn, Ian, to your role. In 2006, you wrote a really significant briefing paper on access to native title records.

II: It came about because the … it was for a rep body conference. It was because, from memory, Louise said, 'Can you address this?'. It was actually … I thought it was Indigenous rep bodies. Rep bodies being concerned that their connection reports, their expert reports, were going to be made available to absolutely anyone who asked for them. That's how it came about.

LA: It did come about a bit before. It was actually native title lawyer Andrew Chalk and someone else saying, 'You've got this incredible body of material. We want it to be available. And we want it to be available for best practice. But we know that there's a whole lot of …'.

AG: … problems …

LA: That ran parallel with some consideration we'd had internally, because dealing with some of the anthropologists and the rep bodies and dealing with Ron [Levy] actually in the Northern Land Council. Ron was really instrumental in that.

II: So that's how that came about; so it was actually asking, 'Well, let's just start at the beginning and look at what is actually accessible and not accessible, and what happens to records once they're in the court and all the rest of it'; 'How do we deal with archives?', *et cetera*.

AG: Because the Federal Court hadn't really been worried about it in those terms before you undertook the briefing paper, from our investigations.

KR: In the sense of when you were coming in to the court was there anyone that you thought, 'Oh, I'll go and speak to so-and-so' because, of course, a court with records would have to have think about records.

II: Within the court?

KR: Yes.

II: No. It was talking to you, Louise, I think. That was it.

LA: And I was talking to Justice Mansfield and that was it. [Laughs].

KR: I mean, this is what our project is about in the sense of how much had the court thought about managing its own records before.

LA: No, it hadn't. Hardly at all. It was native title that really pushed that.

AG: That paper was 10 years ago now, but the actual movement of the native title materials between institutions goes on. Obviously the politics of what repatriation looks like, and the replication of things that are evidence or submissions or not, which you covered in the paper, goes on. That's not over. But the Record Disposal Authority that sends native title matters to the National Archives when every single other thing at the Federal Court is still exempt—can you offer any comment on how that happened?

LA: So there were a few things pressing. I mean, one was just the physical … the space that we needed. So we had the Miriuwung Gajerrong Room in Perth. We had the Yorta Yorta room in Melbourne, you know? We had the …

II: … sending things offsite, and then the places offsite saying, 'We're not taking them' and they're wanting to send it back and …

LA: Yes. So we had a real pressure around just the cost of storage. Then we had the cultural kind of questions around what's our responsibility with this material? Are there ways that we could make it available to others to both benefit from as a researcher, but also the nature of what we've got, particularly in those expert reports. I mean, they were …

AG: Extraordinary.

LA: … extraordinary. You don't want them lost in the bottom of an archive box in the basement of a Federal Court—not that we had basements—but the concept of being lost. Yes. So we started some discussion. In fact, we had a couple of archivists, but none of them had engaged with this. So that work came with Grace [Koch] and Toni [Bauman] from AIATIS

[Australian Institute of Aboriginal and Torres Strait Islander Studies]. Toni and I worked very closely on how we could … First of all, it was AIATIS who wanted to be the holders of it and then there was just some concern about that, because from our judges, well, AIATIS is for Aboriginal and Torres Strait Islanders. Whilst that might be appropriate, it doesn't send the message that if these documents are going to be available …

KR: Information.

LA: Yes. Exactly. So that's when we started the discussion with the National Archives and then there was a lot of concern around just the protocols and things—I mean, I don't know how many papers I had to write on Judge's Orders in Perpetuity, and what was the enforcement principle, and if a judge died and what the protocol archives would have? It sounds simple.

KR: All that work that you did. It's important too.

II: Whereas I came at it from the other angle, which was having done *Rubibi* and been in the KLC. So there was a big debate within the KLC about, well, what happens to all of our knowledge and our material? There was a library that was in Derby. Was everyone going to send all their stuff to Derby for it to be in library? Was that going to last? Come to the court …

LA: Because you were closing Derby office, I remember.

II: … by this stage the Yawuru had won *Rubibi*, so they wanted to be independent of the KLC. They were saying, 'Well, we've asked the KLC for the the copies of our stuff. They won't give it to us. Can we get it from the court?'. So then you had …

LA: … Indigenous people coming here to access their own materials.

KR: That is so interesting, isn't it, in terms of ownership?

II: And also that thing about, you know … but that Indigenous people actually trying to mine the archive for the purposes of their cases and coming up with nothing or pretty well nothing, or not much, or really having to see and read in a lot to the archive and the silences within the archive to say, 'Wow, there's something so rich here that actually represents Indigenous people speaking the way that they want to talk to an extent, to the way that they want to talk and its importance'.

AG: The court record does something that other records do not?

II: Yeah, absolutely. Yeah.

KR: Were there key people at the National Archives at the time who you …

LA: The archivist. Grace and Toni would know from AIATIS.

II: Well, Grace kept on saying, 'Have you done anything more about that archive policy and the issue?'. You'd be, like, 'Oh, God. Got to get back onto that and trying to talk'. A lot of it was actually trying to get the judges to actually agree, well, what are we going to keep? If we're going to keep it, there's no point in keeping it unless we've got an access arrangement. What are our rules around access going to be?

AG: So now there are kind of different historiographical conventions going on about those discussions; what is part B of the record …

KR: I think, probably, it takes time because there is an interpretive element that the judges then feel they're responsible for. What is the record for the purposes of judicial review as opposed to archival practices?

AG: That's the part A – part B demarcation.[13]

LA: Yes, it is.

KR: And part B revolves around what is the significance to the nation?

II: Yeah. So there's one thing about the record that determines let's keep it, which is great. It's kept, but then, it's then what? The management of it, accessibility arrangements … The only other thing that I just wanted to say really quickly, even whilst we're grappling the actual record: there's a whole other series of documents and materials that courts have, which is far harder to work out.

AG: The file.

II: Yes.

AG: Exactly, because the record is not the file.

II: Or if we choose to save in native title matters: the correspondence; those digital diaries; the tapes of the transcript; so people singing; people's actual voices; those gifts that the court gets given—which, to me, is like, you know, well, what is the significance of those gifts? How do we understand them? Should we have them as a collection? All of those things. But they are not part of the physical …

---

13 See Warwick Soden and Lyn Nasir, interview by Kim Rubenstein and Ann Genovese; Chapter 7 in this volume.

AG: ... file. So if you're talking about what should happen with a file. You've got a set of kind of understood procedures and practices and processes around trying to decide what should happen with those, and how to access those things, but you've got these other things, objects, songs that, in some ways, that should free the courts up, as in how to curate them. The point is now I think, because of the negotiations that you've all done, they are safe, right? They're with the National Archives? Or the court? In any event, native title remains unlike other important matters, in which the materials are definitely not 'safe'. So ...

LA: Yeah, but I think that it's absolutely important to keep that alive really and we should probably have some conversations reminding people, and I think ... that it is so important. I mean, generationally you need to move on and there needs to be an uplift of other capability. But going back, I suppose, to where I started, at the anniversary celebration, I just felt like the court was at risk of forgetting itself a bit. The statements at a senior level are still about passion and the importance. I mean, CJ Allsop, in the 40-year anniversary, was talking again about the incredible importance of the native title ... the intersection between ... this is about the development of a nation.

II: Well, he's an historian.

AG: Exactly.

LA: But to me, what that said was, well, is the Federal Court now seeing itself as an administrative vehicle no more in a way? It seems that it has fallen back from how critical courts are to do this. Now, whilst that might be relevant and appropriate now, in those early days, it wasn't. We were much more instrumental in making and breaking the system. I'm just not sure if all of those questions are going to remain alive. For example, the 2006 to 2007 amendments to the *Native Title Act*, the 2009 amendments and now, of course, the most current coming out of the Noongar claim issues, and we were instrumental in driving or reacting to or trying to inform those amendments. There's so much documentation around all of that. Some of it, whether it's ever appropriate to see the light of day ... That is a whole other administrative record sitting in the Federal Court that's now ...

KR: Yeah. It's, well, this is the active citizenship and the legislative citizenship experience.

LA: Yeah, exactly. Yes.

As discussed in the introduction to this collection, and to this chapter, the various issues raised in the interview are of continuing relevance to the court and to Indigenous and non-Indigenous scholars and communities. As Louise Anderson notes in the extract, native title represented the recognition of an intersection of two laws by Anglo-Australian law, and it was after the arrival of the native title jurisdiction in 1994 that the Federal Court addressed its public role and responsibilities in new ways. For the purposes of the Court as Archive Project, this included the fact that it became more broadly involved in the content and management of its records and stories, which we think it is important to emphasise.

This interview, as noted, is the first of its kind in Australia to record the work of Native Title Registrars in the early years of a new jurisdiction. We hope it forms the basis for our further work on the encounters between laws and people, and how they changed our institutions, in the years after *Mabo*.

9

Providing Public Access to Native Title Records: Balancing the Risks Against the Benefits

Pamela McGrath

Introduction

Since the establishment of the *Native Title Act 1993* (Cth) (*'Native Title Act'*), Aboriginal and Torres Strait Islander peoples have lodged close to 1,800 native title claimant applications; 360 of these have since been determined, 40 by trial. Many claims were ultimately withdrawn; however, 266 remain on foot.[1] A further 41 compensation applications have been filed. As a result of these many legal proceedings, the Federal Court of Australia and the National Native Title Tribunal (NNTT) are now in possession of an enormous number of records that contain information about many thousands of Aboriginal and Torres Strait Islander persons, both living and deceased.[2]

---

1 As at 5 June 2017, 1,806 claimant applications had been filed since 1993. National Native Title Tribunal (NNTT), *Search Native Title Applications, Registration Decisions and Determinations* (5 June 2017) National Native Title Tribunal <http://www.nntt.gov.au/searchRegApps/NativeTitleClaims/Pages/default.aspx>.
2 The NNTT and Federal Court are not alone in possessing such information; over the years, state governments and respondent parties have accumulated similar collections of native title records. The collections of state governments are likely far larger, as during mediations towards consent determinations, they are provided with copies of evidence such as connection reports and genealogies that are ultimately never submitted to the Federal Court or NNTT.

Native title records are exceptional in both scale and scope and are as unique as the property rights they evidence. As legal records, they are an account of the administration of justice, but they also have broader historical and cultural importance. Collectively, they tell the story of the implementation of one the most significant political interventions in colonial relations since 1788, when Arthur Phillip planted a British flag on the land of the Eora Nation at the place now known as Sydney Cove. Perhaps more importantly, they contain extensive documentation of Aboriginal and Torres Strait Islander peoples' families, histories and cultural practices in relation to land, tendered as proof of asserted rights and interests, and constitute a unique body of research that is not available elsewhere.

Indeed, the onerous evidentiary requirements of the *Native Title Act* have resulted in, albeit unintentionally, one of the most substantial government-sponsored research efforts ever undertaken with Indigenous Australians. At the outset, applicants are required to submit genealogical, cultural and historical information that demonstrates their traditional connections to land;[3] as proceedings progress to mediation or litigation, more detailed evidence is required to persuade both the Federal Court and respondent parties of the veracity of their claims.

How should native title records be managed into the future? Who should be able to access them, and for what purposes? Developing appropriate policies for the management and archiving of native title records is a necessary but onerous responsibility for the Federal Court and NNTT. Part of the challenge lies in the fact that such protocols must address two key imperatives that are not always compatible: the need to ensure public

---

3   Evidence is required to demonstrate that native title exists, as defined by s 223 of the *Native Title Act*, which states that:

>   The expression native title or native title rights and interests means the communal, group or individual rights and interests of Aboriginal peoples or Torres Strait Islanders in relation to land or waters, where:
>
>   >   (a) the rights and interests are possessed under the traditional laws acknowledged, and the traditional customs observed, by the Aboriginal peoples or Torres Strait Islanders; and
>   >
>   >   (b) the Aboriginal peoples or Torres Strait Islanders, by those laws and customs, have a connection with the land or waters; and
>   >
>   >   (c) the rights and interests are recognised by the common law of Australia.

confidence in the administration of justice and the need to respect the concerns of Aboriginal and Torres Strait Islander peoples in relation to personal or culturally sensitive information.[4]

Using the example of a series of research reports produced by the NNTT between 1995 and 2012, this chapter explores some of the intersecting legal and ethical interests that complicate the possibility of making native title records publicly available through either archives or publication. Rather than applying a strictly legal reading of what is or is not permissible, I advocate for a risk-based approach that prioritises the impacts of information management policies on Indigenous Australians and their relationships with others. Identification of attendant risks requires, I argue, meaningful consultation with relevant Aboriginal and Torres Strait Islander peoples and their informed consent for any mitigation strategies.

But is this practically achievable given the potential cost of undertaking consultation and the limited and ever-diminishing resources available to the Federal Court and the NNTT? An alternative approach proposed here is to ensure that native title records held by the Federal Court, the NNTT and the National Archives of Australia (NAA) are at the very least readily *discoverable*. Facilitating public discoverability as the first step in developing comprehensive management protocols will reduce the legal and cultural risks associated with unfettered public access while ensuring that native title records can always be found if and when they are wanted.

Weighing Up the 'Public' Interest

Any decision to make native title records publicly available requires consideration of a broader public interest. At first glance, the cultural, educational and historical significance of native title records implies a public interest that should be supported with public access. Yet the highly personal nature of much of the information these records contain, and the circumstances under which they were obtained, raise some very good reasons as to why their availability should, in fact, be limited.

---

4 Ian Irving, 'The Challenges of Managing Documents Related to Native Title Hearings' in Pamela Faye McGrath, Ludger Dinkler and Alexandra Andriolo (eds), *Managing Information in Native Title (MINT)* (Australian Institute of Aboriginal and Torres Strait Islander Studies, 2015) 53.

The 'public interest' is not a clearly defined legal concept, but, rather, is treated by the law as 'flexible enough to respond to the facts and circumstances of any particular case'.[5] When used in a statute, as it is in the *Native Title Act*, the term 'public interest' derives its content from 'the subject matter and the scope and purpose' of the legislation in which it appears.[6] Among the possible public interest matters that may be relevant in the context of native title, ensuring the proper administration of government and the promotion of open justice are among the most compelling.[7] However, the public interest must also be considered in relation to the subject, scope and purpose of the *Privacy Act 1988* (Cth) ('*Privacy Act*').

Further, there is a need for both privacy and the public interest to be considered against the cultural and customary concerns of Aboriginal and Torres Strait Islander peoples. Ultimately, it falls on the Native Title Registrar to decide on this balance.

Under the *Native Title Act*, the Native Title Registrar may keep other records and information as he or she considers appropriate, and make those records available to the public.[8] The Native Title Registrar must *not* make information available to the public if he/she considers that it would *not* be in the public interest to do so. And when considering the public interest, the Native Title Registrar must take into account 'the cultural and customary concerns' of Aboriginal peoples and Torres Strait Islander peoples.[9] The term 'cultural and customary concerns' is undefined in the *Native Title Act* and can reasonably be interpreted as potentially including concerns about the management of personal or culturally sensitive information.

This raises a critical question about the extent to which the interests of Aboriginal and Torres Strait Islander persons and peoples are usually accommodated within consideration of a broader 'public' interest. Aboriginal and Torres Strait Islander persons are undoubtedly members

---

5   Law Institute of Victoria, Submission 22, cited in Australian Law Reform Commission, *Serious Invasions of Privacy in the Digital Era*, Discussion Paper 80 (2014) 116 <https://www.alrc.gov.au/publications/serious-invasions-privacy-dp-80>.
6   *Hogan v Hinch* (2011) 243 CLR 506, [31], cited in Australian Law Reform Commission, above n 5.
7   For a list of common values, freedoms and matters of public interest, see Australian Law Reform Commission, above n 5, 30.
8   *Native Title Act* ss 98A (1) and (2).
9   *Native Title Act* s 98A.

of the public, but as a social category, they are a 'persistent minority'.[10] Persistent minorities rarely have their way in processes of democratic decision-making, which has profound consequences for their ability to 'make the larger world in which they live a home for themselves'.[11] In the words of Noel Pearson, it is the structural problem of the 3 per cent 'mouse' of Indigenous Australia contending with the 97 per cent 'elephant' of the rest of the population: 'The 3 percent can never really get the 97 percent elephant to behave in a way that treats the mouse with dignity as citizens'.[12]

It appears that the *Native Title Act* is in fact structured towards addressing this demographic disadvantage. The obligation for the Registrar to consider the cultural and customary concerns of Aboriginal and Torres Strait Islander people as a matter of public interest is clearly aimed at supporting Indigenous Australians to have a greater say over the fate of information about themselves, their families and their land. It follows that the assumption at the heart of this intention—namely that Aboriginal and Torres Strait Islander peoples are a segment of the Australian public whose interests, in this context, are to be given priority—should be a central consideration in the development of protocols for the management of native title records into the future.

But what does this look like in practice? Drawing on the lessons learned from developing management protocols for the NNTT research reports, I am advocating for a process that puts the opinions and perspectives of Aboriginal and Torres Strait Islander peoples at the centre of any analysis of the risks and benefits associated with creating public access to native title records. The discussion that follows does not reflect current NNTT or court policy in relation to managing and creating access to native title records.[13] Rather, it offers a particular perspective on the issues that is grounded in my many years of research and policy experience in this area.

---

10   Thomas Christiano, 'Democratic Equality and the Problem of Persistent Minorities' (1994) 23(3) *Philosophical Papers* 169.
11   Jeff Spinner-Halev, *Enduring Injustice* (Cambridge University Press, 2012) 133.
12   Noel Pearson, 'Keynote Address: An Agenda for Indigenous Empowerment' (Speech delivered at the Royal Australian and New Zealand College of Psychiatrists Annual Congress, Brisbane, 6 May 2015) 9 <http://capeyorkpartnership.org.au/news/an-agenda-for-indigenous-empowerment/>.
13   A small number of the research reports are subject to directions from a Tribunal Member restricting their disclosure made under s 94L or s 136GD of the *Native Title Act*. This special category of report requires a unique management regime and is not dealt with in any detail here.

The NNTT Research Reports

Among the many thousands of native title records held by the NNTT is a small but significant collection of 280 research reports that were produced by NNTT researchers (employees of the Australian Public Service) during the period between 1995 and 2012. These research reports were generally commissioned for one of two statutory purposes: to assist parties in relation to native title proceedings under s 78 of the *Native Title Act*; and to assist the NNTT with the mediation of applications under s 108(2) of the *Native Title Act*.

The research reports are substantial documents that bring together, often for the first time, copies of publicly available historical and ethnographic ('ethno-historical') sources about particular Aboriginal or Torres Strait Islander groups in relation to particular areas. The ethno-historical items they include were authored by many different kinds of people—explorers, anthropologists, linguists, pastoralists and the like—the vast majority of whom were non-Indigenous. Typically, the sources range from extracts of early maps of 'tribal' or 'language' boundaries, journals and field notes, mission and government records, books, newspaper articles and academic papers to published oral histories of Aboriginal and Torres Strait Islander individuals and families.

For each research report, the ethno-historical materials are accompanied by a summary chapter written by NNTT researchers. These provide background information about the authors of the ethno-historical materials and the circumstances in which they collected their data. Some of the summary chapters include focused discussion about specific matters of contention—for example, the location of a boundary between two groups or the identity of a local ancestor.[14]

The amount of information contained in the research reports is substantial. To give a typical example, a research report prepared in 2001 relates to three different native title groups and includes items spanning a time period of 102 years. Specifically, it contains:

---

14 Each summary chapter also typically includes a list of sources viewed but not cited and a bibliography. Some of these bibliographies have already been published by the NNTT as standalone documents and are currently available on the NNTT website (although the summary chapters themselves are not); see National Native Title Tribunal, *Publications* (2016) National Native Title Tribunal <http://www.nntt.gov.au/News-and-Publications/Pages/Forms-and-Publications.aspx>.

- a summary chapter of 52 pages
- 32 ethno-historical map appendices
- three maps showing relevant native title claims
- 33 ethno-historical document appendices, ranging between one and 30 pages in length.

This particular report also names 90 different Aboriginal persons, some of whom are still living, and includes numerous statements about the location of traditional territorial boundaries, sites of ritual significance and commentaries on the practice of culture and custom (including references to gender-restricted ceremonies). The unpublished ethno-historical sources included in the report came from five different archives located in four different Australian cities and previously published ones were obtained from a number of different libraries and secondhand booksellers.

With the hard work of locating, scanning and aggregating all this material already done, each research report provides immediate access to a research literature that, even though already publicly available, was previously out of reach to anyone without the necessary time, money and expertise to search for it themselves. In this sense, the potential value of the research reports to Aboriginal and Torres Strait Islander people and their researchers, lawyers and advocates, as well as respondents to their claims, cannot be understated. They are also of potential value to academics and members of the public who, for other reasons, are interested in understanding the indigenous social and cultural landscapes of particular areas.

That said, the research reports are not without their flaws. The ethno-historical materials they contain are not comprehensive and vary considerably in scope and quality. There are some national sources, such as Norman Tindale's *Aboriginal Tribes of Australia* and David Horton's *Encyclopaedia of Aboriginal Australia,* that are prominently featured in almost every research report, while other significant but less well-known and accessible materials are overlooked.[15]

---

15   A number of research reports include transparency maps showing the location of the underlying native title claim in relation to both Tindale and Horton's accounts of group boundaries; Norman Tindale, *Aboriginal Tribes of Australia: Their Terrain, Environmental Controls, Distribution, Limits and Proper Names* (University of California Press, 1974); David Horton (ed), *Encyclopaedia of Aboriginal Australia* (Aboriginal Studies Press, 1994).

Further, the analysis contained in the summary chapters does not take into account the perspectives of contemporary native title claimants. This was a deliberate decision on the part of the NNTT, aimed at ensuring that the objective neutrality of the NNTT was preserved and that the reports did not stray into the territory of providing expert opinion. As a consequence, the sources are presented without critical assessment of their reliability or the weight they should be given when considering any underlying native title rights.

The NNTT was alert to these shortcomings at the time they were drafted and acknowledged them with disclaimers that nicely highlight some of the attendant risks and benefits associated with their possible publication. Among other things, the disclaimers note that the research reports were prepared within short time frames, are not comprehensive, and that the inclusion of particular ethno-historical items does not constitute an endorsement of those items by the NNTT. Where the research reports contain names of deceased Aboriginal people or culturally sensitive information, warning statements are also included.

Despite these limitations, the research reports were, and remain, a valuable if sometimes problematic resource for claimants and respondent parties alike. The preparatory research undertaken for native title claims during the early years of the *Native Title Act* was extraordinary and involved intensive documentary discovery. Scores of researchers and traditional owners were simultaneously tasked with the job of locating and reviewing thousands of potentially relevant records. The demand on libraries, archives and museums was so intense that the Commonwealth Government funded the Australian Institute of Aboriginal and Torres Strait Islander Studies (AIATSIS) to establish a Native Title Access Unit to deal with the surge in requests from native title groups and respondent parties for searches of their collection.[16]

The NNTT research reports were of great assistance in this effort, saving everyone involved considerable time and money. Despite their variable reliability, they were useful for examining the factual basis of applications, preparing documentation for registration testing and negotiating boundaries between overlapping claims. A crucial starting point for native title applicants, they also provided reassurance to non-Indigenous

---

16 Copies of many of the ethno-historical materials included in the NNTT research reports were provided by the Australian Institute of Aboriginal and Torres Strait Islander Studies (AIATSIS).

respondent parties sceptical of the very fact of prior occupation ('yes, there is evidence that Aboriginal people actually lived here'). In light of this utility, the research reports were usually distributed widely to everyone involved in a matter—anthropologists, claim lawyers, respondents and state government officials alike.

They were especially valuable to researchers located in remote areas during the early years of native title when digital technologies had yet to become commonplace. When I worked as a researcher in the Tom Price office of the Pilbara Native Title Service in the early 2000s, Google was barely two years old, broadband internet was in its infancy and our unreliable dial-up connection was torturously slow. All the archives I needed to access for the claims I was researching were located many thousands of kilometres away in Perth, Adelaide and Canberra, and the native title representative body I worked for could only afford to employ a single historian, who undertook background research for more than 30 different claims. In these circumstances, the NNTT research reports were a godsend, providing my colleagues and me with access to crucial pieces of evidence that would otherwise have been beyond our reach.

However, these reports undoubtedly mean the most to those Aboriginal and Torres Strait Islander peoples whose histories are contained in their pages. For many groups, the research reports were the first time that a survey of ethno-historical sources about their people had been undertaken, and/or the first time they had access to these sources themselves. Far from being neutral documents, the collective knowledge they contain about country, culture, kin and the impact of colonial settlement affords them a degree of emotional and political power that resonates well beyond their original purpose. Their contents have the potential to confirm or deeply disturb an individual's fundamental sense of self and where they belong in the world, generating joy, grief, shame, anger and argument in turn and altering both an individual and shared sense of social reality. Disclaimers mean little in such circumstances. Rather, sensitive and respectful attention is required in the development of any plans for the future management of these valuable assets.

Managing Valuable Native Title Records

It is now 25 years since the first NNTT research report was produced, and there is a pressing need to have them archived. This requires consideration of, among other things, the level of public access allowed once they are lodged with the NAA. For many reasons, this will not be a straightforward undertaking.

The research reports remain sought-after assets, even though the NNTT has not produced a research report since 2012 and many of the older research reports are now effectively redundant because native title has been settled in the areas they discuss. They continue to be used by parties involved in native title proceedings, and every year the NNTT receives a number of requests for copies of existing reports from members of native title groups, their legal representatives, respondent parties and the Federal Court. Requests also occasionally arrive from other interested Aboriginal and Torres Strait Islander persons and members of the public. Once archived, such requests will also be received by NAA.

There are some significant differences in the obligations of the NNTT and the Federal Court in relation to archiving of legal records, despite an overlap in the records they hold (both hold some of the same kind of records, as well as records relating to the same proceedings).[17] The NNTT and the Federal Court operate under different NAA record authorities and are dealt with differently under the *Privacy Act*. Consequently, each organisation must develop its own approach to archiving and accessing native title records, and responsibility for developing management policies for the NNTT's research reports lies with NNTT alone.[18]

The NNTT's policy for managing access to the research reports has been revised a number of times over the course of the last two decades. At times, the research reports have been made widely available, including on the NNTT website, with little control over their distribution.[19] At other

---

17   Prior to legislative amendments to the *Native Title Act* in 2012, the NNTT was responsible for case management of native title claims and, therefore, both organisations are in possession of case management files. Similarly, as it currently stands, the NNTT undertakes registration testing for native title applications for which the Federal Court provides case management, leading to a situation where both organisations are in possession of records relevant to a particular matter.
18   Federal Court of Australia, *Annual Report 2014–15* (Federal Court of Australia, 2016) 21, 60 <http://www.fedcourt.gov.au/digital-law-library/annual-reports>.
19   Copies of some of the research reports are held in the AIATSIS collection.

times, a very cautious approach has been taken, and their distribution has been carefully controlled and monitored. The current NNTT policy deals with requests for access on a case-by-case basis, but, in principle, aims to provide native title groups and their representatives with all relevant information held by the NNTT. Facilitating access requests from members of the public is complicated by the absence of a direct interest.

Developing appropriate access protocols is an issue that NNTT continues to wrestle with. When I was appointed NNTT Research Director in 2015, I was given responsibility for reviewing the access policy for the research reports and developing a plan for their longer term management. Pre-armed with firsthand experience of their great utility and value as tools for native title researchers, I embraced the task with enthusiasm and immediately started exploring the possibility of making them more readily available, perhaps through open-access online publication. It seemed to me that such useful documents should be made more widely available and that this could be done in a way that encouraged self-service and reduced the administrative burden of the NNTT.

After 12 months of scoping the possibilities, delving into countless layers of legal, cultural and ethical complexity, I was prepared to admit that my initial enthusiasm for an 'open access' approach to publishing the NNTT research reports may have been pre-emptive. I had come to appreciate that, even though copies of most of the research reports are already in circulation and contain information that is already publicly available, increasing public access to these unique knowledge assets is not without risk. These risks are for the most part borne by Aboriginal and Torres Strait Islander people alone. Moreover, it has become increasingly clear that the attendant risks will not be effectively mitigated or resolved by simply applying a strict interpretation of what is legally permissible. A different approach is required that more fully considers the possible social impacts of the research reports within their home communities.

Assessing the Risks and Benefits of Creating Public Access

While most of the information contained in the research reports is freely available elsewhere, this fact alone does not diminish the potential risks associated with allowing public access to them, and the task of developing appropriate policies for their ongoing management has proven to be complex.

There is a degree of ambiguity in the *Native Title Act* that may be interpreted as providing for, or at least not preventing, public access to the research reports. As previously noted, the Registrar alone is empowered to make decisions about the provision of native title information to the public, and, when doing so, must take into consideration matters of public interest.

Given the historical and educational value of the research reports, there would seem to be a clear public benefit to making them available. However, the *Native Title Act* does not confer any specific *educational* purpose on the NNTT or Native Title Registrar, and the original purpose for which research reports were prepared was not educational. Nevertheless, the *Native Title Act* does not necessarily preclude publication of the research reports for educative or research purposes, and ss 78(1)b and 78 (2)(a) provide for the Native Title Registrar to provide assistance, including research assistance, to any person at any stage of a proceeding in matters relating to that proceeding.

But do the potential benefits of providing public access to these records for educational reasons justify the potential risks such access poses to Indigenous Australians? One way of approaching this question, I suggest, is to engage in a process of risk analysis aimed at identifying how the publication of native title records will impact on Aboriginal and Torres Strait Islander peoples and persons, their communities and their relationships with other Australians. The explicit intention of such an analysis should be to inform the development of policies that not only minimise risk but also empower and strengthen key relationships to fully realise the conciliatory intent of the *Native Title Act*.[20]

---

20 The preamble of the *Native Title Act* makes it clear that the intention of the legislation is to 'rectify the consequences of past injustices' and 'ensure that Aboriginal peoples and Torres Strait Islanders receive the full recognition and status within the Australian nation to which history, their prior rights and interests, and their rich and diverse culture, fully entitle them to aspire' and to 'further advance the process of reconciliation among all Australians'.

Risk management in government is a highly specialised area that is guided by its own set of rules and requires expertise in its own right.[21] The approach that I present here does not represent the current policy and practice of the NNTT or the Federal Court, nor is it a definitive assessment of all the attendant risks, their likelihood and/or their potential consequences. Rather, it sets out some basic principles of risk assessment that might be usefully brought to bear on the development of policies for the management of native title records.

A common approach to assessing risk involves applying a framework that identifies the possible consequences of a particular course of action, articulates the likelihood and severity level of risk for particular stakeholders, and develops strategies to mitigate those risks. Risk oversight and management are a key part of the corporate governance of both the Federal Court and NNTT. Both institutions are committed to an organisational culture that supports the identification, analysis, assessment, treatment, monitoring and review of all strategic, professional, reputational, personnel, political and operational risks. These include not only risks to the institutions themselves, but also to their stakeholders.[22]

Needless to say, when it comes to native title matters, it is Aboriginal and Torres Strait Islander peoples who are the primary stakeholders, and the strategic, reputational and political risks they face should be paramount in any consideration of the impacts of creating public access to native title records. This requires consideration not only of impacts internal to Indigenous families and communities, but also risks posed to Indigenous people's relationships with others. In the context of native title, those relationships are between Aboriginal and Torres Strait Islander individuals (as represented by their prescribed bodies corporate) and the rest of the world, with the NNTT and the Federal Court (as representatives of government) playing a central role in the mediation of that relationship.

To put it another way, the failure of relationships between native title holders and the NNTT or the Federal Court will have ramifications for the broader relationship between Indigenous Australians and government, and, as such, any actions that potentially undermine this relationship warrant thoughtful consideration.

---

21 The Federal Court and NNTT are guided in their approach to risk management by the *Australian/ New Zealand Risk Management Standard* (AS/NZS ISO 31000:2009) and the *Commonwealth Risk Management Policy 2014*. Federal Court of Australia, *2016–2020 Corporate Plan* (Federal Court of Australia, 2016) 39 <http://www.fedcourt.gov.au/about/corporate-information/corporate-plan>.
22 Ibid.

Even though they are just a fragment of the entire collection of native title records held by the Federal Court and the NNTT, assessing the risks associated with creating public access to the NNTT research reports is no small task. The risk profile of each research report will vary because each is unique in purpose, scope and methodology and deals with a distinct group or groups of Aboriginal and Torres Strait Islander peoples with their own unique laws and customs. And although much of the information they contain is already available elsewhere, and many of the native title proceedings they relate to have been finalised, the multidimensional nature of the information they contain means that there are potentially many legal and cultural issues to be considered. For the purposes of this paper, I focus on four: copyright, personal information, culturally sensitive information and out-of-date or inaccurate information.

Copyright

Copyright is perhaps one of the more straightforward issues to be considered in relation to making native title records publicly available. Nevertheless, for reasons explained below, copyright is a potential impediment to publication (ie, reproduction as opposed to access) and has a significant impact on the ability of the NNTT to reproduce the research reports in their entirety in a public forum.

As previously noted, the summary chapter of each research report is an original piece of work that is copyrighted to either the NNTT or the Commonwealth of Australia, and which the NNTT, therefore, has the right to publish. However, each of the appendices has its own unique provenance and copyright remains with the original copyright holder (except where they are out of copyright). The NNTT has never sought permission to use these materials for any purpose other than for their original purpose—namely, to assist with native title claim applications or mediations—and therefore, cannot republish them without first obtaining the permission of the copyright holder.[23]

---

23   The NNTT operates under the Federal Court's GovCopy licence. The GovCopy licence is for organisations that are not part of, or have not been authorised by, the Crown but are characterised as administrative bodies that are funded by taxpayers. Organisations with a GovCopy licence may use up to 10 per cent of copyright material. This includes reproductions and communications, including internal emailing and uploading of copyright material to intranets. For more information, see: Copyright Agency, *Your Organisation and Copyright* (2015) CopyrightAgency <http://copyright.com.au/wp-content/uploads/2015/05/CopyrightAgency_GovCopy_FactSheet.pdf>.

With the total number of appendices in the thousands, it is simply not feasible for the NNTT to seek permission to republish ethno-historical sources from all copyright holders. However, this does not preclude the possibility of making them publicly available through an archive, or publishing the summary chapters as standalone documents (as the copyright for these is held by the NNTT). Although the utility of the summary chapters would be somewhat constrained if they were published without copies of the ethno-historical items to which they refer, for some language groups they remain the only summaries of ethno-historical materials ever prepared and are potentially of value in their own right.

Personal and Sensitive Information

One of the more complex issues that arises when considering the consequences of creating public access to the research reports, and native title records generally, relates to the management of personal privacy. 'Personal information' as it is defined in the *Privacy Act* refers to information or opinion about an individual that enables that individual to be identified. 'Sensitive information' is a category of personal information that includes information or opinion about, among other things, an individual's racial or ethnic origin, political opinions and religious and philosophical beliefs.[24] The Australian Privacy Principles apply to this kind of information, regardless of whether the individual concerned is alive or deceased.

The research reports are replete with information that is of a personal nature. In some cases, they contain photographs of named individuals, living and deceased, and opinion about their racial origins. Others include lists of individuals named in ethno-historical sources, some of whom are still living, alongside facts about language and tribal affiliation. Needless to say, such information is related to the race, ethnicity, political attitudes, and religious and philosophical beliefs of those identified and falls under the category of sensitive information.

---

24 Office of the Australian Information Commissioner, *Australian Privacy Principles* (January 2014) Office of the Australian Information Commissioner <https://www.oaic.gov.au/privacy-law/privacy-act/australian-privacy-principles>.

As is the case with copyright, there are differences in the privacy obligations of the Federal Court and the NNTT in relation to the records they hold. The *Privacy Act* does not apply to documents and other materials relating to court proceedings; these are dealt with under the *Federal Court of Australia Act 1976* (Cth) and the rules made by Judges of the Federal Court. However, unlike the Federal Court, the NNTT and the Native Title Registrar are bound by the *Privacy Act* and the Australian Privacy Principles in relation to the collection, use, disclosure, management and access of personal information.[25]

The court has considered privacy issues specifically in relation to the NNTT research reports. They determined that, while it is clear that the NNTT may provide research reports to persons outside of the NNTT to assist with a native title application compatible with the *Privacy Act*, making research reports available to the general public involves a secondary purpose that *may* invoke the Privacy Principles. In light of this, the Federal Court's current Privacy Policy states that:

> The disclosure of [the NNTT research reports], in whole or in part, *may* be subject to the Privacy Act and/or specific directions made by the NNTT under section 94L or the former section 136F of the Native Title Act.[26] (emphasis added)

Given this legal uncertainty, one of the options open to the NNTT is to seek a public interest determination from the Information Commissioner in relation to the publication of the research reports.[27] This would provide clarity on the matter and, if publication were deemed to be compatible with the Australian Privacy Principles, would enable the NNTT to proceed with publication of the research reports indemnified against the risk of legal action over the publication of personally sensitive information.

---

25 Federal Court of Australia, *Privacy Policy* (31 March 2014) Federal Court of Australia <http://www.fedcourt.gov.au/>.
26 Ibid.
27 'A public interest determination (PID) may provide that an act or practice of an APP entity that could otherwise breach an Australian Privacy Principle (APP), or a registered APP code that binds that entity, shall not be regarded as having done so (s 72(2)). An APP entity undertaking that act or practice will not be taken to have contravened s 15 of the *Privacy Act* (or s 26A if an APP code)': Office of the Australian Information Commissioner, *Privacy Public Interest Determination Guide* (June 2014) Office of the Australian Information Commissioner <https://www.oaic.gov.au/agencies-and-organisations/guides/privacy-pid-guide>.

However, such indemnity does not mitigate the risks for those Aboriginal and Torres Strait Islander persons whose personal information is published. It is precisely in such a situation—where the legality of a particular course of action is unclear or ambiguous and does not adequately accommodate the risks of key stakeholders—that it is useful to shift the focus onto the relationships underpinning the proposed transaction, and the potential risks that any particular course of action poses to those relationships. The failure of the NNTT and the Federal Court to appropriately acknowledge and mitigate such risks may in fact undermine the level of trust between Aboriginal and Torres Strait Islander peoples and government (as represented in this instance by the NNTT and the Federal Court), and is a political risk in its own right.

Despite the fact that most ethno-historical sources used in the research reports are already publicly available, the potential for the personal information they contain to damage an individual's or group's reputations and relationships is very real. This risk is intensified by the fact that the research reports increase the ease with which such information can be discovered. Consider, for example, the potential impact of a single snippet from an ethno-historical source that identifies a particular ancestor as belonging to language group X, despite the fact that their descendants actively identify that person as belonging to language group Y. It won't matter whether the reliability of that particular 'fact' has been debated in court and found wanting; out of context and in the absence of detailed analysis of its veracity, that 'fact' has the potential to damage the status and standing of an entire family, both within their community and more broadly within the Australian society.

Not all native title records containing information of a personal and sensitive nature will carry such risks, and it may be the case that in some instances creating public access to the research reports would be welcome and celebrated by the Indigenous persons and native title groups concerned. But while there are certain kinds of information that are more likely to be of concern than others, there are no fixed criteria by which the likelihood of risk or consent can be predicted by a third party. The only way to identify the likelihood and severity of the substantive risks associated with exposing sensitive personal information for any particular matter is to consult the individuals directly involved; given the amount of personal and sensitive information contained in the research reports, this will be a time-consuming and expensive undertaking.

Culturally Sensitive Information

As with information of a personally sensitive nature, the task of identifying and mitigating risks associated with exposure of culturally sensitive information is a complex proposition. Bureaucrats employed by the Federal Court and the NNTT are generally not well placed to understand and assess the attendant risks and, as with personally sensitive information, consultation with relevant Indigenous parties will be required.

The types of culturally sensitive information that are commonly problematic in the public domain are relatively well-known and include, for example, the names or images of deceased individuals; references to male initiation practices; out-of-date terminology; and information that identifies the location of sacred sites. However, the great diversity of cultural practices and historical experiences among the many hundreds of Aboriginal and Torres Strait Islander groups around Australia makes it is impossible to predict the potential for any particular details to breach local cultural protocols.

The hurt individuals and families may experience as a result of the publication of culturally sensitive information is very real. Individuals' relationships with cultural information are profound, as are the possible consequences of failing to control its' distribution appropriately. Breaches of traditional law and custom in relation to cultural information may result in pain, anxiety, illness and, potentially, death, and the people deemed responsible for a breach may be punished by their community. The loss of information and authority in relation to both culture and country, in turn, undermines an individual's cultural status and impedes their ability to reproduce their traditions and, therefore, themselves in very fundamental ways.[28]

The significance of the impacts of exposure and loss of cultural information is underscored by a recent Federal Court decision in the Timber Creek native title compensation case. In 2016, the Ngaliwurru and Nungali peoples were awarded a *solatium* of $1.3 million for hurt arising from damage caused over the loss of their native title rights in an area of approximately 79 hectares in and around the town of Timber

---

28   Benedict Scambary and Gareth Lewis, 'Sacred bodies and ore bodies: Conflicting commodification of landscape by Indigenous peoples and miners in Australia's Northern Territory' in Pamela F McGrath (ed), *The Right to Protect Sites: Indigenous Heritage Management in the Era of Native Title* (AIATSIS Research Publications, 2016) 224.

Creek. Crucial in consideration of the *solatium* were multiple dimensions of social effect—namely, 'loss of amenities', 'pain and suffering' and 'reputational damage'. Central to the judge's decision was the hurt caused by a loss of cultural reputation among members of neighbouring groups and 'the sense of failed responsibility for the obligation … to have cared for … that land'.[29]

The consequences of exposing cultural information to the public can only be identified and assessed by people who are familiar with it and can contextualise its social effect. The only way to be certain that the publication of native title records containing cultural information will not have undue negative consequences is to seek advice directly from the Aboriginal or Torres Strait Islander people concerned. Consultation not only guards against potential hurt or pain, but it also puts control over cultural evidence back in the hands of the people to whom it belongs, reinforcing respectful relationships between Indigenous peoples and government and delivering on the basic intent of the *Native Title Act*.

Inaccurate, Incomplete or Out-of-Date Information

The final significant issue associated with creating public access to the NNTT research reports is that they can present a partial or inaccurate impression of the native title rights of a particular group if they contain out-of-date, incorrect or misleading information. The misunderstandings such information may perpetuate can have a significant impact on relationships and reputations, and can generate argument and conflict among and between individuals and groups.

The NNTT research reports were prepared for a very specific task—namely, to provide information to assist with the mediation and resolution of native title claims. They were designed to be used and considered alongside other forms of evidence—namely, the testimony of contemporary claimants. They were not written with a general public readership in mind, and as noted above are limited in scope and variable in quality. The inclusion of ethno-historical sources in the NNTT research reports is no endorsement of their reliability, and the most accurate and persuasive historical records for a native title claim will not necessarily have been included. Rather than a fulsome account, each research report

---

29 *Griffiths v Northern Territory of Australia (No 3)* [2016] 900 FCA 318.

offers only a glimpse of the reality of Aboriginal and Torres Strait Islander connections to country as understood through only a fraction of the total body of relevant evidence.[30] Additionally, as soon as there is any change to the status of the underlying claim, the research reports are effectively out-of-date and are unlikely to reflect the facts of native title as the Federal Court has subsequently determined them to be.

All of this makes for a knowledge asset that, despite its inherent value, is nevertheless highly problematic and open to misinterpretation. The possibility for NNTT research reports and other native title records to contribute to social conflict is often raised during public forums and private discussions about the management of native title information.[31] As an Aboriginal colleague who has been closely involved in her own family's native title claim explained:

> I have seen traditional owners have different views on research materials and in most cases have seen conflicts created due to the lack of proper understanding of the research material [in circumstances where] traditional owners and community doubt the reliability of the primary and secondary sources.
>
> All that [the research reports] provide is a snapshot analogy of cultural and historical bibliographic research that was done on their traditional country and I believe it gives a very marginal understanding of the authenticity of the research.[32]

---

30 This broader body of evidence would usually include oral testimony of claimants; genealogies; contemporary maps of boundaries and sites of significance; and difficult-to-obtain but more in-depth ethno-historical materials, such as anthropological field notes held in international archives. The Federal Court and NNTT do not hold copies of all the evidence that may have been submitted in relation to native title applications resolved by consent determination. However, state governments will hold copies of this material. Given the large number of native title claims to date that have been resolved through mediation rather than litigation, the collections of native title records held by state governments will be much larger than those held by the Federal Court and NNTT. They too, presumably, are struggling with the challenge of how to manage them.
31 For example, see proceedings of a workshop on native title information management hosted by AIATSIS in 2015; McGrath et al, above n 4.
32 Email to author, 10 February 2016. The source wishes to remain anonymous.

It is difficult to assess the likelihood of public access to the NNTT research reports or other native title records creating or aggravating social conflict.[33] In each instance, the possibility will be context-dependent and will be influenced to a great extent by the circumstances of those concerned at any given moment in time. Even if the likelihood of social conflict is low, the potential severity of its consequences warrants careful consideration as to whether the educational benefits that potentially flow from creating public access ultimately outweigh the associated risks.

That the contents of research reports may be unreliable, incomplete or misleading raises a compelling argument that on that basis alone they should *not* be made publicly available. That their publication may also contribute to social conflict and damage to the reputations of Aboriginal and Torres Strait Islander peoples and their relationships with others tips the scales even further in that direction.

Nevertheless, it should not be presumed that native title groups will always want to prevent the publication of NNTT research reports. The same colleague who raised concerns about their potential to generate arguments also expressed a belief that they should be made publicly available in some form so that traditional owners can use them to help locate, review and understand historical information relevant to their people and country.[34] The issue is, then, one of consent.

Informed Consent and the Need for Meaningful Consultation

On the face of it, the risks associated with creating public access to the NNTT research reports are likely much reduced because most of the information they contain is already in the public domain. However, this assumption fails to consider the circumstances in which that information was initially collected, and, in particular, whether free, prior informed consent for recording and distribution was provided by the original informants.

---

33 For further discussion of the generative role of native title research in social change and conflict, see Simon Correy, 'The Reconstitution of Aboriginal Sociality through the Identification of Traditional Owners in New South Wales' (2006) 17(3) *The Australian Journal of Anthropology* 336; Eve Vincent, *Against Native Title: Conflict and Creativity in Outback Australia* (Aboriginal Studies Press, 2017).
34 Correy, above n 33; Vincent, above n 33.

Since the introduction of the *Native Title Act* in 1993, many thousands of Aboriginal and Torres Strait Islander people have willingly shared information of a personal or culturally sensitive nature with third parties to progress their native title claims. However, the NNTT research reports also include cultural and personal information that was not collected with the consent of named individuals or groups. While this may not be an issue when using this information for a native title claim, it becomes one when it is to be made available for public use.

Determining the existence of prior consent requires examination of the expectations of the informants at the time that the information was originally collected. Establishing consent in circumstances where everyone involved in the original exchange—researchers and informants alike—may have long since passed away is especially difficult. Even when information has been more recently gathered and from a consenting individual for the express purpose of providing evidence for a native title claim, agreement to use that information for a secondary purpose—namely public education—cannot be assumed.

The impossibility of establishing consent does not negate the need for consultation with relevant persons or groups. Rather, circumstances where consent is either absent or ambiguous call for more, not less, consultation about the risks of making sensitive information publicly available. For although it may seem that any damage would already have been done as a result of someone else publishing the material, the *repetition* of that injustice may still impact directly on Aboriginal and Torres Strait Islander peoples.

What does a meaningful and effective consultation look like in the context of native title? In 2010, the then Aboriginal and Torres Strait Islander Social Justice Commissioner, Mick Gooda, suggested that at a minimum it requires that:

- consultation processes should be products of consensus
- consultations should be in the nature of negotiations
- consultations need to begin early and should, where necessary, be ongoing
- Aboriginal and Torres Strait Islander peoples must have access to financial, technical and other assistance
- Aboriginal and Torres Strait Islander peoples must not be pressured into making a decision

- adequate time frames should be built into consultation processes
- consultation processes should be coordinated across government departments
- consultation processes need to reach the affected communities
- consultation processes need to respect Aboriginal and Torres Strait Islander representative and decision-making structures
- governments must provide all relevant information and do so in an accessible way.[35]

Designing and implementing processes that pay heed to the above criteria and are agreed to by all parties will be neither straightforward nor quick. Key informants may have passed away or be difficult to locate, and other native title groups may hold divergent views about publishing ethnohistorical sources relevant to both. Similarly, descendants of a particular named individual may hold different opinions about how best to manage personal information about a shared ancestor. Like native title claims themselves, the process of figuring out the fate of the many thousands of records they have produced is likely to be a long and expensive one.

Discoverability: A Possible Way Forward

In the context of limited resources available for consultation and risk mitigation, how should the NNTT and the Federal Court proceed with the challenge of managing the research reports into the future?

One course of action would be to simply deposit them, along with all other native title records, with the NAA under the strictest possible access conditions. The disadvantage of this approach is that it limits the potential educational and historical value of native title records by making it very difficult for members of the public—Indigenous and non-Indigenous alike—to locate and access them. Of greatest concern is that traditional owners and prescribed bodies corporate who do not hold their own copies of these materials may have difficulty accessing them, as will other Aboriginal and Torres Strait Islander persons who, for whatever reason, are not actively involved in their relevant native title group.

---

35 Australian Human Rights Commission, *Native Title Report 2010* (Australian Human Rights Commission, 2011) 60.

One way to preserve the broader educative and historical value of native title records while minimising the risks associated with their exposure is to make them publicly *discoverable*, but not publicly *accessible*. By 'discoverable', I mean that information about what records exist and the conditions under which they may be accessed can be easily and readily found by anyone who is looking for them. This approach would ensure that until such time that meaningful consultation with individuals and groups can occur, circulation of the records themselves is limited but knowledge of their existence is not lost.

To this end, the NNTT has recently investigated the feasibility of creating an online map-based search tool that would enable users to generate bibliographies of native title research assets, including the research reports and the ethno-historical items they contain. Copies of the assets themselves would not be provided unless the consent of the native title group, identifiable persons and copyright holders has been obtained.

Online technologies and reliable standardised metadata will be crucial to the success of this strategy. Much of the contextual information currently contained in the research reports—namely, background information about the identity and qualifications of authors and the circumstances in which they collected their data—could readily be included in the metadata for each record, without risk of exposing personal or culturally sensitive information. This would assist the reader with assessing the reliability and relevance of particular documents without having to view the originals.

The ambition to create discoverability does, nevertheless, raise a critical question about the extent to which the act of collating and publishing metadata about native title records is in and of itself an act that requires consultation with Aboriginal and Torres Strait Islander peoples. The risks are certainly much reduced; however, any consequences will still be experienced almost exclusively by Indigenous Australians alone, suggesting some form of consultation—perhaps with prescribed bodies corporate and/or native title representative bodies—may be warranted before proceeding with this strategy.

Conclusion

All of the issues discussed above in relation to the management of NNTT research reports are relevant to the development of management policies for other types of native title records held by the NNTT and the Federal Court—for example, court transcripts, genealogies, preservation evidence and connection reports. Because these documents were created exclusively for native title proceedings and contain original historical, cultural and personal information unavailable elsewhere, these particular records are potentially of far greater value than the research reports. The potential benefits of making them publicly available will be greater, but then so too will the associated risks, and these risks will be disproportionately experienced by Aboriginal and Torres Strait Islander peoples.

In the development of policies to identify and mitigate these risks, the possible impacts of any particular course of action on the relationships and levels of trust between Indigenous Australians and government should not be forgotten. For when these relationships fail, it is invariably Aboriginal and Torres Strait Islander people who suffer. The recent report *Overcoming Indigenous Disadvantge: Key Indicators 2016* noted that 'stronger relationships between Aboriginal and Torres Strait Islander Australians and non-Indigenous Australians build and sustain mutual respect, while mutual respect contributes to stronger relationships—[it is] a virtuous circle'.[36] The report further noted that participation in decision-making was a key element of self-determination, which, in turn, is a critical part of governance. Effective governance, leadership and recognition of culture are essential to the social and economic development of Aboriginal and Torres Strait Islander Australians and have the potential to influence virtually all other indicators of wellbeing.[37]

If we recognise that a fundamental intention of the *Native Title Act* is to provide for the advancement and protection of Aboriginal and Torres Strait Islander peoples, and to progress the process of reconciliation among all Australians, then it is incumbent on those of us who are responsible for developing policy to put those interests and relationships at the centre of all decisions about the fate of native title records.

---

36 Productivity Commission, *Overcoming Indigenous Disadvantage: Key Indicators 2016* (Commonwealth of Australia, 2016) 7 <http://www.pc.gov.au/research/ongoing/overcoming-indigenous-disadvantage/2016#thereport>.
37 Ibid 25–6.

A robust approach to developing policy to assess and mitigate risks associated with creating public access to native title records is one that prioritises the interests of Aboriginal and Torres Strait Islander peoples. It is one that recognises that what is legally possible is not necessarily the most appropriate way forward, and, instead, invests in consultation towards achieving informed consent. However, where the resources are not available to facilitate this level of engagement, providing for public discoverability of native title records is a viable alternative that will ensure the inherent value of these precious knowledge assets is preserved until issues of public access can be resolved.

10

Archiving Revolution: Historical Records Management in the Massachusetts Courts

Andrew Henderson

Introduction

The Court as Archive Project is unique in its consideration of the records of Australian superior courts in centring the fundamental value of court records as more than simply a collection of process, but as a social and cultural archive. As the editors discuss in the introduction to this volume, historical court records have assumed an increasing significance as a primary source for researchers across a range of disciplines. Engagement with the substance of court records has opened opportunities to develop more diverse and more complete narratives of individuals' relationships with one another and with the state.

As an inheritor of English legal tradition, Australian courts share features with other former colonial possessions, including the practice and traditions of adversarial, common law courts of record. Therefore, international experience provides a valuable source on which to draw in the development of retention and maintenance practices.

As part of the process of drawing together those experiences for the Court as Archive Project, the experience of United States courts—particularly those of its oldest colonies—has become increasingly relevant.

Figure 1: Massachusetts Supreme Judicial Court, Boston, Massachusetts.

Source: Author's photograph.

10. ARCHIVING REVOLUTION

Massachusetts is one of the oldest colonies in North America, having been claimed by British adventurers in 1602, armed with letters patent from Queen Elizabeth I.[1] Massachusetts is also the landing site of the *Mayflower*, carrying the Pilgrims to the new world,[2] and the site of the 'shot heard around the world'[3]—the confrontation between British soldiers and colonial militia at Concord in Middlesex County—that heralded the War of Independence.

The lengthy history of Massachusetts courts and their establishment as courts of record means that their records of proceedings contain a wealth of information about the development and growth of the colony as part of a nascent United States. Hidden among the records of the Massachusetts courts are proceedings that include the names of a number of the United States' 'founding fathers', including John Hancock, Paul Revere, Samuel Adams and President John Adams; the biographical value of this collection, it has been argued, is 'difficult to exaggerate'.[4]

Although Massachusetts courts are much older than the Federal Court of Australia, they have confronted similar issues regarding records retention and the vexed question of what constitutes a 'significant' record that requires permanent retention. However, through a process of determining historical context, sampling and inspection, Massachusetts found that a definition of 'significance' was largely unnecessary.

'Significance': Context and 'Fat Files'

Two inspections conducted in the 1970s assessed the significance of Massachusetts courts records as one of several potential sources of historical and cultural information. Those inspections found that pre-1859 court forms contained important biographical information about the parties that, as a result of changes to the forms, was omitted after 1859. For records after 1859, the historical and cultural value of the record to researchers could be preserved by retaining only a small, random sample and an oversample of

---

1   John Stetson Barry, *The History of Massachusetts: The Colonial Period* (Phillips, Sampson & Co., 1855) 10. Interestingly, there was also a competing claim to Massachusetts by the Dutch East India Company under a Charter from William of Orange.
2   Ibid 80–1.
3   Ralph Waldo Emerson, 'Concord Hymn' in Edward Waldo Emerson (ed), *The Complete Works of Ralph Waldo Emerson* (Houghton Mifflin, 1904) 159.
4   Robert Brink, 'Deferred Maintenance of Court Records' (1980) 73 *Law Library Journal* 997, 1001.

any file larger than two inches in thickness or which had been the subject of an appeal. As a result of a large-scale sampling and inspection process, a determination of the 'significance' of a record did not require the physical inspection of every file, but a high degree of confidence could be taken that the larger the file, the more 'significant' the record was likely to be.

Despite now being more than 40 years old, the same process of random sampling and an additional oversampling of large files remains in place in Massachusetts today.[5] The practice is the subject of little complaint or comment. On occasion, researchers find that a record important to their research has been destroyed. However, the court's experience has been that the instances are rare and, when the practice is explained to researchers, it is accepted.[6]

This chapter provides an overview of the origins of the Superior Court's approach, adopted as a result of the Colonial Courts Record Project and, subsequently, the Superior Courts Record Project. It also draws together some of the lessons and concepts from both projects as a means of providing an analysis of how a project of this size came into being, and how it reached what many might consider an unusual approach to determining the question of 'significance'. In doing so, it suggests that Massachusetts courts' approach to the development and implementation of records retention practices may be valuable in approaching similar superior courts' collections in Australia.

Massachusetts Court Records: History in an Unbroken Line

The origins of the justice system in Massachusetts are almost as old as the colony itself. The *Research Guide to the Massachusetts Courts and their Records* goes as far as to argue that the justice system 'traces its history in an unbroken line' to 1630.[7] Until 1639, records of judicial proceedings were

---

5   *Supreme Court Judicial Rules* (10 February 1995), r 1.11; see also Executive Office Trial Court, *Guide: Trial Court Record Retention Schedule* (n.d.) Mass.gov <https://www.mass.gov/guides/trial-court-record-retention-schedule>.
6   Interview with Bruce Shaw, Director, Massachusetts Superior Judicial Court, Archives and Records Preservation (Boston, Massachusetts, 5 July 2017).
7   Catherine Menand, *A Research Guide to the Massachusetts Courts and their Records* (Supreme Judicial Court Archives and Records Preservation, 1987) 7.

'irregularly kept'.[8] However, in arguably one of the very earliest directions on the maintenance of judicial records in the colonies, the Massachusetts General Court directed that all evidence was to be kept 'to posterity'.[9] All courts, including a superior court to exercise the same powers of the Courts of Common Pleas in England, were subsequently re-established as 'courts of record' in 1691 when William III appointed a governor to the colony.[10]

The significance of 'courts of record' is discussed elsewhere in this volume.[11] However, the designation of Massachusetts courts as courts of record brings with it two important signifiers—one affecting the status of the court and the other affecting the status of its record.

First, and according to English practice at the time, Massachusetts courts transformed from being informal or ad hoc tribunals to adopting a permanent existence and developing a transparent and consistent body of law.[12] Second, and more importantly, in the context of courts as archives, the establishment of a perpetual record meant that the record's contents became immutable and incontrovertible. As early as the 13th century, the oral history of proceedings in the King's courts in England were considered to be authoritative and above question. With the advent of a written record, the same character was attached to those records. The court record was not required to be further proved or supported by reference to oral evidence.[13]

Despite the political upheaval of the War of Independence, and the successive realignments of colonial boundaries to both amalgamate[14] and then separate the colonies and, subsequently, states,[15] Massachusetts courts

---

8   Emory Washburn, *Sketches of the Judicial History of Massachusetts* (Charles C Little and James Brown, 1840) 89.
9   Ibid.
10 Ibid. Interestingly, the Governor was styled as a 'president' with a deputy president and elected assistants to provide advice, similar to an executive council.
11 See Chapter 1, this volume.
12 Enid Campbell, 'Inferior and Superior Courts of Record' (1997) 6 *Journal of Judicial Administration* 249.
13 SE Thorne, 'Courts of Record and Sir Edward Coke' (1937) 2(1) *The University of Toronto Law Journal* 24; Gaillard Lapsley, 'The Court, Record and Roll of the County in the Thirteenth Century' (1935) 51 *Law Quarterly Review* 299.
14 Alan Taylor, *American Colonies* (Viking, 1st ed, 2001) 277.
15 For a detailed account of the waxing and waning of Massachusetts' boundaries with the surrounding states, see Franklin Van Zandt, *Boundaries of the United States and the Several States* (United States Department of the Interior, 1966) 95.

have remained in a similar tiered structure.[16] The current Massachusetts General Law establishes a Supreme Judicial Court, an Appeals Court, a Trial Court (consisting of a series of specialist jurisdictions), a Superior Court and District Courts.[17] The establishment of each tier under the General Law places the administration of the court largely under the supervision of the court itself.

Record Retention in Massachusetts

By the mid-1970s, there were approximately 2.7 million court files stored in locations all over Massachusetts. No preservation or conservation work had been done on the materials, and there was no designated central repository. Clearly, the Massachusetts courts' extensive history contributed to the volume of the materials. At the same time, that history also meant that the records constituted an invaluable archive of economic, social and political disputes stretching back more than 200 years.

As a result of a substantial records inventory, assessment and sampling exercise, supervised by a board comprised of judges, historians and other scholars, the Massachusetts Superior Judicial Court[18] adopted a unique approach to the management of its records. Rather than developing a definition of 'significance' as a means of determining which files should be retained, the project found that the thickness of the file and whether it had been taken on appeal were the only consistent indicators of historical significance. Only those files that were greater than two inches in thickness, or were appealed, were recommended for permanent retention.

---

16 Menand, above n 7, 21.
17 *Massachusetts General Law* (MGL) ch 211, 211A, 211B, 212 and 218.
18 Michael Hindus, Theodore Hammett and Barbara Hobson, *The Files of the Massachusetts Superior Court, 1859–1959: An Analysis and a Plan for Action* (GK Hall and Company, 1979) (the 'Hindus Report').

Origins of Massachusetts' Records Management

The origins of efforts to adopt a structured approach to the management of court records in the United States can arguably be found at the intersection of two significant events during the 1970s: Chief Justice Burger's 'deferred maintenance' address and the consequent creation of the National Center for State Courts; and the bicentenary of the United States.

Deferred Maintenance

In 1971, President Richard Nixon and Chief Justice Burger of the United States Supreme Court spoke at the first National Conference of the Judiciary. The *American Bar Association Journal* acknowledged that the occasion was a rare one to have brought the head of the executive and the judiciary to the same conference platform.[19] Both the President and the Chief Justice addressed delays in the justice system and the need for reform to improve public confidence.[20] However, while the President's remarks were addressed to procedural reform, the Chief Justice adopted a different approach. Acknowledging that delays in litigation were something on which even Roscoe Pound had expressed concern,[21] he also drew attention to the ageing administrative practices of courts, particularly in the context of their records administration. Commenting specifically on the increasing complexity of litigation, Chief Justice Burger noted that:

> In terms of methods, machinery and equipment, the flow of papers ... most courts have changed very little fundamentally in a hundred years or more. I know of no comprehensive surveys, but spot checks have shown that the ancient ledger type of record books, sixteen or eighteen inches wide, twenty-four or twenty-six inches high, and four inches thick are still used in a very large number of courts. These cumbersome books, hazardous to handle, still call for longhand entries concerning cases. I mention this only as one symptom of our tendency to cling to old ways.[22]

---

19 'Williamsburg Cradles Another Revolution—This One in the Administration of Justice', (1971) 57 *American Bar Association Journal* 421.
20 Richard Nixon, 'Reforming the Administration of Justice' (1971) 57 *American Bar Association Journal* 421; Warren Burger, 'Deferred Maintenance' (1971) 57 *American Bar Association Journal* 425.
21 Burger, above n 20.
22 Ibid 427.

As a means of addressing the diverse methods of administration consistently, Burger proposed the development of a National Center for State Courts as a 'national clearinghouse or center to serve all the states and to co-operate with all the agencies seeking to improve justice at every level'.[23]

The National Center for State Courts (NCSC) that Burger had proposed commenced operation less than 12 months later.[24] Among its earliest projects was a survey of records management practices in state courts nationally.[25] The survey found that a large number of courts held records more than 100 years old, but that 'many states [had] allowed these records to be relegated to attics, basements, and closets with little selectivity and virtually no management'.[26] Importantly, the NCSC survey was subsequently submitted as a successful proposal for seed funding to undertake records management activities in courts to the National Historical Publications and Records Commission—the significance of which is discussed further below.[27]

Bicentennial Fever

The push for a better approach to the management of courts' historical records, in particular, was assisted by a significant historical milestone. The bicentenary of the United States in 1976 brought with it an enthusiasm for historical information, just as the Canadian centenary had done nine years earlier.[28] Planning began some 10 years before and, based on recommendations of the American Revolution Bicentennial Commission, the United States Congress established a national coordinating body—the American Revolution Bicentennial Administration[29]—and a number of institutions were gripped by 'bicentennial fever'.[30]

---

23 Ibid.
24 Warren Burger, 'The State of the Federal Judicary—1971' (1971) 57 *American Bar Association Journal* 855, 856.
25 National Center for State Courts, *Court Records Retention Survey and Guidelines Project Proposal* 627, cited in Brink, above n 4, 998.
26 Ibid 998; see also Robert C. Harrall, 'Court Records Management: "The Mitten" Revisted' (1976) 2(1) *Justice System Journal* 77.
27 Brink, above n 4.
28 Gabrielle Blais and David Enns, 'From Paper to People Archives: Public Programming in the Management of Archives' 31 *Archivaria* 101, 102.
29 Act of 12 November 1973, Pub Law No 73-179, 87 Stat 697 (1973).
30 Richard Baker, 'Reflections on the Modern History of Congressional History' in Glenn Gray, Rebecca Johnson Melvin and Karen Paul (eds), *An American Political Archives Reader* (Scarecrow Press, 2009) 6.

To mark the bicentenary, the American Association of Law Libraries (AALL) held its national conference in Boston with a focus on the legal history of the American Revolution and the management of historical records.[31] A number of speakers at that conference drew attention to the absence of a collected history of colonial administration as well as the value of the historical records that many institutions and private collections held.[32] However, they also emphasised the difficulty of building a complete picture of America's legal history, referring to the sources being contained in an 'immense and scattered mass'[33] and being 'diffuse'.[34] David Flaherty, who had published work on a history of Massachusetts as told through court records, noted that there was a significant inconsistency in the way in which court clerks had marked or catalogued court records across time, making it difficult for the historian to determine not only the content of the record but whether a particular record even existed.[35] He also noted that he had, in effect, had to travel to every colonial county seat to determine what records were available.[36]

In addition to the difficulty of locating material, concerns were also expressed about the manner in which valuable records were being kept. Records were being stored in basements and decommissioned cells in environments that did not suit long-term preservation. Speakers at the AALL conference also emphasised the need for a 'carefully planned and rigidly supervised program of housekeeping'[37] to ensure that materials did not continue to be lost as a result of age.

---

31   Amercian Association of Law Libraries, 'Association News' (1975) 7(1) *Newsletter* 1, 2.
32   Kinvin Wroth, 'Documents of the Colonial Conflict: Part I—Sources for the Legal History of the American Revolution' (1976) 69 *Law Librarians Journal* 277; Gerard Warden, 'Commentary on Sources for the Legal History of the American Revolution: Part II—Documents of the Colonial Conflict' (1976) 69 *Law Library Journal* 292.
33   Wroth, above n 32.
34   Morton Horwitz, 'Documents of Constitutional Development' (1976) 69 *Law Library Journal* 295, 296.
35   David Flaherty, 'The Use of Early American Court Records in Historical Research' (1976) 69 *Law Library Journal* 342.
36   Ibid 344; see also Michael Hindus, 'Designing Projects for Maximum Impact: Saving the Early Court Records in Massachusetts' (1979) 42(3) *The American Archivist* 307.
37   George Cunha, 'Preservation and Conservation of Legal Materials' (1976) 69 *Law Library Journal* 300.

THE COURT AS ARCHIVE

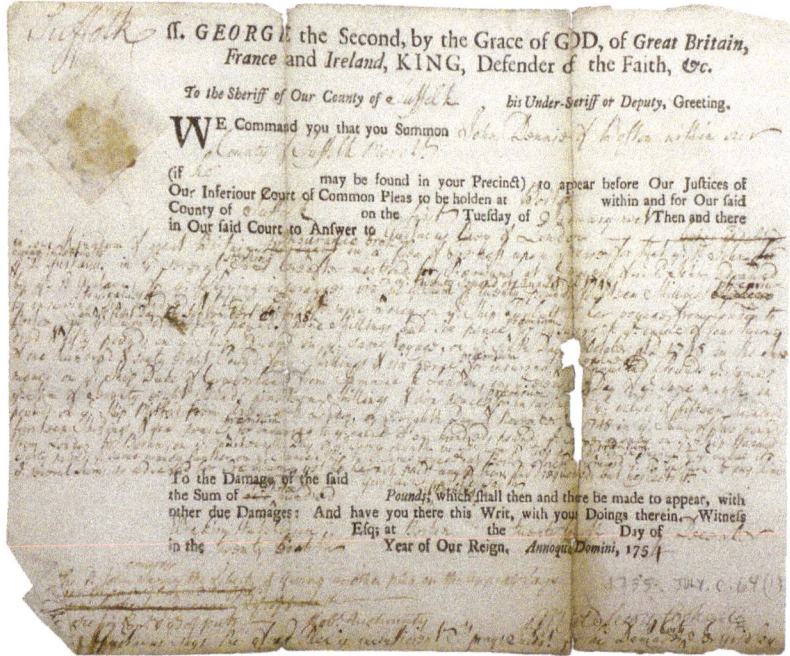

Figure 2: An example of court records held by Massachusetts courts—Writ of Summons dated 1775.
Source: Author's photograph.

A New Wave of Users

While the concerns of scholars and court staff about the scattered and imperilled historical records of Massachusetts courts are cited as the principal origin of the development of Massachusetts court record practices,[38] part of those concerns also related to the interests of a new and growing body of users. A lack of administrative structure is clearly a cause for concern, but it was not the objective in itself. Many of the concerns expressed by scholars related to their inability to find materials to support their research. Among court staff, it related to the inability to *help* researchers by finding the material for which they were searching.

The concerns of the materials' *users* rather than their keepers also reflected a new movement in archival and library management occurring at the same time, prompted, at least in part, by a renewed interest in history. The bicentenary introduced a new 'wave' of users to archives—genealogists

---

38 The Hindus Report, above n 18; Brink, above n 4.

spurred on not only by the bicentenary, but also by the broadcast of historical miniseries like *Roots* a year later[39]—and coincided with more popular awareness in North America of the availability of historical information.[40] Attempts were made to provide a more 'user-friendly' approach to archival records and to move away from the understanding of archives as the domain of the expert archivist, as had been the subject of debate among North American archivists during the 1970s and 1980s.[41] However, the impetus given to the public's interest in historical material by the bicentenary prompted a renewal of the debate.[42]

The National Historical Publications and Records Commission

Important for the development of a number of projects during the bicentenary was also the expansion in 1974 of the National Historical Publications Commission (NHPRC), which had been established in 1934, to now include records.[43] The expansion allowed the National Archives and Records Authority (the equivalent of the National Archives of Australia) to make funds available to state and private archival collections for their preservation—some of which was made available to Massachusetts courts.

Sampling and 'Significance'

The current records management practice was not the first attempt to introduce a method of structured record-keeping to the court's historical records. In 1976, the Colonial Courts Records Project commenced under the supervision of a judicial committee appointed by then Chief Justice Edward Hennessy to undertake a survey and inventory of the courts' records to be conducted by lawyer and legal historian Michael Hindus.

---

39 Heather MacNeil and Terry Eastwood, *Currents of Archival Thinking* (ABC-CLIO, 2nd ed, 2017) 229.
40 Ibid.
41 See, for example, Mary Pugh, 'The Illusion of Omniscience: Subject Access and the Reference Archivist' (1982) 45(1) *American Archivist* 33; Bruce Dearstyne, 'What Is the Use of Archives? A Challenge for the Profession' (1987) 50(1) *American Archivist* 76; Francis X Blouin Jr and William Wallach, *A Decade of Sponsored Research: The Research Fellowship Program for Study of Modern Archives* (University of Michigan, 1994) 17.
42 Edward Weldon, 'Lest We Forget: Setting Priorities for the Preservation and Use of Historical Records' (1977) 40(3) *The American Archivist* 295, 295; Howard Applegate, Richard Brown and Elsie Freigovel, 'Wider Use of Historical Records' (1977) 40(3) *The American Archivist* 331.
43 44 USC § 25 (1974).

The principal objective of the Colonial Courts Record Project was to locate, identify and microfilm the hundreds of thousands of scattered records for Suffolk County, within which Boston lies.[44] The project was supported by a grant from the NHPRC and eventually produced a survey of the records published in 1977: *The Records of the Massachusetts Superior Court and its Predecessors: An Inventory and Guide*.[45] Chief Justice Hennessy considered the project to be his most significant contribution as Chief Justice.[46]

The judicial committee responsible for the Colonial Courts Record Project recommended permanent retention of all pre-1859 files for two key reasons. The survey had identified some 40,000 cubic feet of records stored in various locations across the state. However, only 5,000 cubic feet contained pre-1859 materials.[47] The survey suggested that the change in volume was due to changes in the administrative practice of courts and the legal profession. The advent of printed forms, rather than bespoke process, meant that the rate at which material could be produced had increased.[48] It also suggested that the increase in volume, particularly in the early 20th century, appeared to relate to motor vehicle torts—a cause of action previously unknown.[49] Storage requirements for pre-1859 files were, therefore, significantly less onerous.

Second, from about 1859 onwards, the practice of Massachusetts courts changed so that court records contained substantially less sociological and biographical data. Pre-1859 materials commonly contained addresses, gender, occupational and other data that made them a valuable and unique source. Post-1859, that data was omitted but was also available from a range of other sources.[50]

The Colonial Courts Record Project and the survey provide some important direction and advice about the scoping of any form of management strategy. First, the records need to be seen in a much broader context

---

44   Interview with Bruce Shaw, Director, Massachusetts Superior Judicial Court, Archives and Records Preservation (Boston, Massachusetts, 5 July 2017).
45   Michael Hindus, Superior Court of Massachusetts and Judicial Records Committee of Massachusetts, *The Records of the Massachusetts Superior Court and its Precedessors: An Inventory and Guide* (Archives Division Office of the Secretary of the Commonwealth, 1978).
46   Interview with Bruce Shaw, Director, Massachusetts Superior Judicial Court, Archives and Records Preservation (Boston, Massachusetts, 5 July 2017).
47   Hindus, above n 45.
48   Hindus Report, above n 18.
49   Ibid.
50   Ibid 7.

than simply a collection of process; it is a social archive. Approaching the initial assessment of the records process from the perspective of the *value* of the records from *different perspectives* rather than an inward-looking assessment of importance to the court or legal history is fundamentally important.

Supporting this assessment is a sound understanding of the content of the records not in isolation but in connection with other archives. The 1977 survey identified the content of pre-c1859 records as unique in telling a much wider story about the colony and state as a whole. From the perspective of the Australian Federal Court, it is arguable that the management of native title court records, their uniqueness having been explored in other chapters in this volume, and acknowledged in the Federal Court's existing Disposal Authority, fall within the same category.

A Proposal for Sampling

While the judicial committee responsible for the 1977 survey had recommended a clear approach to pre-1859 records, it made no recommendations about the much larger collection of post-1859 materials. However, rather than leaving the matter, the committee chose to undertake a further project to determine what to do with the more recent records.

The Superior Courts Records Project began in 1977, still under the supervision of the judicial committee but now to be conducted by a larger team including Michael Hindus, lawyer and historian Theodore Hammett and historian and sociologist Barbara Hobson. The project's objective was to attempt to find a way to rationalise the large body of post-1859 files in a cost-effective manner that would not devalue the collection for researchers. Very early on, the committee agreed to a process of 'selective retention',[51] but which files to retain and which to keep was a sensitive question.[52]

What is important about this observation of 'sensitivity' is that one of the underlying concerns of the committee and the court was the level of risk that both were prepared to accept: by destroying a certain proportion of

---

51 The Hindus Report notes that 'this is, of course, a euphemism. We use this term to refer to the destruction of files': ibid 5.
52 Ibid.

files, historically significant material would be lost. That is, the committee and the court had made the initial, fundamental decision that everything could not be kept and that material would clearly have to be destroyed. Therefore, the project's objective was to find a point of compromise. How much historical material were the committee and the court prepared to lose in the interests of managing such a massive collection before the risk and rate of loss became unacceptable?

Hindus and his co-authors proposed a method of selective retention based on a sampling methodology: a random sample was proposed to be taken from the collected body of files with the balance to be destroyed. Underpinning this approach was the concept that by selecting an appropriate sample, conclusions could be drawn about the population as a whole.[53]

A random sample was selected from two counties—Suffolk and Hampshire—based on a randomly generated set of file numbers. The choice of counties was deliberate: Suffolk being predominately urban (it includes Boston and other major urban centres) and Hampshire being predominately rural.[54] The sample was split again across civil and criminal matters as being substantively different classes of matters with different characteristics.[55]

A randomly generated set of numbers was chosen instead of a set number series from each period or a sample from specific jurisdictions to avoid distorting the sample. For example, Hindus notes that if a predetermined number range were used, it would skew the sample towards a particular period.[56] File numbers tend to be assigned in all courts in numerical order so to set a range would, consequently, predetermine a period in time.

The sampling methodology also took into account the volume of matters and historical interest. Once the number of post-1859 matters was identified, a total sample size was selected that would provide a statistically significant result. However, a sliding scale of the proportion of matters within years was also identified. Hindus notes that this was done for two reasons: older matters were considered by the committee to be of greater value and, because the total number of matters commenced in the

---

53   Ibid 42.
54   Ibid 45.
55   Ibid.
56   Ibid 13, 42.

Massachusetts Superior Court increased over time, a smaller proportion could be taken while producing a similar number of physical files as for earlier years.[57]

This approach, as an alternative to the physical of *every* file, has some clear advantages. It is clearly more time- and cost-effective. However, Hindus acknowledges that it may not be appropriate for all matters or all jurisdictions. For example, Hindus notes that while undertaking the project, the committee was also approached for advice on sampling with respect to probation files. Ultimately, sampling was not recommended based on the absence of important identifying information, which would allow a sample to be taken as representative of a set, the unique nature of the records and their sensitivity.[58]

Therefore, the application of a sampling methodology as a starting point for determining an approach to selective retention is not entirely random. As Hindus explains, the nature and size of the collection need to be considered and understood at the very start. Factors such as geographical, temporal and jurisdictional spread need to be taken into account in determining the overall size of the sample, and this cannot be done without adequate identifying data. Within that spread, factors such as the increase in total filings or filings of a particular type need to be identified and taken into account in setting the parameters of the sample.

However, once those parameters are determined, then the method of selecting the sample needs to be as random and objective as possible. For example, Hindus and his team used a random number generator to determine file numbers within the predetermined objectives. The advantage here is to avoid skewing the nature of the sample. In such a sensitive context as the preservation of records in which members of the committee may have an interest, it also avoids skewing in favour of individual members' interests that, ultimately, might not be representative of, or shared by, researchers 10, 20 or 50 years later.

---

57 Ibid 13.
58 Ibid 14.

Testing the Sample: Historical Significance Within the Sample

As acknowledged earlier in this chapter, the process of selective retention requires an assessment of, and compromise on, the risk of the 'wrong' records being destroyed. As a means of testing the sampling process and providing a sense of what Hindus refers to as 'comfort' to the committee responsible for supervising the project, the project took the additional step of developing a methodology to determine how many records contained information of real historical interest.

Eighty-two different variables were established as a means of identifying the characteristics and historical significance of each file. The codes, signifying important legal, social, historical and cultural factors, were determined by a committee composed of nine scholars prominent in the fields of legal history, social history, criminology, law, demography, minority history and statistics.

For example, in relation to civil files, codes were assigned to the basic information of jurisdiction, the identity of the plaintiffs and the defendants (grouped by social or economic interest) and the cause of action. Additional codes were assigned to reflect the procedures on the file (eg, claim, counterclaim and appeal) and, very simply, its size. A third set of codes was then applied to identify historical elements of interest (eg, if the matter dealt with issues of ethnicity, race, labour or family).[59]

The process also allowed for an overall rating of historical interest based on a simple low-to-high scale. The variables upon which this ranking could be based were not listed to remain flexible, but might include variables such as social context, detailed descriptions of social practices or the political context within which a matter was occurring.

Hindus and his co-authors acknowledge that, while the process of settling on a list of codes and assigning them to files was as robust as it could be made, it cannot be argued that a different group of scholars, or even different scholars, may have agreed on the same variables.[60] This is a weakness in the process. However, the broadly representative nature of the committee, looking outside just the judges and court staff, and,

---

59 Ibid Appendix B.19.
60 Ibid 59.

thereby, reflecting a much broader range of perspectives, arguably makes the list of codes more defensible. The importance of the contents of the file was not being determined from a purely legal or administrative perspective, but, at the same time, those elements were not ignored.

While the initial sample identified was up to 6,000 files, time constraints and the amount of material on some files meant that, ultimately, a sample of 3,500 files was inspected—1,422 criminal files and 1,968 civil files— and the variables present in the files identified.

Once the files were coded for characteristics and significance, the project was then able to produce data on the extent to which the sample, and, therefore, the complete collection of files, held material of historical value. Surprisingly, the sampling process revealed two key findings:

- Only 6.8 per cent of sampled civil files and 8.1 per cent of criminal files were of historical interest, and the majority (4.6 per cent and 6.6 per cent, respectively) were ranked of 'low' historical interest.[61]
- Out of the 82 different variables, the study found that the size of the file (literally thickness), whether the matter had been taken on appeal to a superior court and (in the case of civil matters) whether the matter was one in equity were the only consistent indicators of historical interest.[62]

Implementing Hindus: Summary and Lessons

As discussed earlier, the results of the Superior Courts Record Project and the recommendations of the Hindus Report were consequently adopted as records retention policy in Massachusetts and continue to be applied today.

However, the Hindus Report was also written with the intention of providing a set of principles or practices for courts to follow in emulating the records management practices of the Superior Court of Massachusetts.[63] While the methodology is summarised in this chapter, there are some broader lessons and concepts that also need to be taken into account.

---

61   Ibid 62, 66.
62   Ibid 62, 64, 71.
63   Michael Hindus, Theodore Hammett and Barbara Hobson, 'Preface' in ibid.

The Importance of Timing

The management of historical court records, both in Massachusetts and across the United States, was not something on which the courts or the NCSC had haphazardly or accidentally focused in the early 1970s. As Chief Justice Burger and the AALL had highlighted, courts' records were generally in a parlous state by the early 1970s and management had remained fundamentally unchanged 'for a hundred years or more'.[64]

Records and records management was therefore hardly a new issue or problem. However, what appears to provide the motivation for it to be addressed is increasing community awareness of the value of the courts' records, driven by external events coupled with an acknowledgement by courts of the value of their records to the community as a whole. Massachusetts was able to take advantage of Chief Justice Burger's call for the establishment of a National Center for State Courts and additional resourcing from the NHPRC to give impetus to its own efforts.

In the context of the records of Australian superior courts, it is difficult to identify an event or events that might provide the same level of national focus and motivation as the country's bicentenary. However, given the nature of the Federal Court's collection of materials in particular, events such as the 30th anniversary of the *Mabo* decision[65] or the introduction of the *Native Title Act 1993* (Cth) might provide the basis for a renewed focus by the community and by the government on the value of those materials.

Nevertheless, there is an important and perhaps perennial issue bound up within the issue of timing, which is also worth noting.

Content and Purpose of the Records

The development of a records management policy for Massachusetts courts was not something that was compelled or forced by the bicentenary or the clamour of researchers. Just as with Australian Commonwealth courts, Massachusetts courts are constitutionally separate from the other arms of government, and any decision to change its practices was required to be made by the courts themselves. What is critical to understanding how comprehensive the process becomes is the overall commitment by the courts to that process.

---

64 Burger, above n 20.
65 *Mabo v Queensland (No 2)* (1992) 175 CLR 1.

As noted above, while the initial Colonial Courts Records Project was prompted in part by an acknowledgement that administrative practices needed to change simply as a matter of efficiency, it also acknowledged the value of court records to the community as a whole. That is, the project, survey and Hindus Report all acknowledged that the records were more than merely records of process, but were also invaluable historical, social and cultural records that might form part of a larger narrative about the colony, state and, ultimately, the nation. For example, the former Director of Archives and Record Preservation at the Massachusetts Superior Court, Bruce Shaw, notes the purpose of court records retention is not 'warehousing dead and static paper', but the retention of materials that 'are living historical documents'.[66]

This acknowledgement is also evident in some of the decisions made about permanent retention. For example, the decision to preserve pre-1859 records was in part made on the basis that as biographical (and not process) records, they formed an invaluable part of a wider narrative, whereas other elements of a resource 'community' took up the same story after 1859.

It is also evident in the decision that the project and the Hindus Report be overseen by a committee drawn from a diverse array of interests. It is not only the diversity of interests that is important. It is also that the process of drafting rules about the records to be retained was overseen rather than conducted by that committee. This is an important distinction. To have the same committee review samples or attempt to develop a definition of 'significance' rather than to review the outcomes of the sampling process avoids compromise or confusion in decision-making and drafting.

In the context of the Australian Federal Court's records, there is a need to acknowledge that its records have more significance than simply a record of process. As is discussed elsewhere in this volume, the records have the same historical, social and cultural value, and the same integral role as a part of a larger narrative, as the records of Massachusetts courts. However, that acknowledgement must also come with an understanding that to determine how to approach the management of that resource, lawyers and judges represent only one perspective.

---

66   Interview with Bruce Shaw, Director, Massachusetts Superior Judicial Court, Archives and Records Preservation (Boston, Massachusetts, 5 July 2017).

Significance and Sampling

One of the most challenging aspects of the Hindus Report and the implementation of Massachusetts record management practice is the seemingly simplistic manner in which the issue of 'significance' was ultimately determined. Without context, the practice of random and oversampling based on physical size of files can appear to be only a few steps above simply tossing files down a set of stairs and keeping those closest to the top.

However, as has been summarised in this chapter and is discussed at length in the Hindus Report, the manner in which the practice was developed was based on an understanding of the nature of the records being surveyed and objective testing of the proposed method against a substantial section of the existing files. Put another way, the random sampling of files was not a practice arrived at randomly.

As noted much earlier in this chapter, the practice is, and has been, the subject of little complaint and even less discussion. It was also one developed by taking into account the nature of the records themselves. Hindus and his co-authors acknowledge that the same methodology may not be appropriate for every set of records. This is very similar to the decision taken, for example, by the Federal Court of Australia to keep *every* native title court file but to keep only a smaller proportion of other matters.[67]

However, there is a further interesting sidenote to the Hindus Report that reinforces the extent to which a similar process might apply. In an Appendix to the Hindus Report entitled 'Historical Interest and the Front Page', Hindus and his co-authors discuss steps taken to address concerns that had been expressed by the committee overseeing the project that the sampling process would lead to the destruction of matters of 'unusual interest'.[68]

As a means of assessing the extent to which matters that might have been the subject of significant community or media interest, the Hindus Report reviewed front pages of the *Boston Globe* for 1933 and traced matters mentioned through the Superior Court's files. What the process identified was that the focus of media attention was predominately on

---

67   Records Authority No 2010/00315821, Federal Court of Australia (FCA), 19 October 2011.
68   Hindus Report, above n 18, 185.

criminal matters, which was not representative of the bulk of the court's overwhelmingly civil work. Second, and perhaps importantly for public organisations with limited resources, the process of historical media review and tracing was found to be time-consuming and labour-intensive, particularly in the case of matters that might have a number of related proceedings.[69]

Ultimately, there are no recommendations made about retention practices and 'unusual interest'. That is not to suggest that a court considering a similar approach might not find a need to address media interest. One of the issues identified in the Hindus Report, though, is the demand of a historical media review. However, in relation to current or prospective records, the same issues would not be applicable. A current or prospective matter might be marked for permanent retention as a result of ongoing media discussion.

What the Hindus Report does warn against is the potentially distortive effect of relying on media attention as an indicator of significance. One of the key concerns of the Hindus Report was to ensure that the sample taken was truly representative of the work of the relevant court. As a result, a larger sample of civil matters compared to criminal matters was taken, as well as a smaller proportion of modern proceedings, given the similarity of their content. The case file numbers selected for any one year were also randomly generated to avoid taking a sample that reflected any one part of a legal year than another.

The distortive effect of media attention is something that needs to be considered in the context of the work of each court to which a similar methodology might be applied. The Federal Court of Australia, for example, has a diverse jurisdiction. To the extent that media interest was to be taken into account in a determination of significance, it would be necessary to review that criterion in terms of the effect that it has on the sample collected for any particular year. In a year in which there is a large degree of media focus placed on television broadcast rights[70] or the enforcement of intellectual property rights against 'torrent' downloading websites,[71] care needs to be taken to ensure that it does not produce a sample of matters that are not representative of the work of the court as a whole.

---

69 Ibid 186.
70 *Seven Network Ltd v News Ltd* [2007] FCA 1062.
71 See, for example, the extensive litigation leading up to *Dallas Buyers Club LLC v iiNet Limited (No 5)* [2015] FCA 1437.

Washing Records: Record Preservation versus Record Retention

What is not apparent from the work discussed in this chapter and the implementation of the Hindus Report's recommendations is the substantial commitment that Massachusetts was required to make not only to the proper identification of records, but also to the process of their physical preservation.

Although discussed as early as the 1970s, the poor physical state of court records was as much of a concern to researchers as the poor identification of their location.[72] The former Director of Archives and Records Preservation at the Superior Judicial Court noted that from the start of the Colonial Courts Record Project, it was necessary not only to identify where records were kept but also to begin a process of repairing and preserving those records.[73] Consequently, Archives and Record Preservation has a large document-preservation facility in the Superior Judicial Court Building.

Figure 3: Document preservation facility, Superior Judicial Court.
Source: Author's photograph.

---

72 See, for example, Brink, above n 4; Harrall, above n 26; Wroth, above n 32.
73 Interview with Bruce Shaw, Director, Massachusetts Superior Judicial Court, Archives and Records Preservation (Boston, Massachusetts, 5 July 2017).

Archives and Records Preservation has continued to work on the painstaking process of preservation since the 1970s, and continues on that work today. By virtue of the sheer volume of materials, the process of recovering and repairing records means that the end of the process may still be some years away.

The effort required in the case of Massachusetts records is principally the result of almost 200 years of inattention—a problem that the Federal Court of Australia does not face. However, what the experience of Massachusetts does highlight is that the practice of records retention, and their acknowledgement as a valuable source, does not stop at the point of selecting records but incorporates everything required to maintain that record permanently. The National Archives of Australia has the necessary expertise and facilities to ensure that that occurs. However, while a decision on 'significance' by the Federal Court is outstanding, and records remain in its possession, there is a need to ensure that appropriate steps are taken to ensure those records' physical integrity before additional remedial measures are required.

Conclusion

As examples of English colonial legal systems, the United States and Australia share a common heritage. They are steeped in the concept of superior courts' records providing a perpetual and incontrovertible record of their contents. Both legal systems also share aspects of a common experience in developing awareness of the wider significance of those records as a social and cultural resource. Although the origins of Massachusetts courts and the Federal Court are separated by almost 300 years, that same common experience is nevertheless evident.

As this chapter has endeavoured to summarise, because of internal and external pressures, Massachusetts courts were compelled to find a way of balancing the value of their collected records with the administrative and financial cost of simply retaining everything. The practice adopted of random sampling and oversampling based on the physical size of a file might, on first look, appear to be haphazard and potentially dangerous in terms of the potential loss of important historical material. However, what this chapter has attempted to make apparent is that the current practice developed based on an understanding of Massachusetts courts' role as part of a larger narrative of the nation's history—both in terms of those records that might not be found elsewhere and those records in which information might be duplicated.

It would also be incorrect to assume that the practice equates significance to size—it does not. Through a careful survey and sampling process, Massachusetts has been able to identify that, in that particular jurisdiction, file size provides a clear and consistent indication of the potential significance of that record into the future.

What this chapter does not suggest is that another court, seeking to apply Massachusetts' experience, adopt file size as an indicator of significance. What is instead required is a careful sampling and survey of records to determine what indicators might provide the same level of confidence and consistency in identifying appropriate records for retention as a permanent archive.

11

Sentencing Acts: Appraisal of Court Records in Canada and Australia

Trish Luker

Introduction

In archival theory and practice, sentencing is the process of identifying and classifying information, potentially resulting in its destruction. It is a surprising homonym to judicial pronouncement of criminal punishment, despite the emotive association with censorship and book burning. In archival science, as in law, sentencing is the result of evaluative judgment. In the case of archival science, these judgments about historical and social value, institutional accountability and resourcing have a powerful impact on social memory because they determine which 'creators, functions, and activities in society will be represented in archives'.[1]

In the practice of archival appraisal, records are sentenced in accordance with a disposal authority—a documented appraisal framework for decisions about preservation or disposal of records. However, disposal does not necessarily mean that the records are destroyed; it may mean that they are transferred to another institution or even to a national archive to

---

1 Terry Cook, 'Documenting Society and Institutions: The Influence of Helen Willa Samuels' in Terry Cook (ed), *Controlling the Past: Documenting Society and Institutions—Essays in Honor of Helen Willa Samuels* (Society of American Archivists, 2011) 2.

be retained. Particularly from the mid-20th century, the proliferation of documentation resulting from bureaucratisation and rapid technological developments has meant that 'choices had to be made about what to maintain'.[2] It is now generally acknowledged that not all records can, or should, be preserved and that resources should not be wasted on keeping records longer than necessary.

In Australia, federal government agencies cannot dispose of records without authorisation from the National Archives of Australia (NAA).[3] This is also the case in Canada, where permission for destruction of Canadian government records must be obtained from Library and Archives Canada (LAC).[4] However, in both jurisdictions, courts are subject to archives legislation only to a limited extent,[5] resulting in uncertainty about responsibilities and rights in relation to court records. In the absence of obligations under archives legislation, courts have drawn on a range of frameworks to make decisions about preservation and disposal, including legal principles and obligations, information management requirements, administrative needs and constraints, and jurisdictional obligations. However, attempting to reconcile these (sometimes competing) obligations has resulted in incoherent and inconsistent decisions about preservation and disposal of records. In some instances, it has also resulted in contentious public debates, legal conflict and litigation.

This chapter considers the role of courts as archives through an examination of approaches to appraisal and disposal of court records. Drawing on fieldwork conducted in Canada and Australia, I will demonstrate how superior courts of record in these jurisdictions have attempted to address their legal and institutional responsibilities, to varying points of resolution. I begin by identifying a number of disputes over the preservation and destruction of records from legal inquiries and court processes, drawing

---

2   Sue McKemmish, Barbara Reed and Michael Piggott, 'The Archives' in Sue McKemmish, Michael Piggott, Barbara Reed and Frank Upward (eds), *Archives: Recordkeeping in Society* (Centre for Information Studies, Charles Sturt University, 2005) 175.
3   *Archives Act 1983* (Cth) ('*Archives Act*'). Section 6(1) of the Act gives the NAA power to authorise the disposal or destruction of Commonwealth records; s 24 gives agencies responsibility for destruction, transfer or alteration of Commonwealth records, subject to the authorisation of the NAA.
4   *Library and Archives Canada Act*, SC 2004, c 11, s 12(1) ('*Library and Archives of Canada Act*').
5   In Australia, the *Archives Act* s 19(1) specifies that the legislative provisions concerning Commonwealth records, including disposal and destruction, do not apply to records in the possession of a court or court registry, unless Regulations so provide. In Canada, the *Library and Archives of Canada Act* applies only to government institutions, as defined in the *Access to Information Act*, RSC 1985, c A-1, Schedule 1. No courts are covered by this legislation.

on examples from the Australian and Canadian contexts. These disputes highlight the importance of some of the questions posed by the Court as Archive Project; questions that courts in both jurisdictions have been attempting to grapple with over recent years. What responsibilities do courts have, as institutions of legal authority and record, to preserve, curate, store and provide access to records of their adjudication? What principles should guide and determine appraisal decisions about what to keep and what to dispose of? How should courts balance the (sometimes competing) obligations to the principle of open justice and litigants' right to privacy and confidentiality? Are some court records so significant as to be preserved in perpetuity and, if so, what principles should guide the selection of these records?

I have chosen to highlight disputes over the destruction of records concerning Indigenous and First Nations, Inuit and Métis peoples. These records, and disputes about them, bring into stark relief some of the competing public, institutional, political and ethical demands faced by courts and other legal bodies concerning their responsibilities as archives. Rather than seeing these disputes as exceptions to general principles and challenges, in the Court as Archive Project, we regard them as paradigmatic examples that can assist courts to develop appropriate institutional archival policies and practices. As Australian archivist Michael Piggott argues, more attention to archival histories, such as histories of acquisition and destruction of records, could help explain current community views of the past and benefit current social debate, especially in relation to Indigenous records.[6]

In Australia, from the early 1990s, the development of native title jurisprudence, as well as other areas for Indigenous claims, including litigation concerning the legality of genocide, cultural heritage claims and compensation by members of the Stolen Generations, resulted in the production of an extensive body of evidentiary and litigation materials for the purposes of legal action. Under the *Native Title Act 1993* (Cth), for example, claimants must provide evidence that they possess communal, group or individual rights and interests in relation to land or waters under traditional laws and customs. This is an onerous burden of proof, requiring that claimants demonstrate an ongoing connection to the land in question, dating back to the assertion of colonial sovereignty. In addition to witness

---

6   Michael Piggott, *Archives and Societal Provenance: Australian Essays* (Chandos Publishing, 2012) 238, doi.org/10.1533/9781780633787.

statements, it may include genealogies, anthropological, historical and linguistic reports, maps, photographs, artworks and other material. The Federal Court has been conscious of the historical value of the records produced for the purposes of litigation and its responsibilities for them as a court of record with obligations to the national interest. However, for many years, it did not have a suitable archival appraisal framework on which to base decisions about what to preserve and what to destroy. This points to the significant interrelationship between the development of the Federal Court's approach to its record-keeping obligations alongside developments in its native title jurisdiction.[7]

Where Australian and Canadian courts of record have attempted to resolve questions about record-keeping responsibilities, they have drawn primarily upon legal principles and obligations, including the need to preserve records of judicial decisions for the purposes of precedent; the civil law principle of 'open justice'; the rights of individual litigants to privacy; the maintenance of legal professional privilege; and the need to protect certain groups, such as children. Further, as for all public institutions, decisions by courts about record-keeping have been driven by rapid changes and developments in technology, as well as increasing constraints on financial resources and storage space. As a result of these imperatives, and despite the lack of legislative coverage, superior courts of record in both Canada and Australia have engaged in negotiations with national archives institutions, the NAA and LAC, seeking arrangements for custodianship of case file records, once the case is closed.

Legal principles and obligations are necessary and important requirements for courts' approaches to decisions about appraisal and disposal of records. However, federal supreme courts of record should also consider their archival responsibilities in terms of the deeper public law issues underlying their institutional role. Courts can benefit from approaches reflected in contemporary archival theory, where it is recognised that appraisal choices are political and ethical because they 'shape the future of our jurisdiction's documentary heritage'.[8] Drawing on such a framework will assist courts in developing their archival responsibilities beyond consideration of the need to preserve legal records of individual disputes, but rather as records that are of public interest and importance because they reflect societal

---

7 See Chapter 7, this volume.
8 Terry Cook, 'Macroappraisal in Theory and Practice: Origins, Characteristics, and Implementation in Canada, 1950–2000' (2005) 5 *Archival Science* 101, 103.

dynamics and public issues. As Canadian archivist Terry Cook explains, 'archivists should focus on the mechanisms or *loci* in society where the citizen interacts with the state to produce the clearest evidence of societal dynamics and public issues, and thus of societal values'.[9] This is a valuable framework for informing the development of archival principles for federal superior courts of record because of their important role in adjudicating claims and disputes of a democratic society, and as a legal archive of national value.

The aim of the Court as Archive Project has been to clarify the institutional purposes and civic responsibilities of Australian supreme courts of record through their archival role. In particular, we have focused on the unique role of the Federal Court of Australia as a site for production of significant national archives. We have also ventured to develop principles to inform the administration of the court's records, as a responsive civic institution in 21st-century Australia. The chapter concludes with an account of the development of the Federal Court's records authority that sets out the current framework for the management and disposal of its case file records. I focus, in particular, on the rationale for the definition of what constitutes a 'court record' and the identification of a 'significant' case. This history importantly reveals the extent to which the negotiations between the Federal Court and the NAA have provided the defining context for the meaning of the 'court record' in Australian superior courts of record. It demonstrates the importance that histories of archives theory and practice play in defining legal and court practices.[10]

Gaps in the Records

Appraisal has been described as the 'critical archival act', the archivist's 'first responsibility',[11] but also as 'the most vexed issue in archival practice in the early twenty-first century'.[12] Perhaps, as Sue McKemmish, Barbara Reed and Michael Piggott suggest, because appraisal has not always been part of archival practice, 'pragmatic and practice-based approaches became the core guides'.[13] However, it is now well-recognised among archival thinkers

---

9   Ibid 125–6.
10   The interview with Warwick Soden, CEO, Federal Court of Australia, in Chapter 7 of this volume, provides an account of this history from the Federal Court's perspective.
11   Cook, above n 1, 2.
12   McKemmish, Reed and Piggott, above n 2, 175.
13   Ibid.

that appraisal, like other areas of archival work, involves decisions about far more than the availability of storage space and financial resources. Archival appraisal results in the creation of archives as institutions and, for this reason, decisions about what to keep and what to destroy requires sensitivity to the 'political, social, philosophical and ethical nature of appraisal'. Indeed, Terry Cook goes so far as to suggest that, as a society, 'we are what we do *not* keep, what we consciously exclude, marginalize, ignore, destroy'.[14]

The truth of this aphorism is clearly demonstrated in settler colonial polities, such as Australia and Canada, when contentions over the reliability and interpretation of state-produced archival records have come into sharp relief, notably as a result of legal avenues and processes of reconciliation with Indigenous peoples. For example, in Australia, research conducted during the 1990s for the National Inquiry into the Removal of Aboriginal and Torres Strait Islander Children from their Families revealed destruction, under authorised procedures, of a range of records, including adoption and fostering case files across state jurisdictions.[15] The inquiry received a number of submissions concerning the difficulties Indigenous people experience in gaining access to archival records held by the various record-keeping agencies.[16] Some stated that 'government agencies had destroyed or lost particular classes of records relating to adoption, foster care or personal information, either through deliberate culling or through fires in the buildings that housed the records'.[17] There was also an unexplained gap in Aborigines Welfare Board files for an entire decade: 1938–48.[18] Further, as the inquiry pointed out, records made and held by non-government organisations, including churches that ran children's homes and orphanages, are neither required to retain records nor to provide access to these records under Freedom of Information legislation.[19] As a result of these revelations, the inquiry made a number of recommendations in relation to changes to archival records management

---

14   Terry Cook, '"We Are What We Keep; We Keep What We Are": Archival Appraisal Past, Present and Future' (2011) 32(2) *Journal of the Society of Archivists* 173, 174.
15   Human Rights and Equal Opportunity Commission, *Bringing Them Home: Report of the National Inquiry into the Separation of Aboriginal and Torres Strait Islander Children from Their Families* (1997), 325–6.
16   Ibid 348.
17   Sonia Smallacombe, 'Accessing Personal and Family Records: Contesting the Gatekeepers' [1998] *Indigenous Law Bulletin* 2.
18   Above n 15, 325–6.
19   Above n 15, 333–4.

practice, including a moratorium on destruction of records relating to Indigenous individuals, families or communities held by government or non-government agencies.[20]

This was not the only time recommendations have been made in relation to record-keeping after legal inquiries. Kim Eberhard points out that in at least eight key inquiries into various aspects of the welfare of children conducted in Australia since 1989, recommendations were made in relation to record-keeping, even when the terms of reference did not mention these matters. She argues that commissioners conducting these inquiries have been 'confronted with the centrality of records to their inquiries, and that a lack of records has been the most critical factor leading to recommendations concerning record-keeping in both public and private sectors'.[21]

In Canada, there have also been controversies surrounding the destruction of government and legal records. During the late 1980s, a furore emerged in the context of the Royal Commission of Inquiry to investigate the charge that Canada was a haven for Nazi war criminals.[22] The National Archives of Canada was called to give evidence about its records management policy and processes, and many government officials were surprised to learn that not all immigration and security case records were retained in perpetuity.[23] Terry Cook, one of the archivists from the Canadian National Archives involved in the appraisal decisions resulting in the destruction of the records, has written extensively about the impact, personally and professionally, of the revelations that valuable historical records concerning human rights violations had been destroyed. He argues that this marked the beginning of a new approach to appraisal and disposal at NAC with national and international impact.[24]

---

20 Above n 15, Recommendation 21: Destruction of Records Prohibited, 347.
21 Kim Eberhard, 'Unresolved Issues: Recordkeeping Recommendations arising from Australian Commissions of Inquiry into the Welfare of Children in Out-of-Home Care' (2015) 43(1) *Archives and Manuscripts* 4, 6.
22 Commission of Inquiry on War Criminals in Canada, *Report and Findings* (Privy Council Office, Canada, 1986).
23 Terry Cook, '"A Monumental Blunder": The Destruction of Records on Nazi War Criminals in Canada' in Richard J Cox and David A Wallace (eds), *Archives and the Public Good: Accountability and Records in Modern Society* (Quorum Books, 2002).
24 Ibid 62.

More recently in Canada, disputes have arisen about responsibility for contemporaneous records of testimonial and documentary evidence produced in proceedings under the Indian Residential Schools Settlement Agreement.[25] This agreement provided for two avenues of reparations, one of which was for previous students who wished to pursue compensation claims for serious assault and sexual assault. The Chief Adjudicator of the Independent Assessment Process (IAP), Dan Shapiro, sought an order for destruction of the documents at the end of the process to protect the privacy of the survivors and perpetrators.[26] However, the Truth and Reconciliation Commission sought an order that the documents be archived at LAC on the basis that the narratives produced for the hearings are an irreplaceable historical record of the Indian Residential School experience.[27] The court granted the Chief Adjudicator's request that the IAP documents be destroyed after a 15-year holding period by the Canadian Government. However, it also made an order that with the consent of the claimant, and subject to redaction of identifying personal information about alleged perpetrators or affected parties, the records may be archived at the National Centre for Truth and Reconciliation.[28] On appeal, the Ontario Court of Appeal upheld this decision and a further appeal to the Supreme Court of Canada (SCC) was dismissed.[29] In a unanimous Full Court decision, the court rejected the argument that the documents were subject to federal access, privacy and archives legislation.[30]

These disputes clearly demonstrate, sometimes in poignant ways, the competing legal, ethical and political demands and expectations associated with decisions about preservation and destruction of legal records. The obligations of courts and other legal entities to maintain records of proceedings may come into direct conflict with the right of individual

---

[25] The Indian Residential Schools Settlement Agreement was agreed to on 8 May 2006. It is a multiple court–approved settlement resulting from approximately 150 individual and class actions taken by former students of Indian residential schools: <www.residentialschoolsettlement.ca/IRS%20 Settlement%20Agreement-%20ENGLISH.pdf>.

[26] *Fontaine v Canada (Attorney General)* 2014 ONSC 4585. The application by the Chief Investigator was supported by the Assembly of First Nations, the Twenty-Four Catholic Entities, the Nine Catholic Entities, the Sisters of St Joseph and Independent Counsel.

[27] The application by the Truth and Reconciliation Commission was supported by the Canadian Government and the National Centre for Truth and Reconciliation.

[28] The National Centre for Truth and Reconciliation, based at the University of Manitoba, was established 'to preserve the memory of Canada's Residential School system and legacy' as the permanent home for all statements, documents and other materials gathered by the Truth and Reconciliation Commission of Canada: <http://nctr.ca/map.php/>.

[29] *Fontaine v Canada (Attorney General)* 2016 ONCA 241.

[30] *Canada (Attorney General) v Fontaine* [2017] 2 SCR 205.

litigants to privacy or the need to respect Indigenous control of cultural knowledge. At the same time, the record of the court's proceedings produced by the court is of significant national archival value, as it records the claims and disputes of a democratic society. They are rich records of public interest and importance about the relationship between the individual and the state that are not readily accessible elsewhere.

Further, these disputes highlight the unique characteristics of records produced by courts in the course of litigation, which may include transcripts of oral testimony, expert witness reports, evidentiary materials, photographs, affidavits and other court records. As Cornelia Vismann argues, files are the foundation of legal activity, but they 'remain below the perception threshold of the law'.[31] Records presented in litigation may have been sourced from established state- or privately owned archives, or they may have been created specifically for the litigation on the basis of new research or investigations. These records may subsequently be incorporated into or associated with new records, being records of disputes between parties. As records of court processes, they are generally subject to the legal principle of open justice. However, this is not always the case, as some proceedings are held in closed courts or are subject to confidentiality requirements. The specific characteristics of court and legal records suggest the need for an approach to archival appraisal that recognises their value not only as records of proceedings of claims and disputes, but also as archives documenting changes in understandings of political demands, and democratic expressions about rights and values.

Archival Appraisal

In Australia and Canada, archives legislation provides the legal framework for preservation and disposal of government records through the establishment of national archives institutions.[32] In both jurisdictions, the legislation was introduced as part of the administrative law packages

---

31 Cornelia Vismann, *Files: Law and Media Technology* (Stanford University Press, 2008) 11.
32 In Australia, the *Archives Act 1983* (Cth) ('*Archives Act*'), established the NAA to 'ensure the conservation and preservation of the existing and future archival resources of the Commonwealth' (s 5(2)(a)). In Canada, the *National Archives of Canada Act*, RSC 1985 (3rd supp), c 1 ('*National Archives of Canada Act*') established the National Archives of Canada 'to conserve private and public records of national significance' and 'to be the permanent repository of records of government institutions and of ministerial records' (s 4(1)). The *National Archives of Canada Act* was repealed by the *Library and Archives of Canada Act*, which established the LAC.

in the 1970s, including Freedom of Information legislation that was intended to provide improved access to government information. However, based on the principle of the separation of powers between the executive and the judiciary, the records of courts are specifically exempt from the operation of archives legislation.[33] Nevertheless, faced with exponentially increasing case loads and decreasing availability of archival storage space, superior courts of record in each jurisdiction have engaged in negotiations with national archives for transfer and custodianship of court archives, including case file records.[34]

Under the Australian *Archives Act*, the NAA has power to authorise the disposal or destruction of Commonwealth records,[35] giving government departments and agencies responsibility for destruction, transfer or alteration of Commonwealth records, subject to its authorisation.[36] The *Archives Regulations 1984* (Cth) provide the framework for appraisal and disposal of records, including the requirements for consent to destruction from both the NAA and the Commonwealth institution.[37] In Canada, archival appraisal is conducted by the national archives institution, LAC, in consultation with federal government agencies. The consent of the National Archivist must be obtained for destruction and disposal of records.[38]

In an article that considered disposal practices under the Australian *Archives Act* from an administrative law perspective written some 20 years ago, Kim Rubenstein argued that the legal framework for records destruction is sparse. While the NAA has the responsibility for determining the practices and procedure appropriate for disposal, the Act does not provide clear direction because it does not contain an objects clause that sets out

---

33 *Archives Act* s 19. In Canada, the *Library and Archives of Canada Act* does not cover federal courts. In Australian states and territories, New South Wales alone specifically excludes court and tribunal records from obligations under the *State Records Act 1998* (NSW) ss 9(1)(c) and (2), 26(1)(c), 49(1)(c) and (2). In most Canadian provinces, records legislation includes provisions for archiving of court records. For example, the Saskatchewan *Archives and Public Records Act*, SS 2015, c A-26.11 provides for management of Court of Appeal records, including administrative records. However, in some jurisdictions, provisions specify a long period for court retention prior to transfer.
34 See Chapter 4, this volume.
35 *Archives Act* s 6(1).
36 *Archives Act* s 24.
37 *Archives Regulations 1984* (Cth) regs 3–7.
38 *National Archives of Canada Act* s 3; *Library and Archives Canada Act* s 12(1).

fundamental principles to guide the decision-makers in what is worthy of disposal. She suggested that there was not enough guidance in the Act and that there was a lack of accountability.[39]

Since this time, responsibility for government record-keeping practices in Australia has devolved even further to the agency level, through the extensive use of records retention and disposal authorities (RDAs).[40] The NAA has tasked itself with responsibility for the selection and preservation for retention of the most important information identified as being of permanent (or continuing) value due to its national significance or public interest. All other records are the responsibility of the agency that created or controls the information, although decisions about what to retain, and for how long, are made through the development and implementation of RDAs. These allow government authorities to make decisions about preservation, destruction or transferral of records at the department or agency level, in accordance with frameworks established by the agency in consultation with the NAA. Some RDAs are general and apply to areas such as administrative functions across agencies, others are agency-specific. The framework outlined by the NAA for records management stresses the need to reduce business risk, increase accountability and improve operational efficiencies. It identifies the context of limited financial resources and storage space as rationales for records destruction.[41]

Despite lack of legislative requirement, RDAs have been established by courts and tribunals with federal jurisdiction, including the Federal Court of Australia, to cover specific areas of operation. For example, disposal of the administrative files is authorised by a general Administrative Functions Disposal Authority, applying to all federal government activity and covering an extensive range of records of administrative practices.[42] Under the authority, government departments and agencies are permitted to dispose of certain 'low-value and short-term information' considered

---

39   Kim Rubenstein, 'Erring on the Side of Destruction? Administrative Law Principles and Disposal Practices under the *Archives Act 1983* (Cth)' (1997) 4 *Australian Journal of Administrative Law* 78, 82.
40   *Archives Act* s 24.
41   National Archives of Australia, *Records Authorities* (2018) <www.naa.gov.au/information-management/records-authorities>.
42   National Archives of Australia, *Administrative Functions Disposal Authority (AFDA), (Revised March 2010)* (2018) <www.naa.gov.au/Images/AFDA2010-7Feb2013-revision_tcm16-44429.PDF>.

part of normal administrative practice, including draft notes, temporary materials and such.[43] It is only once an RDA is established that sentencing can occur, performed by the agency itself, but authorised by the NAA.

Notwithstanding the proliferation of RDAs, archival appraisal is ultimately an interpretative act. The decision as to whether a record is appraised as worthy of retention and preservation is a process that results in only some records being attributed status as archives. As Canadian archivist Tom Nesmith argues:

> The destruction or exclusion of non-archival records 're-creates' the surviving records by repositioning them in the archives vis-à-vis related records, or by removing aspects of their context of interpretation. The records elevated to the status of archives then become the focus of the meaning-making or interpretive process, which in turn makes and remakes them.[44]

In this way, archival practices of appraisal shape records and selectively establish relationships among records that did not necessarily exist before archivists created them and, thus, foster some interpretive possibilities and diminishing others.

Similarly, the framework drawn upon to establish principles and approaches to appraisal and sentencing have been subject to change and have themselves been influenced by theoretical developments in archival theory, history and other disciplines. For most of the 20th century, archival appraisal based its decision-making on what to keep and what to destroy 'primarily on assessing actual or anticipated research uses of records, particularly for writing academic history'.[45] However, 'value through use' is now recognised as an inadequate basis for archival appraisal. Fundamental changes in understandings of history and historiography that developed during the late 20th century have contested the historical authority attributed to archivally based history, identifying the way it reflects the history of hegemonic, rather than the marginalised, oppressed and subaltern.[46] There has also been a significant expansion of conceptual

---

43 National Archives of Australia, *Normal Administrative Practice* (2018) <www.naa.gov.au/information-management/managing-information-and-records/disposal/NAP/index.aspx>.
44 Tom Nesmith, 'Seeing Archives: Postmodernism and the Changing Intellectual Place of Archives' (2002) 65 *The American Archivist* 24, 34.
45 Cook, above n 23, 59.
46 Francis X Blouin Jr and William G Rosenberg, *Processing the Past: Contesting Authority in History and the Archives* (Oxford University Press, 2012).

understandings of 'the archive' and increased use of archival sources by disciplines outside academic history, including law.[47] In settler colonial contexts such as Canada and Australia, this has notably included the use of archival sources as historical evidence in legal actions in relation to land rights, treaty rights, cultural heritage and compensation for loss in relation to stolen children and wages. Importantly, the court case file records of these actions themselves provide valuable accounts of the claims and disputes that reflect the changing nature of society.

Appraisal at Courts of Record

Developments in archival theory recognise the outdated notion that archivists simply and invisibly process records for future use. As Tom Nesmith points out, within postmodern understandings of communication, archivists are co-creators and shapers of knowledge in records, and 'thus help form society's memory'.[48] Records are not inert but are continually evolving. He argues that archives-making is a type of authoring or creating:

> Some of what makes a record meaningful is inscribed in it by those who literally made it, but most of what makes a record intelligible lies outside its physical borders in its context of interpretation. Archivists, who do much to shape this context, therefore share in authoring the record.[49]

The increased sophistication of theoretical approaches to archival appraisal has had a significant impact on records retention policies internationally. New conceptual and methodological approaches to archival appraisal, such as 'macroappraisal', attempt to reflect 'a broader spectrum of human experience in society and to mirror more closely therefore society's own values, rather than more narrowly the values of powerful records creators or those derived from anticipating use patterns'.[50] Macroappraisal has been adopted in Canada as the official appraisal strategy at LAC and has been very influential at the NAA, employed as a 'functions-based' approach, in conjunction with individual agencies. It is a top-down approach that

---

47 See contributions to 'Evidence and the Archive: Ethics, Aesthetics, and Emotion' (2014) 40(1) *Australian Feminist Law Journal* 1.
48 Nesmith, above n 44, 31.
49 Ibid 32.
50 Cook, above n 23, 62.

requires assessment of the value of records not at the level of the individual document or file, but, rather, at the level of the organisation, department or government.

While superior courts of record in Australia and Canada have been included in the ambit of application of RDAs for general records, they have encountered obstacles and delays in developing and obtaining agreements for authorities in relation to case file records. The overriding principle of the separation of powers, the absence of imprimatur under archives legislation, competing demands for financial and space resources, as well as the unique characteristics of court records are all factors that have contributed to these challenges. In particular, when engaged in the process of developing frameworks for archival appraisal through records RDAs, superior courts of record in Canada and Australia have been confronted with a question that goes to the heart of their identity and ultimately defines their record-keeping responsibilities—namely 'What *is* a court record?'. In the following section, I will explain how superior courts of record in Canada and Australia have engaged with archival appraisal, with particular attention to the question of what constitutes a court record.

What is a Court Record?

During 2015, I conducted fieldwork for the Court as Archive Project in Canada, with attention to developments in records management at the key federal courts of record, the Supreme Court of Canada and the Federal Court of Canada, as well as the federal archival institution, LAC.

Supreme Court of Canada[51]

The SCC is the highest court in Canada's federal court system, adjudicating approximately 80 cases per year; it deals only with appeals, and no evidentiary material is presented. As the court with final judicial authority in the nation, its decisions establish legal precedent. For this

---

51   The information contained in this section is based on communication with David Rajotte and Michael MacDonald, archivists from Library and Archives Canada on 9 September 2015; Etienne Perras, Manager, Library and Information Management Branch, Supreme Court of Canada on 9 September 2015; and Barbara Kincaid, General Counsel and Director-General, Court Operations Sector, Supreme Court of Canada on 3 November 2015, and her subsequent participation, via Skype, in the Court as Archive Symposium, The Australian National University, 17 February 2016.

11. SENTENCING ACTS

reason, since its establishment in 1875, the court's policy in relation to record-keeping of case files has been to 'keep everything'.[52] Until 2009, case file documents were maintained in paper form and stored in the court's records centre. Starting in the 1980s, the court began producing microfilm of case files, progressively establishing a comprehensive record dating back to 1875. In 2009, the court introduced electronic document management and records management and, since this time, has made available to the public live and archived webcasts of its hearings.

In 1977, the court signed an agreement with LAC to transfer case file records for preservation once the court file was closed. One copy of the microfilm is maintained at the court registry and the original files, together with a second microfilm copy, are transferred to LAC. This transfer arrangement occurs every two to three years, but it does not include cases from the most immediate past years. In 1991, a transfer agreement between the SCC and LAC was signed, which meant that all publicly filed documents contained on the case files from 1875–1945 were transferred to LAC for care and custody, although the court continued to own the material. LAC provides unlimited public access to all Supreme Court files unless the material has been identified by the court as restricted. Public access is available at LAC via the online catalogue and includes the video recordings of hearings.[53]

In 2003, the court began negotiating a comprehensive agreement with LAC for permanent transfer of records deemed to be of enduring value. Barbara Kincaid, General Counsel, SCC, explained that the protracted negotiations to develop the court's retention policy raised for the court important questions about how to define the court record: questions that, as a court of record, it was imperative the court resolve because the answer to this question determines what records the court is required to preserve permanently. For example, in attempting to balance the open court principle with individual rights to privacy and security, is it acceptable for the court to place limits on public access to court records, media and parties to the proceedings where there are statutory publication bans, sealing orders or statutory restrictions on access to case files? In keeping with its vision of making its collection accessible to the Canadian public,

---

52 Interview with Barbara Kincaid, General Counsel and Director-General, Court Operations Sector, Supreme Court of Canada (Ottawa, 3 November 2015).
53 Email from Barbara Kincaid, General Counsel and Director-General, Court Operations Sector, Supreme Court of Canada, to Trich Luker, 3 November 2015.

LAC would like to digitise the microfilm collection. However, what happens to sensitive information in older case files? What is the risk given that personal identifiers and other sensitive information may be contained in closed case files? Further, how does the court distinguish between judicial information, such as records of judicial deliberations, and public information—namely, what is on the official court record?[54]

In 2017, a comprehensive agreement between the SCC and LAC was finalised. It provides the terms for the provision of perpetual care and public access to SCC 'information resources of enduring value' (IREV). Under the agreement, 50 years following closure of the case file, the Supreme Court will donate to LAC records identified as case-related operational documents that are IREV. This includes the court records filed by litigants or produced by or on behalf of the court; specifically, applications for leave to appeals, appeals and reference documents identified as case files, docket information, judgments, statistical reports concerning the variety of cases heard before the court, and audio, video or web recordings of hearings.[55] Under the agreement, the SCC is responsible for identifying records that, as a result of a legal obligation, court order or administrative classification, result in limits on accessibility or dissemination. LAC must consult with SCC before providing access to restricted information.

Different conditions apply to collegial judicial documents, including correspondence, memorandums and notes created by a justice, chambers' personnel, law clerks or legal counsel of the SCC in relation to judicial proceedings before the court. Once operational use has ceased, these will be transferred to LAC. However, they will remain closed for 50 years after the case file for the proceeding is closed (with the SCC maintaining control), after which time they become open to the public.[56]

The agreement took 15 years to be negotiated. It appears to provide a comprehensive arrangement for archival appraisal of the case file and administrative records of the SCC, as well as arrangements for public access to these documents. In navigating the question of what is meant by the 'court record', the SCC has taken a broad ambit by including all

---

54   Barbara Kincaid, 'Administration of Legal Records: Institutional Experiences' (Speech delivered at the Court as Archive Symposium, The Australian National University, 17 February 2016).
55   Agreement between the Office of the Registrar of the Supreme Court of Canada and Library and Archives of Canada, Appendix B, on file with author.
56   The agreement also provides for the donation of the Supreme Court of Canada's administrative records, including registrar and senior management documents, services to justices, legal services and communications, once operational use has ceased.

of the court's case file records. This is enhanced further by the inclusion of collegial documents, providing access to a rich source of judicial deliberations that illuminate how and why these decisions were made. However, the court has taken a cautious approach to issues of privacy and confidentiality by imposing a 50-year embargo on the collegial files.[57]

Federal Court of Canada[58]

The Federal Court of Canada was established in 1971, with a separate appeal division, the Federal Court of Appeal, established in 2003. It is a superior court of record with civil and criminal jurisdiction to hear and decide legal disputes arising in the federal domain, including claims against the Canadian Government, civil actions in federally regulated areas and challenges to the decisions of federal tribunals. As the national trial court, it has a very large volume of cases, with approximately 3,000–4,000 proceedings heard in court per year.[59] The magnitude of the court's caseload means that it faces significant challenges in relation to document management strategies. This is demonstrated by the court's failure, to date, to reach an agreement in relation to archival appraisal. In 2006, a report was produced with recommendations for a records retention schedule; however, this has not been implemented. As Andrew Baumberg, Legal Counsel, put it, the report itself became 'an archived document'.[60] He suggested that one of the key drivers for the court in relation to the development of records retention policies has been the amount of storage space available. As he explained, until around 2013, the court kept everything:

---

57 The Supreme Court of Canada is the first jurisdiction in Canada to establish an institutional treatment of collegial documents. The decision to impose a 50-year closure period took into account principles of deliberative secrecy, determining that this time period would ensure that judges were unlikely to still be alive when the records were made available: Email from Barbara Kincaid to Trish Luker, 10 November 2017.
58 The information in this section is based on interviews with Andrew Baumberg, Legal Counsel, Federal Court (Ottawa, 6 November 2015) and Lise Albert, Information Management Specialist, Information and Records Management Division, Courts Administration Service (Ottawa, 3 November 2015).
59 Courts Administration Service, *2016–17 Annual Report* (2017) 9.
60 Interview with Andrew Baumberg, Legal Counsel, Federal Court (Ottawa, 6 November 2015). In fact, the court found it necessary to amend the Court Rules to allow for establishment of a retention schedule: *Federal Courts Rules*, SOR/98-106, 23.1.

> I think it's really been something that's ingrained in the judicial culture ... you don't throw things out ... We're in a paper culture which I think has actually really started to shift in the last five years.[61]

As a trial court of record, the Federal Court of Canada has a legal obligation to maintain the court records to support the common law requirement to follow precedent. However, as Baumberg explains, 'precedent doesn't seem to require you to keep all the records that were relied on in order for the judge to write their reasons', particularly in modern legal practice. Given the court's enormous volume of cases, many of which do not go to a full oral hearing, it is attempting to grapple with concerns about the availability of storage space and costs of retaining court files. In 2015-16, the Federal Court of Canada consulted with the Canadian Bar Association. The Bar acknowledged that court records and files might have historical and longer term litigation value. It provided some guidance as to retention periods, according to different areas of practice.

In December 2017, the Federal Court of Canada endorsed key parameters for a retention schedule based on a policy framework that includes specified retention periods for different types of proceedings, with some court documents to be retained in perpetuity.[62] The court is considering an open approach to its sentencing decisions, with the possibility for members of the public to make submissions justifying extended retention, as well as a small-scale sampling of files for extended retention. Finally, the Federal Court of Canada anticipates that the transition to electronic records will provide lower cost and more efficient archiving.[63]

Federal Court of Australia

The Federal Court of Australia was established in 1976 as a superior court of record with trial and appellate divisions. It has extensive jurisdiction to deal with most civil disputes governed by federal law

---

61 Interview with Andrew Baumberg, Legal Counsel, Federal Court (Ottawa, 6 November 2015).
62 The Federal Court of Canada has endorsed a policy of a seven-year retention period for proceedings that were dismissed at leave stage or abandoned/discontinued (ie, not adjudicated on the merits); a 15-year retention of documents in other proceedings; and all docket, judgments, orders and minutes of hearings to be retained in perpetuity: email from Andrew Baumberg to Trish Luker, 20 February 2018.
63 Ibid.

(other than family law) and a limited number of criminal matters.[64] In 2015–16, approximately 5,700 causes of action were filed with the court. As discussed in other chapters in this collection, the Court as Archive Project has focused specifically on the Federal Court's archival practices. The decisions this court makes in relation to record-keeping, including appraisal, preservation, custodianship and access, are themselves of public importance, acting as a key indicator of how federal superior courts of record might meet their constitutional mandate and broader democratic responsibilities.[65]

In 1994, the first formal agreement between the Federal Court and the NAA facilitated the transfer of all court administrative and case matter files for storage to the NAA.[66] As in Canada, in the absence of a legislative requirement, one of the key incentives to establishing an agreement was the depletion of storage space within court buildings, resulting in the need for off-site facilities. However, in 2000, the NAA informed the court that, due to its own depleting storage space, it would no longer be able to accept all material.[67] At this time, the court was developing its electronic court filing system. These two factors were important drivers for the court to enter into negotiations with the NAA in the development of an RDA. Importantly, the development of the RDA reveals the evolution of the court's own understanding what is meant by 'the court record'.

During the 1990s, the NAA advocated a methodology for records management, referred to as DIRKS (Developing and Implementing a Record Keeping System), based on business functions, activities and transactions.[68] Over a seven-year period, the Federal Court attempted to implement the DIRKS system, with limited success. Other government agencies were also performing poorly in relation to record-keeping because

---

64 The court's civil law jurisdiction includes administrative and constitutional law, human rights, employment and industrial relations, native title, intellectual property, taxation, trade practices, corporations, appeals from immigration decisions and bankruptcy.
65 See Chapter 4, this volume.
66 National Archives of Australia, *Records Disposal Authority for the Federal Court of Australia, Principal and District Registries, Court Records other than Bankruptcy* No 1124, 1994. Prior to 1994, files were transferred from the Federal Court to the NAA under less formal arrangements; see Chapter 4 of this volume for a detailed discussion.
67 Lyn Nasir, 'Presentation on the Records Authority' (Speech given at the 9th Australasian Institute of Judicial Administration Librarians Conference, Sydney, 21 August 2015); see also Chapter 7, this volume.
68 This methodology was developed for the implementation of the international principle of the Australian standard for *AS4390-1996—Records Management*, a codification of ISO15489 for international best practice for record-keeping.

the DIRKS system was complex and resource-intensive. In 2008, the NAA changed its approach to appraisal, requiring organisations to take greater responsibility at the agency level for identifying documents that defined its 'unique business'. The Federal Court determined that as a court of record, it was court records, rather than administrative records, that fulfilled this role. Further, as a court of record, it determined that the whole of a file constituted the 'record' that should be retained permanently.[69]

However, the NAA has resisted accepting all the Federal Court's case file documents. This has meant that the court has had to consider which court records it believes should be preserved at the NAA as part of the national heritage. It has led to the identification of the criterion of 'significant cases' as the basis for appraisal. However, giving meaning to this criteria has required the court to consider not only its common law role and obligations as a court of record, but also how it sees its responsibilities as a national institution with obligations to the public record.[70] Importantly, this has been driven by consideration of some of record-keeping issues raised by the unique characteristics of the court's native title jurisdiction.[71] As Ian Irving, previous Native Title Registrar at the Federal Court points out, court files for native title matters may include 'a rich repository of historical and contemporary cultural and other information', including 'claimant genealogies, expert anthropology, history and/or linguistic reports, witness statements, photographs and other material'.[72] In considering its archival responsibilities, the Federal Court has had to consider the historical and research value of these records, as well as questions about access to the records.

---

69   At one stage, on the basis of legal advice obtained from the Australian Government Solicitor, the Federal Court considered an amendment to the Court's Rules to define 'the record' and the retention period, but this was abandoned.

70   Our research into the Federal Court records indicates that, at different times, the court has considered the possibility of the concept of 'significant' to refer to a discretionary approach based on precedent, historical interest (ie, who were the parties, what were the issues), media interest or 'special circumstances'; alternatively, a representative sample, limited to 10 per cent, to be selected by the judges according to different practice areas, has been proposed. Most recently, the court's new approach to case management, the national court framework, is being considered as a framework for identification of significant cases.

71   For further discussion of these issues, see also Chapters 8 and 9, this volume.

72   Ian Irving, 'Information Held on Federal Court Native Title Files' (Speech delivered at the Native Title Conference 2006, Darwin, 1 June 2006) <http://aiatsis.gov.au/publications/presentations/information-held-federal-court-native-title-files> ; see also Chapter 9, this volume.

In 2011, the NAA endorsed the Federal Court's records authority, which sets out the framework for the management and disposal of its case file records.[73] The authority delineates the requirements for 'keeping and destroying records for the core business area of case management', as well as for the purposes of national preservation. The authority states:

> in the interests of accountability and consistent decision making and preservation of the archival resources of the Commonwealth, records identified as 'retain as national archives' are to be transferred to the custody of NAA by mutual agreement.[74]

The authority covers all records of the 'core business of deciding disputes according to law', including judges' *coram* books, papers and all administrative tasks performed in the function of deciding a dispute, as well as judicial committee matters, a master set of judgments and other administrative records.[75] Importantly, it specifies that 10 per cent of 'significant non–native title Court files' that have been nominated by the judges are to be retained as national archives. The decision to retain a case file is made on the basis of its value as precedent, high media profile, public interest and case diversity, and that it should represent a cross-section of cases within a year.

The separate identification and treatment of native title court files, all of which are to be preserved and transferred to the NAA, recognises the historical and archival value attached to the information contained in these records. As Pamela McGrath discusses in another chapter in this collection, as a result of native title legal proceedings, the Federal Court is in possession of an enormous number of records that contain information about thousands of Indigenous people, both living and deceased. The onerous evidentiary requirements imposed by the legislation have resulted in 'one of the most substantial government-sponsored research efforts ever undertaken with Indigenous Australians', including genealogical, cultural and historical information that is often personal or culturally sensitive.[76] As McGrath argues, providing public access to native title records raises

---

73 National Archives of Australia, *Records Authority: Federal Court of Australia*, No 2010/00315821, 19 October 2011.
74 Ibid 4.
75 Also exhibit administration, file inspection arrangements, legal assistance, development of policy and procedures, research, reviewing and reporting, taxation of costs, remitted or transferred matters, judges' meetings, development of court rules and practice notes, and consultation with stakeholders.
76 Chapter 10, this volume.

significant and intersecting legal and ethical interests that 'complicate the possibility of making native title records publicly available through either archives or publication'.[77]

The Federal Court is also required to comply with a freeze placed by the NAA on disposal of records affecting the rights and entitlements of Indigenous people. This was in response to the recommendations of the Royal Commission into Aboriginal Deaths in Custody[78] and the *Bringing Them Home* report into the removal of Aboriginal children from their families and communities.[79] These recommendations were intended to assist Indigenous people in the process of re-establishing community and family links with those from whom they have been separated under past government policies.[80] The freeze was extended in 2000 to cover records still in the custody of a range of government agencies; and again, in 2009, to cover records that contain information on policy and procedures about withholding wages, pensions and allowances from Indigenous Australians.[81] The Federal Court is included as one of the agencies responsible for retention of these files, which is reflected in its policy to retain all native title case files.

The Federal Court's records authority establishes 10 classes of records related to case management. Four classes deal with case files—that is, files containing material relating to individual proceedings. The default position for every case file is that material constituting the 'court record', as defined by the Federal Court for the purposes of the authority (referred to as 'Part A' of each file), is retained by the court.[82] This is consistent with the court's status, established under Chapter III of the *Constitution*, as a 'superior court of record'.[83] Material that is not part of the court record (referred to as 'Part B') may be disposed of between 10 and 25 years after the end of the

---

77 Ibid.
78 Commonwealth, Royal Commission into Aboriginal Deaths in Custody, *National Report, Overview and Recommendations* (1991), Recommendation 53.
79 Above n 15, Recommendation 21.
80 National Archives of Australia, *Records Disposal Freezes and Retention Notices* (25 January 2018) National Archives of Australia.<www.naa.gov.au/information-management/managing-information-and records/disposal/freezes/index.aspx#section9>.
81 Ibid.
82 In this category, the authority specifically identifies categories of records: cross-claims and replies; fast-track statements and responses; pleadings; requests for particulars and particulars in response; where the proceeding is an appeal, the notices; where the proceeding is commenced by way of petition, the petition and any answering document; court documents that identify the parties; court documents that record the final orders; reasons for judgment (where published) and copies of orders.
83 *Federal Court of Australia Act 1976* (Cth) s 5.

proceedings.[84] However, certain classes of case files have been identified as so important that their entire contents (both Parts A and B) are to be permanently retained by the NAA as a national archive. These are specified as all native title case files and significant, non–native title files.

The RDA gives the court responsibility for deciding which cases are 'significant', subject to the condition that the number of cases selected not exceed 10 per cent of all cases finalised by the court in any one year. However, there is less specificity about the rationale for identification of what constitutes a 'significant' case, and the process and selection criteria are still to be finalised. During consultation with the court as part of the research for the Court as Archive Project, two general criteria for determining a significant case have been suggested: first, precedential cases, being cases likely to set a new precedent or change an existing precedent; and second, cases likely to have a long-term historical interest due to the parties involved in the dispute or issues involved in the case. Further, the authority specifies that factors for consideration in identifying significant cases should include 'high media profile', 'public interest' and a 'cross-section of cases'.

Preserving cases 'likely to be of long-term historical interest' is a wide and open-ended criterion that begs for clarification. Further, the factors that may be considered in determining the criteria are likely to change, reflecting the social and political problems of a particular time. This should be appropriately reflected in the nature of the cases selected for preservation. As researchers on the Court as Archive Project, rather than identify a definitive list of additional factors (which would require review over the longer term), we have recommended that attention should be directed to the *process* by which the criteria and factors are applied. This process involves the establishment of a committee to oversee the identification of significant cases, with membership drawn from the court's judges, senior executive and key committees. In addition, we recommend that the committee include experts in Australian history, public law, and

---

84 This includes applications for fee waiver or exemption, applications to inspect files, letters to and from parties, minutes of orders for directions, consent orders and final orders, as well as exhibits that have not been returned to parties, list of exhibits, submissions, legal arguments or interpretation of evidence and transcripts of proceedings. Other records included in Part B and subject to disposal include audio recordings of court transcripts (apart from native title matters), which are to be destroyed 10 years after the date recorded; records documenting the court's docket system, which may be destroyed five years after completion; and records documenting the routine operational administrative tasks of the core business of the court, which may be destroyed seven years after completion.

archives and library special collections. The recommendation, in the form of a memo delivered to Chief Executive Officer Warwick Soden, is included in this collection.[85]

Conclusion

Tom Nesmith argues that it is not only decisions about what records to retain as archival but also what is not preserved, what is disposed of through the process of sentencing, that contributes to meaning-making processes based on archival practices.[86] In this chapter, I have investigated the role of courts as archives through an analysis of approaches to appraisal of court records. I have argued that courts must carefully consider their records disposal policies and practices because they are ultimately responsible for the decisions to retain or destroy records. The decision to keep or destroy records can have a significant impact not only on the parties directly involved in the legal process, but also on how law is understood historically and contemporaneously. In Canada and Australia, courts of record, including the Supreme Court of Canada, Federal Court of Canada and Federal Court of Australia, have begun to grapple with these obligations by developing frameworks for archival appraisal through records RDAs. This has raised important questions about their legal and ethical responsibilities in relation to court records and led to consideration of what principles should guide and determine appraisal decisions. It has led them to confront a question that goes to the heart of their identity, and, ultimately defines their record-keeping responsibilities: 'What *is* a court record?'. I have argued that when considering this question, courts should go beyond legal principles and obligations to consider their archival responsibilities in terms of the deeper public law issues underlying their institutional role.

---

85   Chapter 12, this volume.
86   Nesmith, above n 44, 34.

Postscript: A Memorandum to the Federal Court of Australia

The Court as Archive Project has focused on the Federal Court of Australia as a paradigmatic example of a federal superior court of record with responsibility for significant national archives. One of the aims of the project has been to develop principles based on empirical research to inform the administration of the archives held by the Federal Court. The Court as Archive symposium in February 2016 provided an opportunity to engage directly with senior members of the judiciary and administrators of the Federal Court: The Hon Michael Black AC QC, former Chief Justice of the Federal Court; Warwick Soden OAM, Principal Registrar and Chief Executive Officer of the Federal Court; and Ian Irving, then Native Title Registrar, Federal Court.

Following the symposium, and in response to an invitation from the Principal Registrar, we wrote a memorandum to the Federal Court with advice on a process for the selection of significant matters for the purposes of its records authority. The advice is the culmination of our empirical work and thinking on the basis of the research conducted for the project. We include it in the collection as a postscript and in its form as a memorandum, as an official response from us as academic researchers to those charged with the responsibilities of administration of the significant files of the Federal Court into the future.

Memorandum: Federal Court of Australia and the National Archives of Australia — Selection of Significant Matters

The Federal Court of Australia performs a fundamentally important role within Australia's democratic system. The court's records, gathered through its internal workings and the cases that come before it, contain a narrative that shapes contemporary understanding of the rights of the individual and the role of the state in Australia.

In October 2011, the National Archives of Australia (NAA) endorsed the Federal Court's Records Authority (RA) for the management and disposal of the court's records. The RA delineates the requirements for 'keeping and destroying records for the core business of case management' as well as for national preservation.

Court of Record and Significant Matters

The RA establishes 10 classes of records related to case management. Four classes deal with case files; that is, files containing material relating to individual proceedings.

The default position for every case file is that material constituting the 'court record', as defined by the court for the purposes of the RA (referred to in the RA as 'Part A' of each file), is retained by the court. This is entirely appropriate and consistent with the court's position as a 'superior court of record' established under Chapter III of the *Constitution* (*Federal Court of Australia Act 1976* (Cth) s 5). Material that is not part of the court record (referred to as 'Part B') may be disposed of between 10 and 25 years after the end of the proceedings.

Certain classes of case file have been identified as so important that their entire contents (both Parts A and B) are to be permanently retained by the NAA as a national archive, namely:

- all native title files
- significant, non–native title files

The court is responsible for deciding which cases are 'significant', subject to the condition that the number of cases selected not exceed 10 per cent of all cases finalised by the court 'in any one year'.

Selecting Significant Matters

The process and selection criteria for significant cases are still to be finalised. There are some general criteria for determining a significant case suggested by the court:

1. Precedential cases, being cases likely to set a new precedent or change an existing precedent.
2. Cases likely to have a long-term historical interest due to the parties involved in the dispute or issues involved in the case.

Factors for consideration include high media profile, public interest and cross-section of cases.

As researchers on the Australian Research Council–funded project, The Court as Archive: Rethinking the Institutional Role of Federal Superior Courts of Record,[1] we have been invited to offer suggestions on how the protocol for determining significant cases for national retention might be developed by the court. In our opinion, the above two criteria are important and capable of covering most issues and contingencies. We are also of the opinion that the suggested current factors for consideration are relevant, direct and flexible.

However, preserving cases 'likely to be of long-term historical interest' may require consideration of additional factors. These factors will change over time to ensure that social and political problems of a particular time are appropriately reflected in the nature of the cases selected for preservation. This matters as much for the nature and experience of litigants, the conduct of legal practice and changing technologies of court administration. As such, and in lieu of identifying a long list of additional factors (which would require review over the longer term), we believe attention should be directed to the *process* by which the criteria and factors are applied.

---

1 Discovery Project DP130101954, <http://purl.org/au-research/grants/arc/DP130101954>.

Selecting Significant Matters—Process

The process for determining a significant case for retention by the NAA, in our opinion, could be:

1. Utilising the Proposed National Courts Framework

The establishment of the National Courts Framework, and the responsibility for certain jurisdictions by specialist judges, should be incorporated into the process.

The judge responsible for each National Practice Area could take responsibility for the selection process for cases of precedential value, applying the appropriate factors for consideration, including a proportionate limit of 10 per cent.

Additional cases that could potentially be, in the judges' opinion, of longer term historical interest should be flagged and sent to committee (see point 2 below for discussion).

2. Establishment of a Significant Cases Committee

Membership of a Significant Cases Committee could include the Chief Justice (or representative), the CEO (or representative) and members drawn from the court's Planning and Policy Committee.

The committee should also include members from outside the court, in particular, experts in Australian history (legal, cultural and social), public law and archives.

The committee members from outside the court should have the following broad skill sets or experience:

- experience in using court materials for scholarly research
- an understanding of the parameters and shifting values of archival collections
- an appreciation of importance of the relationship between public access and future use of legal materials in fostering public understanding of Australian social and political life.

The committee would meet annually to discuss the additional cases flagged by the National Practice Areas. At these meetings, additional research and preservation considerations could be discussed, reflecting the experience of all members, as outlined above.

We thank you for the opportunity to offer our advice on this important matter.

17 May 2016

Professor Kim Rubenstein
ANU College of Law
The Australian National University

Associate Professor Ann Genovese
Melbourne Law School
University of Melbourne

Dr Trish Luker
UTS Faculty of Law
University of Technology Sydney

Contributors

Associate Professor Ann Genovese
Melbourne Law School
University of Melbourne

Ann Genovese is an Associate Professor at Melbourne Law School, University of Melbourne, and a historian of modern Australian jurisprudence. Trained in two disciplines, her work focuses on how law and history can be brought into better relationship, to address how Australians live with and practice their law. Ann's projects have included histories of feminist jurisprudence and histories of how disciplines meet (in court and in the academy). She has explored these concerns across multiple collaborative and individual research projects, and in her teaching. In addition to being a Chief Investigator on the Court as Archive Project, Ann is also part of the team on the archivally based Australian Research Council Indigenous Discovery Project Lawful Relations from Encounter to Treaty.

Mr Andrew Henderson
ANU College of Law
The Australian National University

Andrew Henderson is the Research Assistant to the Court as Archive Discovery Project. He is a PhD candidate at The Australian National University (ANU) and a sessional lecturer in law at the University of Canberra. Andrew has worked for the Commonwealth Attorney-General's Department in a number of roles including courts' administration and as Official Receiver in Bankruptcy for Western Australia.

Ms Hollie Kerwin
Victoria Legal Aid

Hollie Kerwin is a first-class honours graduate from the ANU College of Law and was awarded the Blackburn Medal for her Honours thesis. She worked as a Research Assistant to the Chief Investigators in the development phase of the Court as Archive Project application. Since graduating she has worked as an Associate to Her Honour Justice Susan Kenny in the Federal Court of Australia, and as an administrative and constitutional lawyer in the Victorian Government Solicitor's Office and for Victoria Legal Aid (VLA). She is currently a senior policy and projects officer at VLA, running strategic public law litigation and supporting VLA's law reform initiatives.

Dr Trish Luker
Faculty of Law
University of Technology Sydney

Dr Trish Luker is based in the Faculty of Law, University of Technology Sydney. Her primary research interests are located at the intersections of evidence law, legal decision-making and documentary practices. In addition to the Court as Archive Project, Trish has been a chief investigator on the Australian Feminist Judgments Project (with Heather Douglas, Francesca Bartlett and Rosemary Hunter) and a project entitled What is a Document? Evidentiary Challenges in the Digital Age (with Katherine Biber).

Dr Pamela McGrath
National Centre for Indigenous Studies,
The Australian National University

A Visiting Senior Lecturer with the National Centre for Indigenous Studies at ANU, Pamela McGrath has been involved with native title claim research, policy analysis and the teaching of native title anthropology for almost two decades. She was a founding collaborator of the Centre for Native Title Anthropology at ANU, where she worked as a Research Fellow until moving to the Native Title Research Unit at the Australian Institute of Aboriginal and Torres Strait Islander Studies in 2012. Pamela's recent research projects have focused on the social and economic impacts of the native title regime, Indigenous cultural heritage regulation and the management of native title information and archives. She has also researched and written about aspects of intercultural sociality, identity and camera culture on the Australian frontier. Between 2015 and 2018, Pamela was Research Director at the National Native Title Tribunal and currently works as a consultant researcher for native title claim and compensation matters.

Dr Narrelle Morris

Curtin Law School
Curtin University

Narrelle Morris is a Senior Lecturer in the Curtin Law School and an Honorary Research Fellow in the Asia Pacific Centre for Military Law, Melbourne Law School. She is the principal legal researcher on the project Australia's Post-World War II War Crimes Trials of the Japanese: A Systematic and Comprehensive Law Reports Series. She is an editor and contributor to *Australia's War Crimes Trials 1945–51* (Leiden: Brill Nijhoff, 2016). This book was shortlisted in 2017 for the New South Wales Premier's History Award for Australian History. She held an ARC DECRA Award (2014–2017) to conduct research into the Australian war crimes investigator and jurist Sir William Flood Webb. Her most recent publication is 'Sir William Webb and Beyond: Australia and the International Military Tribunal for the Far East', in Kerstin von Lingen (ed), *Transcultural Justice at the Tokyo Tribunal: The Allied Struggle for Justice, 1946–48* (Brill, 2018). She is also the author of the forthcoming guide *Japanese War Crimes in the Pacific: Australia's Investigations and Prosecutions* (Canberra: National Archives of Australia, forthcoming 2019).

Ms Maya Narayan

Victorian Government Solicitor's Office

Maya Narayan is a graduate of Melbourne Law School and Victorian lawyer, practising predominantly in constitutional and administrative law. Since being admitted, Maya has worked as the Researcher to the Solicitor-General for Victoria, Richard Niall QC (now a Judge of Appeal of the Supreme Court of Victoria), as Associate to the Hon Justice O'Callaghan of the Federal Court of Australia and as a Principal Solicitor at the Victorian Government Solicitor's Office. Maya was the recipient of the inaugural Professor Colin Howard Memorial Prize for outstanding student-published research and the 2011 Australian Institute of Administrative Law Essay Prize.

Dr Susan Priest
School of Law and Justice
University of Canberra

Dr Susan Priest is the Associate Dean of Education in the Faculty of Business, Government & Law and a Senior Lecturer in the School of Law & Justice at the University of Canberra. Susan has particular conference participation and research interests in Australian legal history, colonial NSW criminal law and some human rights issues. Susan has published in books and peer-reviewed journal articles in these areas and is currently a Visiting Fellow at the Centre of International and Public Law pursuing postdoctoral archival research into aspects of early Australian judicial biography.

Professor Kim Rubenstein
ANU College of Law
The Australian National University

Kim Rubenstein is a Professor in the ANU College of Law, a former Convenor of the ANU Gender Institute and a Public Policy Fellow at the ANU. From 2006–15, she was Director of the Centre for International and Public Law and co-edited a six-volume series with Cambridge University Press, *Connecting International Law with Public Law*. Her interest in archives stems from her expertise and work on Australian citizenship and her extracurricular activity of writing the biography of her former school principal, Joan Montgomery OBE AM. In addition to being a Chief Investigator on the Court as Archive ARC Discovery Project, she was also a Chief Investigator on the ARC Linkage Oral History Project on Trailblazing Women and the Law.

Mr Ernst Willheim
ANU College of Law
The Australian National University

Ernst Willheim is a Visiting Fellow in the ANU College of Law. Between 1967 and 1998, he worked for the Commonwealth Attorney-General's Department where he headed several policy and professional divisions, led Australian delegations to international conferences and appeared as counsel for the Commonwealth in constitutional and other public law matters in the High Court and other appellate courts. As Head of the Justice and Administrative Law Divisions, his responsibilities included courts and tribunals, and he personally initiated important reforms in judicial administration.

www.ingramcontent.com/pod-product-compliance
Lightning Source LLC
Chambersburg PA
CBHW041924220426
43670CB00032B/2954